OFF THE RAG

*Lesbians Writing
on Menopause*

Edited By
LEE LYNCH
and **AKIA WOODS**

NEW VICTORIA PUBLISHERS

Published by New Victoria Publishers Inc., a feminist, literary, and
cultural organization, PO Box 27, Norwich, VT 05055

Cover design by Claudia McKay

Printed and Bound in the USA
1 2 3 4 5 6   2001   2000 1999 1998 1997 1996

Library of Congress Cataloging-in-Publication Data

Off the rag : lesbians writing on menopause / edited by Lee Lynch
    and Akia Woods.
        p.   cm.
      ISBN 0-934678-77-4 (pbk.)
     1. Lesbians' writings, American. 2. Lesbians--Biography.
3. Menopause--Fiction 4. Women--Biography. 5. Women--Fiction.
6. Menopause. I. Lynch, Lee, 1945- . II. Woods, Akia, 1954-
PS3509.L47034 1996
810.8'09206643--dc20
                                                                    96-19898
                                                                        CIP

We dedicate this book to
all the lesbians who have gone before us,
often traveling the uncharted territory of menopause alone.

ACKNOWLEDGMENTS:

Many thanks to those who tried to help us find contributors, sent information or simply gave us support. This is a very partial listing.

Stephanie Byrd, Ariel Waterwoman, Chrystos, Latina Health Organization, Sojourner staff, SAGE, Donna Allegra, Lidell Jackson, Brenda Jones, Wewah & Bar Chee Ampe-Native Two Spirits in New York City, International Lesbian & Gay People of Color Human Rights Task Force, Mariana Roma-Carmona, Jerome Zorilla, BLUES, Jennifer Abod, Carmen Corrales, Nancy Bischof, Barbara Summerhawk, Asian Lesbians of the East Coast, Laura Perry, Leslie Burgess, Las Buenas Amigas, Ila Suzanne, Lesléa Newman, Barbara Smith, Andrea Lockett, Dorothy Abbott, Margarita Donnelly, Chea Villanueva, Judith Barrington, Asian Health Organization, Happy Hyder, Ayofemi Folayan, Regina Cash at ESSENCE Magazine, Grace Nam, Saja Greenwood, MD, Carol Seajay, Tee Corinne, D.C. Asian Lesbians, National Women's Health Network, Boston Women's Health Collective and many others.

Thank you also to ReBecca Béguin, Claudia Lamperti, Beth Dingman and Deborah Dudley, for walking us through this process with patience and unwavering dedication in giving this book to lesbians.

TABLE OF CONTENTS

TABLE OF CONTENTS

FOREWORD

When my gynecologist told me I was in perimenopause* I was pleased. When I began to miss whole months of the appropriately named "curse," I was euphoric. The words that came to me, over and over, were celebratory: "I'm getting my body back!" At one point I went four and a half months (gleefully counting each day) without bleeding. I felt like leaping and cavorting, a born again Peter Pan—until the cramps arrived, with a vengeance.

Still, I knew I was on the road to freedom from my loathsome "friend." Until the depression hit. I'd had a slight concussion at about the same time, and will probably never know how much of those six despairing months were due to having my brain rattled and how much to my hormonal tide ebbing. I do know that when a friend suggested an herbal product called Change 'O' Life and told me that her customers bought it by the case, I was desperate enough to try. The depression lifted within a week. At one point I decided it must have been coincidence. So I stopped taking the remedy—and my mood plunged.

Back on the herbs, I was still waiting for my release from the monthlies, and my doctor was talking to me about hormone replacement therapy (HRT). A bone scan confirmed that this skinny white girl is at major risk for osteoporosis. I have no family history of cancer in the various female parts. All of this made me a "safe" candidate for HRT.

---

*Perimenopause is the process that leads up to menopause. It begins when estrogen and progesterone levels begin to decline after age thirty-five and accelerates in the late forties. It is during perimenopause that signs such as hot flashes begin to appear. When our periods stop we are in menopause. We're considered postmenopausal when we haven't menstruated for a year. From *Member News*, HMO Oregon, Winter 1995.

I decided that this menopause business was going to be more of a challenge than I had realized. I needed information and started by asking friends. "You're on HORMONES!?!" a doomsday friend who'd years ago had a hysterectomy posted over e-mail. "My naturopath has me using a yam cream," boasted another. "What about the mares?" I worried.**

"Oh, I might have had a hot flash once," Norma, now seventy-one, told me. "The housewife's disease," scoffed Valerie Taylor. Old lesbians just seemed happy to put those years behind them. A few of the selections in *Off the Rag* have been constructed from letters written by women who "had nothing to tell" and then wrote pages about their experiences. Contributors to *Off the Rag* have given me more of the kind of information I've been seeking than any ten articles by physicians.

Even so, I couldn't decide whether to medicate my change as if it were a disease, or ignore it. Then the *New York Times* reported a study in England where HRT had been used to good effect with Alzheimer's patients. And a second physician recommended HRT to me.

I'd been perusing books about menopause for some time. The most helpful one I'd found by 1993 was the magnificent Crossing Press collection called *Women of the 14th Moon, Writings On Menopause*, edited by Dena Taylor and Amber Coverdale Sumrall. Yet even that included only a smattering of lesbian work, some of which is reprinted in *Off the Rag*. The more books I read, the more tired I became of reading about child-bearing years being over and about husbands finding wives unattractive and the wives, heaven forbid, drying up and destroying marital bliss. Where were the lesbian stories?

It's not that I thought menopause would be physically different for lesbians, but I certainly didn't recognize myself in the words I was finding. Akia and I began to talk about the need for some literature of our own. I wanted to know what other lesbians had decided about HRT. We wanted to know, with our nine-year age difference, what we had to look forward to in our relationship. We wanted the kids coming out now to have some stories about what it had been like for their elders.

**I've called several manufacturers of tablets and patches used in HRT. According to information they provided, most estrogen is derived from yam, soy or corn, not animal sources.

Age difference or not, Akia and I are both from the lesbians-reinventing-the-wheel generation. We came to the conclusion that we'd just have to make it happen. Claudia Lamperti at New Victoria, if my menopausal memory is correct, said yes to the proposal before I finished explaining it.

So we sent out calls for material to all sorts of publications and to every lesbian of *a certain age* for whom we could get an address. We were warned that putting an anthology together is not exactly a picnic, but no one told us that it would be like pulling tampons. Aren't we the most liberated of liberated women? Haven't we cast aside our taboos like so many bras and pledged to talk to one another about our lives? Have menopausal lesbians forgotten consciousness raising?

Claudia once mentioned that the quickest way to get silence in a roomful of lesbians is to bring up menopause. Well, we *tried* to start the conversation. Karla Jay's delightfully affirming piece quickly arrived and soon afterwards we received with great excitement Connie Panzarino's essay. We knew we'd made the right decision, but after that, only a few others dribbled in, often about aging, or menstruation or PMS. All with merit, but very few discussing what we wanted to put out into the world. And worse, we were not getting the diversity we sought. We especially wanted any lesbian who picked up the book to be able to find herself in it somewhere.

We wrote to every organization we could find that would increase our outreach. We spoke with women from faded recesses of our pasts. I called mixed groups and spoke with gay men so helpful and supportive I wondered if we'd hit on a new audience: men-who-have-to-work-with-menopausal-women. Prospective anthologists, be forewarned, editing such a collection falls somewhere between begging strangers for referrals to harassing your best friends for intimacies.

One potential contributor told us that some cultures simply won't talk about menopause. I understand that. In my experience Irish and French-Americans don't even say the word menopause aloud. We postponed the book for over a year trying to create an inclusive body of work. We extended the deadline and extended it again. And again.

The process of editing *Off the Rag* has paralleled my change of life. I was as eager to document lesbian hormonal experience as I was to reach menopause myself. The joys of reading each very special piece equaled the joys of my own maturation. The hand-wringing over finding enough, and representative, material can only be compared to my personal hormone-triggered(?) struggles with depression and panic which at times seemed never-ending and hopeless.

Although we flirted with reprints of scientific information, we ultimately decided that the women's bookstores are full of books and magazines that address the subject. We've included a bibliography to help readers do their own research. *Off the Rag* is stuffed not with treatises and guides, but with our heartfelt stories: intimate, funny, angry, frustrated, honest.

I join Akia in thanking all the people who called or sent us letters, articles, referrals and stories. And I thank Akia herself, for bearing with me through my changes, daily and yearly. I hope to have her patience and understanding if she becomes crabby and self-enclosed, weepy and fearful, or as childishly ebullient as I was when, just turned fifty, hot flashes and all, I successfully flew a kite for the first time in my life.

For the record, I did try minimal HRT for three months. Part of the month I took estrogen and part of the month I took progesterone. It took some research to find medication I could tolerate with my corn allergy, but the pharmaceutical companies were very helpful. Most of them have 800 numbers if the P.D.R. doesn't have enough information. Another resource is your pharmacist, who will have written material available for each drug if you ask for it.

I hated my first experience with HRT. For a week before each chemically-induced period I was wiped out, almost too exhausted to work. I had cramps and a period as heavy as I'd had since adolescence. I was not willing to endure that for the rest of my life if I didn't have to. My gynecologist offered to put me on estrogen and progesterone simultaneously, which would eliminate the bleeding because no buildup occurs on the lining of the uterus. I asked her about the new bone-building drugs on the market and she referred me to an endocrinologist who specializes in this area. (He worked for NASA for a time and told me that astronauts suffer massive bone loss in a gravity-free environment. No wonder a drug was developed.)

At this point I'm waiting another year and a half to see if, without HRT, bone loss is a problem. I am eating green leafy vegetables until they come out my ears. I walk, as fast as I can, for as long as possible, daily, but with two careers, this is limited. I'm using a yam extract as this is supposed to be bone-building, and as soon as I can afford it, plan to visit a naturopath for guidance. (Of course my health insurance doesn't cover such a radical approach.) My gynecologist scoffs at natural remedies as inadequate. I scoff at unnatural remedies that increase my risk of cancer, but may, in the end, resort to them if they make the most sense.

In this treasury of midlife tales I found what I hope other lesbians will find. The simple knowledge that I am not alone in my menopausal miseries or in my excited entry to a new phase of life. I am neither crazy nor perfectly sane. If I'm enjoying a second childhood, if I'm having the same menstrual symptoms of my adolescence, if PMS is exaggerated beyond endurance, if I decide to single-handedly support the pharmaceutical and *"feminine hygiene"* industries once again, if I *hate* doing HRT and am frightened not to, so are you, dear readers. May you find in *Off the Rag*, if not definitive answers, then companionship on this ever-challenging road of being a lesbian woman.

Lee Lynch

INTRODUCTION

When Lee first mentioned that she wished there was a lesbian menopause book, I suggested that she write it. "But I need to *read* it, not write it!" she pouted. Once we'd established that "somebody" should do an anthology, we eventually decided to do it together, so she could read the submissions *now*. When Lee approached New Victoria about the book, they were very encouraging, and so here it is!

Because the idea came without a title, we worked and worked to find the right one. Since then some lesbians have suggested that *Off the Rag* is a somewhat crude and dishonoring term for what is for many of us a complex and sacred passage. Through my life I've heard lots of terms for menstruation, but being "on the rag" is definitely one that stuck with me. Later, when I heard women being told to "get off the rag" or to stop "ragging about" something or "being such a rag," I was able to connect these phrases with premenstrual and menopausal irritability.

Back in my twenties I met a wonderful old crone named Edna. Edna was wise in ways I'd not even considered before. When I complained about the cost of menstrual supplies, she taught me to tear, fold and wear cotton rags which would then be soaked (the blood water used to water plants), washed and reworn. For years I have done this, every month enjoying the fact that I was not lining some man's pocket with money spent to throw away my life blood. And while the end of menstruation, menopause, has in recent history meant the end of paying money to flush our blood into water filtration and septic systems and garbage dumps, it does not necessarily mean the end of paying money to The Man. Many of the writers in this anthology relate their need to buy drugs or other products (yes, even menstrual pads), either transitionally or for the long haul, to help stabilize their bodies through the process of menopause. So when you think of our title, *Off The Rag*, please know that it was crafted with loving respect for Edna and all of the women who have gone before us, sharing their wisdom, their values, their practical solutions and their dreams.

Shortly before I was diagnosed with Chronic Fatigue Syndrome/Multiple Chemical Sensitivity/Fibromyalgia, I began experiencing an amazing array of symptoms. Fatigue, memory loss, night sweats, irritability, depression, interrupted sleep—is any of this sounding familiar? When I started learning more about menopause, I was surprised to see the number of "menopausal" symptoms I had. One year when I went for my yearly exam, my gynecologist thought it was interesting, too. She tested me even though at thirty-seven I was "too young," and so I was officially proclaimed by the medical establishment as still menstrual and not perimenopausal. Somehow that wasn't a surprise to me. What did surprise me happened in the process of working on this book. We received several letters and submissions from women who were still bleeding, but certain they were in perimenopause because of their symptoms—symptoms some of them had been experiencing for seven or eight years already with no change yet in their bleeding!

After we got Carolyn Gage's intriguing piece in the mail, some of my thoughts began to order themselves differently. As a rule, my friends who are comfortable with and have thrived in the male mainstream society (enough to really claim it as their own) seem to have had little difficulty with menopause. Meanwhile, my friends who were not comfortable living their lives in this male society (but doing it anyway) seemed to have their discomfort sharpened by menopause, and a lot more physical symptoms, as well. Although my friends are by no means a valid statistical sampling of lesbians or women at large, I find it a fascinating "coincidence" that this would be true. And, along these same coincidental lines, I find it interesting that many lesbians come out during menopause. (See pieces by Henri Bensussen and Sunlight, for example.) Some realize their lesbianism during menopause and others seem to gain the courage then to act upon what they have long known about themselves. This stuff has just all got to be connected somehow. I guess I am still amazed that the more I learn, the less I seem to know.

And then there's Hormone Replacement Therapy. Oh, I'd heard of it for a long time, but my first intimate understanding of Hormone Replacement Therapy came with one of my social services clients. I had always thought that taking estrogen was something women with certain symptoms or certain doctors did, sort of like taking vitamins. You take a pill most days of the month and that's it. It never occurred to me that those women might have to bleed again. Until a ninety-two year old social services client of mine who could hardly sit on her poor frail butt anyway because of her protruding bones and thin skin started bleeding. I was outraged! Not only that she should have to bleed after having been through all that in her youth (notice that as I get a little older, all bleeding women are "in their youth"), but that she should somehow have to expose her fragile, fragile skin to the abrasion of a thick, wet pad. I was thoroughly incensed and called her doctor to tell him that he surely had made a dosage error and that it had better be corrected NOW. Well, he explained, that's just the way it was going to be from now on. He didn't make an error on the dosage; modern western medicine had divined that in order to be most effective, women had to start bleeding again to take Hormone Replacement Therapy.

That was years ago and since then there have been a lot more opinions about and research on Hormone Replacement Therapy. Many of us are beginning to learn about the different hormones and methods of administration, but I have remained infuriated since that first day when I learned my ninety-two year old client was bleeding. Once I first learned that the hurting, bloody messes would eventually stop, I had looked forward to getting rid of them. I had been promised they would end—promised, of course, by a still-menstruating woman who hadn't been there yet, but was operating on promises given to *her*. Now it looks like getting rid of all the symptoms and the blood may or may not happen, depending on what (if any) treatment I choose to undergo at perimenopause.

Maybe I'm just stuck in an anger phase right now, but I think women have been sold a false bill of goods. Whether the untruth was the part that said we'd be all done with this bleeding nonsense around fifty years of age, or whether it is the promise of better health and eternal youth through the hormone replacement currently being pushed by practitioners of western medicine, it still feels like we got left holding the bag somewhere. Or everywhere. As a boomer worried about Social Security and as a lesbian living in a heterosexual society, this feels unfortunately familiar.

It is really important to talk with each other right now. Tell our truths. Share our stories. Be there for each other. I have great admiration for all the women who sent us work to be considered for publication in this book, a book that could not have been published not too many years ago because of the veils of secrecy around both menopause and lesbianism. And Lee and I both send a hearty "Thanks" and a big round of applause to New Victoria for their constant support of this project. It has been an honor to be involved.

Akia Woods

AN ODE TO ESTROGEN
Karla Jay

At music festivals and women's conferences other radical lesbians danced in circles and sang hymns to the moon goddess mother who had apparently brought on collective menstruation; they delighted in the return of their monthly bleeding. But I was tightly curled in a sweaty ball on my bed, wondering whether enough time had passed yet to down another Motrin. My periods had been an incredibly regular monthly torture from the time I was thirteen (when my mother's version of Motrin consisted of doses of blackberry brandy until I mercifully passed out).

Therefore when my period came to an abrupt halt in 1989 after a traumatic breakup, my friends attributed it to shock, but I was secretly thrilled. I hoped it would never return. I danced under the full moon. I felt immunized during the goddess worshipping events at women's cultural events. But after the novelty wore off, I began to recall that my mother had had such severe osteoporosis that when she died at the age of seventy-two, she had already broken both her hips. Her doctor told me almost all her ribs were broken as well. Always frail, my mother had lived a relatively short life, compared to that of her cousins. My father died in his nineties, as had most of his relatives. What if I had his longevity and her bones? Eeek. Extreme old age is no place for the faint of heart. While more people seem to be living to older ages, I don't see that the quality of living in extreme old age has gone up noticeably. As my father once said, after ninety, it's all downhill, but if you live to be over one hundred, take it.

When I began to wake up every hour of every night with hot flashes, I knew that I was out of eggs, out of estrogen. I drank megaglasses of water every day and drowned in a sea of sweat at night, a sailor wrecked on a reef by my own hormonal tides. A few lesbian friends advised me to swallow capsules of evening primrose, to eat estrogenic vegetables like kale, and to take vitamin E. I tried all these remedies, but to no avail. When I began to consider hormone replacement therapy, they warned that estrogen isn't organic. "Arsenic is," I shot back. "You'll get cancer of the uterus," they threatened. One friend who sounded the alarm about cancer didn't even have a uterus anymore, but she was so concerned that she preferred to sweat it out.

To live almost into eternity as had some of my relations (who were slightly older than God when they died) didn't seem natural to me either. In earlier periods of history, when your estrogen went, you went shortly thereafter. If anything, we have outlived the natural sequence of events in life and now we are paying the cost, just as knees began to buckle not long after the first (stupid) human decided to stand on two legs. If I had over a fifty percent chance of being over ninety, I had best make my mid-life last as long as possible. And then one day as if to seal my thoughts, I bit into a candy bar and spit out a tooth that had shattered into a thousand fragments, as had several teeth before it, all of them unhappy reminders of a virtually milk-free childhood. I studied the deteriorating remains of the candy bar and the white shards of my tooth like decaying tea leaves, in which I saw a future of plastic hips, spinal braces, and a lavender cane. Not if I could help it.

I was encouraged to go on hormones by my lover, Karen. She had been taking hormones for some time herself and was happy with the results. Not only had they cured her hot flashes, but they had also made her skin less dry and had made her hair look thicker. Being a physician, she could also dismiss the negative hype with some medical facts. Most importantly, she pointed out, the level of estrogen women take has been reduced over the years. The packaging even warns the consumer that the dose is not strong enough to prevent pregnancy. Furthermore, adding Provera to the regimen is thought to protect against uterine cancer.

Taking hormone replacement therapy could only help the relationship, too. We met in August, and it couldn't have been much fun for her to curl up against a steaming radiator in the blazing heat. Since I woke up four or five times a night with hot flashes, my sleep was being interrupted, her sleep was being disturbed by my awakenings, and I was getting decidedly cranky.

When a gynecologist confirmed that I was indeed menopausal,

I started hormone replacement. In a matter of days, the hot flashes began to subside, I began to sleep through the night, I began to beam more, and my lover beamed back more. Ahhh. I didn't feel like some younger woman, some chemically altered woman: I felt more like the self I had been before "The Change."

The hormones help reproduce the twenty-eight-day cycle my body had so faithfully followed for so many years. There seem to be as many therapies as there are physicians recommending them, but the cycles are fairly similar, so I waited until my lover started her new cycle to begin taking my estrogen so that our periods would be in harmony.

This was great—we would always be on the same cycle, even if one of us didn't have the "dominant scent" that's supposed to send an entire colony of lesbians onto the rag. And if we were anticipating an important occasion—a family event, a summer party where we hoped to wear white shorts, or a romantic weekend in the country in our bathing suits—we could both delay taking Provera and know that there would be no PMS, no periods. Just fun or romance.

Make that romance and sex. Yes, we've had an incredible amount of sex. Most of our friends seem to be suffering from "lesbian bed death" or terminal marital boredom. The hormones play only a small part in our total relationship, but estrogen keeps the vaginal walls thick and alive, and I have to wonder how many of our friends gave up sex because it became less enjoyable. It's hard to separate biological and psychological factors, but whatever it is, four years into our relationship, our sexual encounters are like we just met the week before. We're hot, horny, wetter than ever, and having more sex than either of us has had in any other relationship. Our friends are tired of our smooching in public.

Once when as we were checking out of our B&B after Women's Week in Provincetown, we ran into the young women who had rented the room above us, just as both they and we were packing our cars to go home. We hadn't met them earlier because we had never made it outdoors for the communal breakfast. I was still packing in our room when Karen came back from her car to complain that the women were sitting in their car in the parking lot and staring and staring at her, jaws agape. I went out to see what was happening, and they began to stare at me. Finally, they pulled out of their spot, but instead of leaving, they pulled into another parking spot and stared some more. Now either I've become so incredibly famous that women recognize me without my American Express Card, or these younger dykes were being—okay let's say it—agist, aghast that the couple they had obviously overheard all weekend (I never said I was quiet) was THAT OLD. Yes, folks, hitting fifty. They looked amazed and stunned. When they finally pulled out of the lot, we blushed a little and laughed a lot. Maybe we'd be role models for them to remember. And we were more than a little relieved that we had told some close friends not to book the room those younger dykes had wound up in!

When not in bed, we try to be physically active. We play some tennis or golf, or we go biking or hiking. In the summer, I bike five miles every day, and for the past two years I've competed in a six-month-long tennis tournament sponsored by the local gay and lesbian tennis league. It involves a match almost every week. In the winters I try to play tennis indoors. Staying fit doesn't come entirely in a pill.

Not everything is an improvement with hormone replacement. PMS is actually worse. For most of my menstruating years, I had never suffered much from PMS; mostly, I would feel an unexplained ache somewhere or a headache that would resolve itself when I got my period. But Provera has given me PMS with a vengeance: "PMS in a bottle," I call it. Grumpy, irritable, trouble sleeping—you name it. And my lover also is taking her Provera at the same time. It's a good thing we live apart so that we can retreat quietly to our cages until it's safe to come out again.

I'm certainly not advocating that everyone take hormones. We each have to weigh the risks and advantages of it and make our own decision. So far, I'm delighted with my choice, but I also know that I can go off the hormones any time I choose: they're not addictive! Right now staying in emotional and chemical sync with Karen works for me and for our relationship. So if you see me taking pills, don't feel sorry for me: Be glad.

THE WISE PROTECTRESS
Tasha Anthony Johnson

The Goddess Hecate is often portrayed as the Goddess of the underworld, though she also has an earth aspect and an astral aspect.

In her underworld aspect she helps those who face death to pass on to that phase of existence so that they can continue their journey to their next life. The word death can be taken symbolically or literally. Death means change, departure. It means something is moving from one place to another. Hecate aids when this movement occurs, be it minuscule or paramount.

One of the parts of Hecate which is rarely discussed is her astral aspect, which I choose to refer to as the living savage. To me the living savage will seek out opportunities to find pleasure, gratification and joy. In this aspect Hecate caters to creativity of all types, since that is one of the main routes to pleasure. This aspect allows women to feel the freedom of experiencing pleasure and joy to their fullest. It is impossible for me to understand any part of Hecate while ignoring another. The living savage is the part of the Goddess who craves passion, who wildly enjoys herself with fierce, intense energy. This can also be explained as innocence, as the ability to enjoy and create devoid of judgement.

Another aspect we hear little about is her earth aspect, which I refer to as the wise protectress. She guides women on their way, gives them strength and direction, helps them to find their inner power. If needed, she can give people a strength with seemingly relentless power but this is tempered with the other aspects of her.

To me, it seems only logical that menopause is when a woman comes into the state of being as close to Hecate as one can be on this plane. It is my belief that a woman is born into that phase of life which is eternal when each element of being female comes together in its fullest. Likewise it is when all three aspects of the Goddess Hecate meet. There is no hoarding one aspect away from another, they all simply co-exist within the woman.

Women give life. Our bodies give us the option every month of doing so, which is regulated by our menstrual cycles. As a young teenager I viewed the world through ungrateful, pained eyes and having a period truly meant to me that I had a "curse." It was a gross and dirty thing to have and all females were in turn gross and dirty. The jail of living in a heterosexual world closed in on me in every way possible, from social acquaintances to the most intimate parts of my being and body. The outlook felt bleak. I would have to marry a man, have babies and then someday endure the horrors of menopause. Menopause gave women yet another reason to be crazy, but this time as old worn out pieces of meat, rather than where I currently stood, a dumb bimbo. The phase in between, of course, was the role of the bitchy mother. None of these phases of development looked attractive to me and rightly so. However, I have been well blessed in my life, and at some point in the bimbo stage, I met a lot of older lesbians.

When I first came out at a mere fifteen years old, the lesbians I came in contact with were all around thirty-five to forty years old. It was a small group of women and they all got to know me well. I was as impressed with them as other teenagers were with movie stars. Things were exhilarating. Those dykes embraced me as one of their own and began teaching me countless lessons about how to be the person I was inside, how to view life, how to treat others and myself, what gay culture was about. I learned from them political and spiritual aspects of what being a lesbian means. They taught me the most important lessons of history that I learned: about the family in the military, about the old gay bars with the red lights above them, about Stonewall and the changes since then. They taught me about safe sex, how to value and love myself and that I had a home.

Mostly I learned these things through watching them, but on many occasions we had long discussions about various topics and the freedom to ask whatever questions I could come up with was granted with ease. The most important lesson I learned from them was that I was loved, wanted, and that I belonged. This was a far different approach and feeling about life than I had before I knew them. It was a far cry from the alienation, loneliness, and feeling of being a social outcast that I had before I met those women. Had it not been for those contacts, I surely would still hold the skewed view of my future that I previously held. I learned that my menstrual blood was not a disgusting thing to be ashamed of, but rather the life force of some grand creator who had divine love for me and who wanted my celebration and happiness of being female to become real. I learned that no phase of development would be shame-based and that the problems along the way inside each stage of development would be solvable and moreover, they would be honorable. I changed the way I naturally viewed menstruation as horrible and shameful, to calling it my moon or moss time, and offering wild creative love during this time. The Goddess was with me, I knew that. I still know that.

With those women I began realizing that life could be a grand adventure, that I would belong in lesbian culture, that I could thrive. I remember being excited about living, about existing, about growing older. I knew that once I hit my thirties, my life would take off. It would be fun, full, happy and creative, just as they had shown me. When I was around those women, I was in the middle of a massive celebration into which they opened their arms and embraced me.

My feelings about those women have not changed terribly much. I still feel pride, honor and belonging. There is something amazing about deeply loving people who have watched each step of your adolescence.

What has changed some is their ages and what they have since gone through. Many of those women are now in menopause. Although I may have an innocent, naive or romanticized idea of their experience, it feels true to me. I have observed women celebrating what is occurring in them as a gift from the Goddess, I have seen them honor their life changes as a rite of passage into solid wisdom, and I have seen a renewed feeling of life in them as they go through this. I have also watched them suffer in depressions and go through various physical trauma. But their lesson still remains: nothing, absolutely nothing is so bad that a woman must be rendered immobile physically, spiritually, mentally or emotionally. They grow through the trials of the problems associated with menopause, and by watching them I am able to witness life working out once again.

The answers to my old questions are different than I used to think they were and I believe that if they had not changed, my life would still be in that rot, fear and loneliness of early adolescence. I will be forever grateful for those women, for their free gifts to me. Some people take growing up more lightly than I did, but for me what lay ahead cannot be described any better than saying it was impending doom, an inherent punishment that all females must endure simply for existing. People notice easily when a person feels that rotten inside, and thank goodness. Those women saw the baby dyke and knew it was not right that I suffered alone. So they showed me how they live. It's really that simple. Passing it along to their young.

I do not believe in the societal myths of what happens to a woman when she goes through menopause. I believe in what I have seen the women I love and cherish experience. I believe in their strength, their calmness, their wisdom, their courage, their excitement and their innocence. I believe in their self-love and compassion for themselves and each other when they feel depressed and out of kilter.

As for the celebration of menopause, it feels to me like the birth of a new self. The reason for this is because I have watched those lesbians support one another, share with each other about the changes and create safe positive energy for one another during this time. Since lesbians do not have ready-made societal rites of passage, we must help one another to create our own. Why shouldn't we? We have our own music, comedians, social norms, sports, newspapers, symbols and even women's bleeding sponges. By witnessing the celebration of this evolution it does not seem to me like menopause will be a loss.

My only doubt (aside from monthly pain) comes from the knowledge that inside my heart I have a spiritual tie to menstruation. Menstruating is the physical, mental, emotional and spiritual manifestation of becoming yourself anew each month. But, my faith in life is strong due to the repeated testaments of the lives of those women who have embraced me, taught me well and allowed me to watch them. I solidly believe that I will learn enough from other lesbians and that by the time I go through my life change I will know how to give myself that manifestation of self as easily as it is regulated by my body now.

I have nothing to fear. Hecate is in each of us and one day I will come into my closeness with her as much as those older women going before me. That is her promise.

MENOPAUSE AND THE GIFT OF HEALING
Elena Sherman

"You better include me in your story. I want credit for my suffering."

So spoke my lover, who one month after I announced I was post menopause, suffered her first real period in three years. She had longingly hoped I had done menopause for both of us. Unfortunately, as much as I wish I could have, we're twenty-three years apart in age, so unless the current arrangement is updated, she'll have to do hers herself. We did, however, make copious notes for her guidance in future years.

I went into menopause with certain ground rules.

1) This was a normal process of life just for me and I was not going to share it with the American Misogynist Association.

2) I was not going to have hot flashes.

3) I was going to keep my sense of humor.

Numbers one and two were easy. I had no trouble staying away from the AMA. I didn't pick up the phone. Fortunately, the menopause police never found me. And I didn't have hot flashes. What I had instead was heat. One sunny day my internal thermostat shot up and stayed there for almost three years. It was bliss, I didn't wear anything heavier than a sweater outside all winter long. I laughed as my lover, the three cats and an 80 pound dog jockeyed for position around the floor furnace in the hall. When all around me were shivering, I was comfortably curled up on the couch with a book. No more screaming from my long-suffering lover when the ten icicles depending from the ends of my feet sought warm territory. And then one day I awakened with a strange sensation. Three days later I identified it. I was COLD. That for me, was the official end of menopause.

My biggest challenge was keeping my sense of humor. I was determined to find good out of all this carrying on. Each cycle was a new adventure, like a complete build-up to the event without any bleeding. The insomnia was a new adventure for this good sleeper. After several months during which nothing helped, I decided to stop worrying about it. I spent my wakeful hours reading cook books and embroidering. Along with the insomnia came a severe loss of energy. Encouraged by Susun Weed's book *Menopausal Years* that both insomnia and energy loss weren't unusual aspects of the process, I decided to commune with my body. We had some very helpful conversations:

"Kid. You want to sleep at night?"

"Of course I do."

"Try exercise."

"I hate to exercise."

"I've noticed. Sneak up on it, start with sex."

Not so dumb, my body. Sex helped a lot. With experimentation we discovered gentle sex, earlier in the evening (when I still had some energy) didn't make me sleep longer, but did provide quality sleep and fun.

For my next act, now that I was warmed up (pun intended), I was beset by tag teams of gremlins providing mood swings with frills and whistles. I was able to slow them down with a combination of a mild generic decongestant and ibuprofen. I mostly limited my use of these to night or when I had to be around someone. (Most specifically my lover. She deserved the best me possible, which sometimes wasn't much.) Alone, I tended to let the gremlins have at it after I discovered the bottom of every swing brought me something from my past which needed exorcising.

"OK bod, what's going on?"

"Remember all those traditions where post menopausal women are tapped as wise women? Well, this is where you make the choice."

"What choice?"

"Your mood swings are helping you get to places that need healing and letting go of. If you choose to allow yourself the cleansing, you can be one of those wise women."

Sounded reasonable to me. Why would men have invented demanding rites for themselves like lifetime vows of poverty, chastity and wearing dresses if they weren't trying to horn in on menopause?

"And while we're at it, what about moving me?"

"Moving? You mean exercise?"

"You said it, I didn't. So, move me, you'll deal better."

"I have too much to do and not enough energy."

"If you don't EXERCISE I can't give you energy or emotional support."

The bod, as usual, was right. So right, that if I don't swim/stretch/move regularly I get stiff, mentally and physically. Each day it gets easier to put my body into motion. Sometimes I even look forward to it.

Accepting and letting go are gifts of menopause. Since taking care of myself has never been my strong point, my lessons tended to be dramatic. At the peak of my most dramatic lesson (and the hardest for my lover to survive) I had crashing mood swings and about four good hours a day into which to cram a living, a life and errands.

I divided my external world into those activities which needed my four good hours, those which just needed me to function and those which weren't going to happen.

It didn't work. I was using most of my energy agonizing over what I should do vs. what I could do.

"HELP!"

"Listen up, Kid. This won't be easy. Forget the lists and work from your instincts. Start with doing something for yourself every day. Something you want to do. Don't devote your life to it. Maybe twenty minutes sketching, or ten minutes sitting in the sun with a cup of tea watching the grass grow, or fifteen minutes of Yoga. Satisfying your needs produces energy."

I timidly tried it. One day I drew a tiny landscape, another I went outside to watch the grass grow. An hour had flown by before I realized I had weeded half of my herb bed. I had satisfied my needs and my body's needs all in one activity. The deep satisfaction I felt gave me a preview of where I was headed. It was those sneak previews that kept me going when the gremlins came back again and again.

I began to monitor how I reacted to various activities. For the first time, I actually saw the gremlins exhausting me while I showered and dressed in the morning. They were the writers and producers of the mindless head arguments that perpetuated my parents' constant squabbling about everything in the world. Giving them the boot was wonderful. The exhaustion was gone. In its place was a solid silence, and I was peacefully ready for the rest of the day.

We celebrated when I announced I had just passed the halfway mark. I can't describe how I knew, I just knew. And little by little things became easier. And I became impatient. I was ready for the mood swings to end before they were, and I started trying herbal remedies. For me, dong quai was like taking speed, even though the friend who recommended it found it very beneficial. Two specific things I found helpful were Schiff's Menopause Nutritional System I and II and Wild Yam extract. The vitamins made such a difference in my disposition that within two days of my running out, my lover would eye me speculatively and inquire if perchance I might be out of vitamins. They were so important to our well-being, she'd go get them for me.

While I wouldn't say I have mood swings anymore (and I'm not about to check and see what she says), I do still have mild cycles. The wild yam calms down the hormone fluctuations.

Now, mostly on the other side, I am reaping the benefits. I'm still learning the importance of putting my needs first, without guilt and without apology. Each time I do I am validated and reinforced by more energy and a very solid feeling of serenity. The more I let go of the social myths and past experiences that trapped me, the more fun I, and we, are having.

"Social myths—humph—why don't you just tell them you're outrageous?"

And so I am…

MENOPAUSE AND THE UGLY DUCKLING SYNDROME
Carolyn Gage

What if it turned out that our problems as women were much simpler than we thought? What if much of the bewildering—and proliferating!—array of seemingly unrelated symptoms and pathologies which afflict women could be viewed as the effect of one single syndrome? And what if that syndrome had a single cause: heteropatriarchy? A staunch reductionist, I am intrigued by the possibility, and in the interests of furthering this line of inquiry, I propose a name for this phenomenon: The Ugly Duckling Syndrome.

As you probably remember, in the fairy tale the Ugly Duckling was tormented by her so-called peers for being different, until the happy day when she discovered that she was really a swan and not a duck at all. In other words, her "differences" were normal and she could stop beating up on herself for not fitting in.

In my own experience, the Ugly Duckling Syndrome has provided an explanation for many of my "maladjustments." First and foremost, I am a lesbian, and although I lived as a heterosexual for many years, I believe I have always been lesbian. My long-term partnership with a man was primarily asexual. My earlier relationships with men were wildly dissociative. And all the time I kept wondering what was wrong with me. In retrospect, I am proudest of the behaviors which caused me shame and embarrassment as a heterosexual. These "aberrant" behaviors were bearing witness to my swaniness, my lesbianism.

I had a terrible time with periods, hating my body and hating my womanhood. This was because duck culture doesn't make allowances for swan cycles. My moontime was a nuisance, a time when my body would exercise a will of its own and when I would have to fight it, drug it, or surrender to it.

Duck culture is linear, based on a definition of progress as steady accretion. Swan culture is cyclical, spiraling. We move forward in rhythmic circling motions which seem to double back to the

23

beginning periodically. Our bloods ebb and flow, our possessions ebb and flow, our relationships ebb and flow. We adopt a grace about our losses and our gains, knowing that the process, not the results, is the focus. Because we live in spirals, not lines, we move in a third dimension and our progress is manifest in upward motion, not in forward or backward lines on the material plane.

Not only does duck culture violate the swan need for moontime withdrawal, but it also does not allow for adjustment to different seasons, climates, or weather conditions. In fact, duck culture has even pathologized the natural tendency of most life forms to slow down in winter! The duck name for this evolutionary adaptation is Seasonal Affective Disorder.

Linear duck culture also pathologizes grief, rage and depression, all of which are necessary circling-back flight patterns essential to swan reconnaissance.

At thirty-six, I developed Chronic Fatigue Immune Deficiency Syndrome. In recovering from this devastating illness, I have had to study up on swan nutrition because, for most of my life, my eating habits reflected duck culture. I also had to notice that duck activities were meaningless and draining to me as a swan, sapping my will to live. I learned that I had been taught social patterns which invited victimization by ducks. I have had to train in swan self-defense. If my natural instincts about territory, environment, and feeding had not been so severely disrupted by exile from my native culture and by a resocialization process which amounted to brainwashing, I am convinced that I never would have contracted the disease.

And now here I am, facing menopause. The "symptoms" look suspiciously familiar: depression, mood swings, irritability, crying jags, suicidality, panic attacks, hypersensitivity, splitting headaches, fatigue, sleep disturbances. Are these really the effects of natural hormonal changes (proof of our ugly duckdom!), or are these traumatic responses to a sudden paradigm shift, as the body throws off the last constraints of an artificially imposed identity?

Could these disorders more accurately be termed the symptoms of captivity? Of exile from a beloved homeland? Of inability to protect or support one's children or one's art? Of identification with other forms of life which are being wiped out? Responses to forced labor? Repressed knowledge of trauma? Systemic poisoning? Pain of reintegrating parts of oneself which have been split off? The agony of remembering the unthinkable? The backlash of terror for breaking a taboo?

Menopause, as I see it, is not so much "The Change" as it is the "End of Denial." For better or worse, at menopause, it is no longer possible to believe that one is a duck. Depending on one's relationship to swanhood, menopause can either be a time of intense disorientation or of profound homecoming.

As lesbians, we began our journey with our coming out. Those same tools which enabled us to resist the institutions of compulsory heterosexuality will stand us in good stead as we sort through the myths and lies about menopause. And who knows? Maybe death, too, is just a final throe of the Ugly Duckling Syndrome.

IN TUNE WITH MY BODY
Connie Panzarino

I have been a lesbian since I was twenty-eight, or probably before, though I didn't know it. I also have had a disability called spinal muscular atrophy since I was born, but they didn't know that until I was about seven months old. It affects the nerve impulse that directs the voluntary muscles, so that I have very little movement, but I have full feeling. In spite of my disability I have been able to achieve a graduate degree in art therapy, publish several books including *The Me in the Mirror*, an autobiography by Seal Press, and maintain a private psychotherapy practice in Boston. In spite of my lesbianism, or rather because of my lesbianism, I'm a happy person, and often an ecstatic woman. In spite of attitudes about my lesbianism I survive.

For many years my disability was fairly stable. My life was fairly stable even with the high level of turnover of personal care attendants which I require twenty-four hours a day for my survival. My relationship was fairly stable for six years, and then I began to have mood swings. I began to cry with my clients, which is not only unethical, but had previously not even been an absurd possibility. I began to be hypothermically cold in the morning, and could not keep up with my respiration. I began to be so hot at night, that my lover was shivering because I continuously had my attendants turn the heat down. I made several trips to the emergency room via ambulance because my pulse rate was over 140 and would not calm down even though I had always been on medication for tachycardia. I hemorrhaged for five days and was threatened with a D&C, which for me would have been life threatening because undergoing anesthesia would probably require a permanent tracheotomy and possibly a permanent ventilator. I was told by several doctors that my symptoms were merely caused by my disability gone wild. Since my life expectancy was two and I was in my early forties, the physicians claimed they did not know what effects the disability had long term.

As it turned out I had an ovarian cyst, but even though that was removed successfully and I was not trached, I was still having all the same symptoms. I was driving my friends crazy pressuring them and all my female cousins to have babies.

As it turns out, I was what is called perimenopausal or pre-menopausal. I ran to my women's bookstore, Crone's Harvest in Jamaica Plain, and bought seven books on menopause. Luckily one of the books was by Susun Weed, an old friend and herbalist from Woodstock, New York. I was able to stop the hemorrhaging using nettles and shepherd's purse as prescribed by an old lover over the phone. Nettle is helped to somewhat regulate my periods although I am back to bleeding every eleven to twelve days now. Nettles are a wonderful herb and helps with the menopausal mood swings, but it is also a severe diuretic, and my body cannot handle too high doses of a diuretic. If I drank two cups of the infusion a day, I would probably not have my period very often and only bleed if I was ovulating. My body can only tolerate a half cup a day. For about eight months a half a cup a day staved my period off for four to six weeks at a time, but as I said, now I'm back to bleeding more often.

In order to stop the palpitations I had to be switched to a drug called Tenormin. When I started taking the nettles, my pulse dropped, so I was able to reduce the Tenormin by half the amount. I still have mood swings, although they are not as severe. I notice that I have some short-term memory problems, which may be due to the Tenormin or may be part of my menopausal symptoms.

My relationship with my lover ended this year. Both of us have disabilities, but only one of us is in menopause. I know that my menopausal highs and lows, forgetfulness, and medical crises that resulted from the interplay of menopause and my disability caused a tremendous strain on our relationship. I tried breaking the silence by talking about menopause at parties and dinners and sharing information with friends. It didn't work very well. Some of the women who were beginning menopause, or were afraid that they might be beginning it, didn't want to talk about it, especially the lesbians. I have found more support with my straight heterosexual friends who are more in touch with the loss of their ability to bear children.

It seems like there is a silent grieving process. Even though I chose not to have children, I kept dreaming of babies and children before I even knew that I was in menopause. Is this grief part of the depression that we feel?

It is difficult to discuss the fact that I'm in menopause in the disability community at times because childbearing is a loaded issue, lesbianism is a loaded issue, and we as people with disabilities who are seen as asexual are constantly in the need to prove how sexual we are. When I say I'm in menopause I am not saying I'm not sexual. If anything I have had a tremendous increase in sexual appetite that I would not want to give up! This is the up side of menopause. Yes, there is fatigue which adds to my already fatiguing disability, but menopause also provides me with power surges. I have learned to trigger hot flashes at times when I am outside and it is cold. I have had to begin using a respirator by mouth or with a small mask on my nose overnight and intermittently during the day. It seems that the fatigue which may be caused by menopause has made it more difficult for my body to keep up with its own breathing. Now that I'm breathing better, I can tolerate the menopausal fatigue better.

Recently I broke my arm. Although I am only forty-six, I am quite osteoporotic because of my disability, and menopause has made that worse. I have been taking calcium, but only 1,000 mg per day. Since I broke my arm I upped my calcium intake to about 1,800 mg per day. This has helped the bones to heal and also has totally eliminated any menstrual cramps. It has been two months now (four periods according to my cycle) and I have had no cramps!

The support I have gotten thus far is from a group called "The Project on Women and Disability," a part of The Boston Women's Health Book Collective. There were monthly think tank and support group meetings of heterosexual, bisexual and lesbian women with disabilities discussing a multitude of topics. Women that were interested in the interplay between disability and menopause and were also interested in some of the attitudes of the lesbian community.

The lesbian community has yet to deal fully with its ableism. We are beginning to deal with racism, but we are still not comfortable enough with our own bodies to be able to accept women whose bodies may be different because of size or shape or ability.

When I speak of menopause, I am calling up my sexuality. My lesbian sisters may welcome me to a potluck if it's accessible or a concert if there are no steps, but talking about my menopause I am sure conjures up more intimate scenes for them, and many lesbians are still not comfortable with thinking about having a sexual relationship with a woman with a disability. Obviously this is not the case for everyone or I would have been loverless all my lesbian life. I have not been loverless and have been very happy with my relationships, but the women with whom I shared my bed were exceptional. I am not exceptional, I am just living my life, but they were exceptional because they faced their own fears and moved beyond them.

The menopausal stage of our lives is about a lot of fears. It's about going back over puberty in a way. When we're teenagers our hormones are constantly shifting and our bodies are changing at a rate that we sometimes can't fully absorb. We go through mood swings, we think life is over, then we have crushes. We have voracious appetites one day and never want to eat for days after that. Menopause calls up a lot of those memories because our hormones are indeed shifting constantly and affecting our entire bodies from physical appetites to sexual appetites, our skin changes, our bones are changing, our energy changes. While things are shifting and scary, for me there has also been an increase of intuition. I feel much more spiritual and much more connected to other people, although for the first time in my life I crave being alone too. I'm not a person who ever enjoyed being alone so this is new for me.

I look forward to becoming a crone and I'm already planning my celebration ritual and party. I look forward to being free from my menses, yet the few times that I did not menstruate for six or seven weeks, I missed it. I've learned to be more in tune with my body than many other non-disabled women seem to be. Having a disability requires self-focus. Now I find that I need to focus on my body even more so. For example, I wait for the nights when my hormones are surging and I cannot sleep to plan my writing. When I feel my hormones shifting and I become more lethargic and sleepy, I use that time to listen to music or watch a video and just "zone out." When the moods spiral downward and I feel the death of every leaf falling off every tree, I use that time to remember friends and family who have died, and I grieve openly. I do not try to stop the pain but let it pour out of me, knowing that it will not last forever. When I forget what I did three hours ago, I let go of it and know that if was truly important I would have written it down, and if I forgot to write it down and the universe finds it important, someone will surely mention it or remind me. I also know that what I did three hours ago will surface two or three weeks from now so that it is not a totally gone memory, but just a misplaced one. I have tried to simplify my life of the clutter so that this transition period can be easier.

I celebrate my menopause, but I would really like to rename it woman-pause because women may need to take time and maybe just stop for a while. As a lesbian this time is more about me, whereas if I were a heterosexual I would imagine it might be more about how men would see me. Although the lesbian community may have their fears about menopause, each one of them will go through it and learn for themselves what body changes are about. It is my hope that this article can make each woman feel more proud of who she is, and where she is at, in the circle of her life no matter what shape she takes, and no matter what her abilities, no matter whether she breathes on her own or with help. A lesbian is a lesbian and she has a right to love who she wants how she wants. We all have the privilege of being on the same planet.

NEARLY, AT LAST
Candis Graham

She smelled the blood. Then she saw it. An erratic trail of bright red spots leading from the sink to the fridge, the fridge to the stove, the stove to the hallway. There was a line of tiny dots along the shiny parquet floor. And, at the end of the hall, a few large crimson puddles.

Standing in the kitchen, too frightened to move, unable even to think, she stared at the trail that led to the bedroom. Blood. Everywhere.

Then she noticed the solitary red footprint outside the bedroom door.

Jovette woke to pain. An excruciating hard knot. Throbbing and cursing in all directions. Her hand moved instinctively to her belly, clutching the loose skin.

The alarm? No. Awake before the alarm went off. Why? A dream. Blood. So strange.

She turned over and felt the bellyache again, at the same time as her hip touched a damp spot on the sheet. The cold wetness pressed against her hip. Noooo. Pain and a mess in the bed.

She opened her eyes quickly and found she was barely able to see in the early-morning darkness. What to do? If she could shake off her sleepiness…and wake up…think. Blood on the sheets. Soaked through? Please, no. Not another stain on the mattress. What to do? Get up…out of bed…to the bathroom. Quickly. Move fast so the blood does not fall. So the blood does not leak out and land on the floor.

"Dale," she whispered, not turning to look at the sleeping woman although she longed to. Any movement could release a fresh flood. "Dale. Are you awake? Listen. I've started my period. I'm getting up. Be careful. I think there's blood in the bed."

"You okay?" Dale's voice was low and sleepy.

Jovette felt Dale's warm hand rubbing her back. She wanted to turn over and hug her. But. There was the risk of more blood in the bed.

How could she have forgotten her period was due? Month after month, without fail, and still somehow she manages to forget. But now that it was here, she remembered yesterday, stretching to reach a package of software diskettes in the back of the filing cabinet, she noticed her breast felt tender as she pressed against the metal. And she has been feeling inexplicably anxious for a day or two, that free-floating anxiety that unbalances every thought and feeling.

"Sure. I'm fine. I'll clean myself up in the bathroom. Go back to sleep. I'm sorry I had to wake you, sweetie."

Some minutes later, Jovette took a bottle of mineral water from the fridge and set it on the kitchen counter. She stood, motionless, with one hand resting on the glass bottle, staring at the open window. Along the fence, the lilac bushes were in full bloom. The scent was strong in the early morning air.

She was surprised to find she felt close to tears. Why? Because her period had started? She took a deep breath, inhaling the sweet lilac smell, before reaching down to adjust the pad in the crotch of her black underpants. She hated wearing pads. The thick wedge between her thighs bothered her, irritated her beyond words for a few days every month. And she hated the stains on her sheets and underclothes. The truth was, she hated everything to do with her periods and longed for them to end no matter what anyone said about menopause.

She looked up at the cloudless sky. She loved the humid summer hotness and today would be another sizzling hot day. That was one good thing. She needed to focus on the good things. She needed to find the inner strength to help her get through the day. Tomorrow would be better. The second day always was.

She envied women who enjoyed their periods. She had a close friend, Germaine, who had thrown a party for her twelve-year-old daughter, Gerry, when she started bleeding. The invitations, delicate silver lettering on red paper, encouraged the guests to wear red clothing. Some women brought gifts for Gerry. Jovette brought her a thick red candle and a beautiful brass candle holder.

Jovette wondered, if her mother had had a party for her when she was thirteen, would she have rejoiced each month thereafter? She unscrewed the cap and poured water into a green-tinted glass. She didn't know one woman who had organized a party to celebrate menopause. She screwed the cap back on and returned the bottle to the fridge. But the idea appealed to her. A party to rejoice at the end of all this bleeding. Now that would be a red-letter day.

She nearly laughed out loud. No pun intended, she said to herself, half apologetically, half delighted with her unintentional humour. She took a long drink of mineral water and decided she would go in early and get a head start at work. She put the green glass in the sink.

Using both hands, she massaged the small of her aching back. Myra was expecting the report by lunch time. It was nearly finished, needing only some statistics and another read-through to tighten the writing.

Again, she felt tears starting in her gut. Don't give in. Keep busy. She turned away from the window, moving quickly, and took a bag of raspberry leaf tea from a glass jar and dropped it into a mug. She would do that first thing, work on the report before the others arrived. She poured boiling water over the tea bag and, immediately, the hot water released a tart sweet smell. Yes. She would go in early. If she could get the report finished by lunch time, the rest of the day would be easier.

She leaned over the mug to inhale the moist smell.

The phone company.

She stood upright. Someone was coming in to install the new phone system today. Today of all days. How could she have forgotten? He would interrupt her all morning long, when what she needed was complete peace and quiet to get the report finished. He would want to know where the main box was and where to install each phone and which ones were to ring and he was bound to have other questions and need all kinds of information she couldn't anticipate. And, of course, he would want to show her how to operate everything.

Why did these kinds of jobs fall on her shoulders? Couldn't someone else in the office look after the phone man?

She lifted the soggy tea bag from the mug and dropped it into the ceramic compost jar. If the installer was a woman, Jovette could tell her that this was the first day of her period and the phone woman would understand. But it wouldn't be a woman. The phone company always sent a man, usually a young one, in jeans and safety boots with heavy gadgets hanging from his thick leather belt. What did the phone company do with the men as they aged? And, more important, why didn't they hire women?

She sipped the hot fragrant tea. How would she ever get the report done by noon? Why did her period have to start today, when she had so much to do? It would be unbearable if Myra was angry at her. Myra had been displeased last week when Jovette was late coming back from lunch. Ten or fifteen minutes late once in a while, what did it matter? How many nights did she stay late to finish something or other? But Myra was a workaholic, no question about it, and obsessed with appearances, and she demanded the same constant dedication from everyone. She was, Jovette suspected, often disappointed. No one could meet her high expectations, not even her own self.

Jovette traced invisible patterns on the mug with her forefinger. She wished her periods would stop. By age forty-four, wasn't it time for menopause? She had read somewhere that recent research shows women start menopause gradually, around thirty-four or thirty-five. Maybe it was already happening to her and had been for years. She couldn't tell. She still had these periods every month, with one day of cramps after a couple of days of free-floating anxiety. But she had noticed that her periods didn't last as long anymore. Some months the bleeding stopped after three or four days, rather than the six days she had endured for most of her life. And the flow didn't seem as heavy after the first day. Was this the beginning of menopause?

Menopause. The word frightened her. All she knew were rumors of hot flashes and depression and bizarre behavior. What would it really be like? Surely, she thought, sipping the soothing tea, menopause would be better than this each month. Or would hot flashes disturb her moods? Would it be worse to wake in a hot sweat? Would she have to climb out of bed, half asleep, to change sopping wet sheets night after night, for months on end or maybe even years? Would Dale stop sleeping with her, in protest?

She reached down to readjust the pad. Could hot flashes be any worse than this tyranny, month after month, year after year, for thirty-one years? Surely hot flashes wouldn't be worse than this. Menopause had to be better. At least menopause, whatever it brought with it, wouldn't last thirty-one years!

But what about the bizarre behavior?

Last month, when Jovette said she was longing for her periods to end, Dale had said she wasn't looking forward to menopause. Jovette asked, "Why not?"

Dale said, "Because my mother went crazy during the Change."

Jovette had heard that some women became depressed, and sometimes they had to be admitted to a psychiatric hospital but no one ever said exactly what the craziness was.

"What do you mean, crazy? What did she do?"

There was silence for a few moments and then Dale said, speaking slowly, "Well, that's when she started drinking, during the Change. She'd have sherry before supper and wine with supper and some days she didn't bother making supper at all. We'd have to make it ourselves if we wanted to eat. She'd sit in the bedroom with the door closed and cry. It was horrible to listen to."

Jovette felt Dale's despair in the word *horrible*. But she felt something more, a sense of deep devastation for Dale's mother. She had to ask, although she tried to choose her words carefully. "But what was happening in the rest of her life? Your father was never home, was he? He's married to his job. He never has time for anyone. She must have been awfully lonely."

"Well, maybe. You know Dad. He's always busy. I don't know what he's going to do when he retires next year. Maybe she was lonely. Janet had moved out. She was at university in Waterloo back then. She'd always been close to Mom. And Frank was gone. He'd always been her favorite, although she insisted she didn't have favorites. He was in Alberta, working in construction, and I know she used to worry about him but she never heard from him. He's always been like that. He never phoned and never wrote to her. He never thinks of anyone but himself. Sharee was gone too, living with her boyfriend, that dumbbell she married. Marcie and I were still living at home. We were in high school, but we had our own lives."

Jovette sipped the tea and stared at the lilac bushes along the fence. She would never hide in her bedroom or turn to drink to console herself. She wouldn't need to. She had a job she liked and a home she liked. She took immense pleasure in the cosy two-bedroom apartment she shared with Dale. And she had a few close friends, good friends, long-time confidants. She loved and was loved by a wonderful woman, a sweet woman who talked to her about every little thing. Jovette breathed deeply, inhaling the sweet lilac scent. Yes, Dale was an extraordinary woman. A strong sense of well-being filled Jovette's body. She loved and felt loved. Her life was full and satisfying. Who could ask for anything more?

She put the mug on the counter and folded her arms over her chest. Surely, for all those reasons, her experience of menopause would be different from Dale's mother. Their lives were completely different. Jovette was an independent and self-sufficient dyke. She had not built her whole life and created a complete identity around providing a home for an ungrateful husband and children.

"So that's when she started drinking."

"Yeah, that's when it all started. And then one night, when my father was complaining about something or other, she picked up a plate of hot food and threw it at him. No one said anything. Not even my father, for once. We sat there like bumps on logs. Oh Jovette, she'd never done anything like that before. He was always complaining, constantly, about everything, you know how he does, he's very particular, but she'd never thrown anything at him before. It was scary."

Frightening for your mother, too. But Jovette didn't share her thoughts with Dale. It was a wonder, as far as Jovette was concerned, that Dale's mother hadn't done something like that years before. And it was a wonder she hadn't thrown something more violent than hot food. It upset Jovette to be around Dale's parents. Dale's father treated her mother like a naughty, no, like a disobedient child with some kind of learning disability.

"Did you remember to get my shirts from the cleaner?" he would ask, saying each word clearly and in a tone that implied it would be a miracle if she had.

Jovette wanted to scream at him, "LOOK AFTER YOUR OWN FUCKING SHIRTS!" She had to resist a strong urge to place herself between them, had to ignore her impulse to try to protect Dale's mother from the constant abuse.

Instead, she avoided visiting Dale's family but without ever telling Dale the real reason. She had no secrets from Dale except this one. She didn't like having a secret, but she feared the truth would harm their relationship. Dale adored her domineering father and had done so her whole life. She was his favorite and, although Dale was a strong feminist, she usually sided with him in any family dispute.

Jovette's sympathies were always with Dale's mother. What sort of hell had she gone through? What drove her to alcohol and the bedroom and solitary tears? No one went in. No arms held her. Her family went on with their lives on the other side of the bedroom door. She must have been terribly lonely and scared. Maybe she felt unwanted and unloved. Her children were leaving home. Maybe she felt old. One thing was certain: she had no one to talk to. She was completely isolated in her spotless suburban home.

Jovette propped her elbows on the kitchen counter and rested her face in her hands. Surely it wasn't menopause that depressed Dale's mother. She had so many other reasons to feel desperate about her life.

Jovette took a deep breath, deliberately, and then another one. As she inhaled the strong lilac smell, she had an idea. A shower. That was precisely what she needed, to make her feel clean and fresh. She placed the empty mug in the kitchen sink.

In the bathroom, she pulled the pad away from her underpants. The smell of menstrual blood filled her nostrils and she felt tears wanting to start in her throat and behind her eyes. She ignored the urge.

She stepped into the tub and stood beneath the full spray of hot water with closed eyes, not moving, and took slow deep breaths, inhaling the moist warm air. She had read a newspaper article the other day that said researchers believed menopause comes earlier for women who have never been pregnant. Millions of women went through menopause every year, had been going through menopause for hundreds of years, maybe thousands of years, and scientists were just beginning to do research now. She supposed they had only recently started to study menstruation, as well. That's what happens when you let men take charge of things. They ignore even the very basic needs and wants of women. If women were in charge, she wondered, would they ignore the needs and wants of men?

She decided she would tell Myra that it was the first day of her period. She would assure Myra that she would do her best to get the report finished by lunch time, but she had to deal with the telephone man, and if the report didn't get done, it didn't get done. It wouldn't be the end of the world. And if it was, tough.

She wouldn't say *tough* to Myra. Not unless Myra drove her to it with one of her sarcastic comments.

Jovette started to cry, small contained sobs that she could barely hear beneath the water. Cry, she told herself, let it all out and get it over with. Bending forward, covering her face with her hands, she sobbed and sobbed. Then she stood up and opened her mouth and howled. The noises sounded loud and painful.

She turned around and held her face up to the stream of hot water. Warm. Comforting. Jovette sniffed a few times as she reached for the soap. She felt better, much to her surprise. She rubbed the soap between her hands and told herself that she must have needed to cry, although she couldn't say why.

There was a knock on the bathroom door, which startled Jovette. She was so absorbed in her thoughts that she believed she was all alone. She dropped the soap.

Dale walked in, rubbing her eyes. "You okay? I thought I heard you crying."

"I was." Jovette pulled the shower curtain aside. "But I'm fine now. Don't worry about me. I was crying, I'm not sure why, but I'm fine now. Go back to sleep, sweetie. Sorry I woke you again."

"You sure you're okay?"

Jovette looked at Dale's face, thinking, I love her. "Yes, I'm sure. Listen, I've decided to go into work early, to get that report done. Shall I let you know when I'm leaving?"

"Yes, thanks. I'll get up then. Want a drive in?"

"No. The walk will do me good. I need the time to think about the report. I wouldn't mind a drive home tonight, though."

"Sure thing."

"I love you, Dale."

Dale smiled and pushed her lips into the shape of a kiss before turning away. She closed the bathroom door behind her.

Jovette pulled the shower curtain into place and bent down to pick up the soap. So much of life is surrounded by myths and half-lies, she thought. What will menopause be like? Hot flashes? What is it like to have hot flashes? Like the way she sweated profusely on hot humid afternoons in July? She smiled. She liked that hot, tropical feeling.

Tonight, after supper, she would phone and ask her mother what menopause had been like. Her mother had had a hysterectomy when she was thirty-nine, five years younger than Jovette was now, and Jovette had a vague memory of her taking a hormone drug for years afterwards. This has been quietly bothering Jovette ever since she read an article about hormone replacement therapy that said artificial hormones are dangerous. The writer admitted that to take the drug or not was a difficult decision for many women. It is possible that oestrogen helps to prevent osteoporosis and may decrease the risk of heart disease, but it is certain that hormones increase the chances of getting breast or uterine cancer. Was her mother at risk because she had taken hormones for years?

Whether or not to take the hormone was not a difficult decision for Jovette. She didn't like the idea of taking drugs of any kind into her body. If she needed any help, she would talk to her naturopathic doctor and try homeopathic remedies or herbs or vitamins or maybe some combination of all three.

She couldn't remember her mother behaving any differently after the operation. The doctor who had removed her mother's uterus told the family the fibroid was the size of a three-month pregnancy. But that doctor, the butcher, had removed absolutely everything—her mother's uterus, both fallopian tubes and ovaries—which was entirely unnecessary when the problem was simply the growth of benign uterine fibroids. That's what Jovette had concluded, based on a magazine article she read many years later. He had inflicted surgical menopause on her mother, without ever consulting her about it.

Her mother didn't seem to mind. Jovette recalled her saying something about it being a relief, because there wasn't the bother of bleeding every month. Not that her mother had minded bleeding every month. But during the last few years, because of the fibroids, the bleeding lasted ten days or longer and was more like a constant hemorrhage than a regular menstrual period.

The other thing she remembered her mother saying was the hysterectomy was a relief because she didn't have to worry about getting pregnant.

Pregnant! That wasn't a concern for Jovette. Noooo. Dale's fingers, amazing as they were, couldn't shoot sperm into her vagina.

Jovette smiled and then gave into her temptation to chuckle.

She lathered soap over her body and scrubbed with concentration. She had never tried to get pregnant, had never wanted to share her life with a child. But she had always believed she had the choice. Menopause would end the possibility of choice. No chance of children from this body. But, if she hadn't had children by age forty-four, was she likely to start now? Noooo. She chuckled. She wouldn't reconsider even if Dale's fingers could shoot sperm! She was perfectly content with her life just as it was.

What did it mean, that she remembered so little about her mother's forced menopause? Her clearest memory was when her mother returned to work five weeks after the surgery, rather than waiting the full six-week period recommended by the doctor. Her mother was proud of her ability to heal and recover quickly. And she was eager to get back to her job.

She had worked at the same government job since a couple of years after Jovette was born and, even now, forty-two years later, she enjoyed her job. She was turning sixty-five in three months, but she had no desire to retire. She was talking about reducing her hours from thirty-five to twenty-five hours a week, so she would have more time to do the volunteer work she loved at the Seniors' Dance and Laugh Institute.

Jovette reached between her legs and created a generous lather in her pubic hair. Enough of this standing around and having a good time. She had to get moving.

She turned around and around, letting the water wash over her and away. It was going to be a busy day and she would have to go to the bathroom umpteen times to pull a soiled pad away from her underpants always hoping she hadn't leaked through to her underpants and, if she had, hoping it hadn't gone through to her trousers. Her only pleasure was the feel of a fresh new pad, but it would be replaced all too soon by that unsettling wet sensation. Within a few hours her pubic hair would be matted with dried blood and clots. She would need a bath as soon as she got home tonight.

Stop! She would get through this day by living in the moment. She would not worry about the rest of the day.

She stepped out of the shower and wrapped a towel around her body, moving quickly to get a pad in place before menstrual blood ran down her thighs and dripped on the floor. Once the pad was in place and held there by a fresh pair of cotton underpants, beige ones this time, she towel-dried her body. Trying to position the pad to catch the flow no matter how she moved—sitting, standing, bending, walking—was guesswork. And she constantly wondered if it was time to change the pad. The monthly experience, year after year, had not made her an expert.

She threw the damp towel over the rack. There was no escape. Except, maybe, menopause. How much longer would she have to wait? Two years? Four years? She had read somewhere (was it the same article that said women start menopause around thirty-four or thirty-five?) that the average age for periods to stop was fifty. That was six years away.

She brushed her hair and looked around the room, at the thin blue bottle of Neal's Yard Remedies Soothing Bath Oil and the taller blue bottle of Crabtree & Evelyn Almond Massage Oil, at the striped blue and green towels folded neatly on the shelf, at the white tube of toothpaste with the illustration of a plump yellow lemon near the cap. She looked everywhere but at the mirror. Would menopause change her body? Would her breasts sag? Would her vagina dry up? Would she no longer feel sexual?

That thought bothered Jovette. She was sure she could cope with almost anything except losing her desire for Dale. Would she stop longing for the woman she loved? She stared at the tube of toothpaste and read the words over and over—*homéoclean* in large blue letters, *lemon* in small white letters.

She shook herself mentally. Better hurry up and get going, if she wanted an early start on the work day. She put her hair brush on the shelf and bent down to reach for the plastic-wrapped pads in the cabinet beneath the sink. She would wear clothes that would make her feel extra special today. But what? She decided to go with her first thoughts. The blue striped trousers, they were loose, and the yellow T-shirt. Both were made of soft cotton. Yes. That would do it.

And she would pamper herself today, she decided. She would go out for lunch, alone, to the restaurant around the corner, the pricey one that had fresh flowers on each table. She would go, even if the report wasn't finished, and have a pot of Lemon Mist tea while she studied the menu. She would order comfort food for lunch.

Maybe the house speciality, cream of cauliflower soup made with nut milk and served with rice crackers. Or maybe the lentil stew with organic brown rice. And afterwards, she would take a dessert back to the office to eat during the afternoon. Apple crumble. Or maybe a heaping bowl of fresh strawberries. Would strawberries be in season yet?

Wasn't it funny that none of her friends ever talked about menopause.

Jovette turned to the naked figure in the mirror and studied the solemn face and slightly swollen breasts and then looked at the two handfuls of pink (pink!) pads. She would start talking about menopause. She had to find women with the truth about it. If she knew what to expect, surely she would be ready. She would start by phoning her mother tonight.

Maybe, she thought as she turned away from the mirror, she would throw a party for herself to celebrate menopause. When? As soon as she didn't bleed for two months in a row, she would start planning the party. Yes.

What a daring idea. She turned back and looked at herself in the mirror and smiled broadly.

"CHANGING BACK"
Azalia Rodriguez

As I begin "the change of life," as my mother calls it, I think back to when I first "changed," when I first started my period. Starting my period when I was twelve was a "change of life." It ended life as I then knew it. I went from being a tomboy to having to be a "lady." After all, it meant I could get pregnant, therefore, I was a young woman. A fate worse than death for a person trying to prove that girls were just as good as boys. I was trying to prove to Dad that I was just as good (or better) than my boy cousins.

Dad owned a bakery in south Texas, also known as the Rio Grande Valley or just the Valley to most locals. Summertime meant that I could go work with Dad. I would wake up at three a.m. and help make bread deliveries of Mexican pan dulce to the many neighborhood stores that were commonplace in the 1950s. Each store had its unique spot where we would leave the bread ready for the early morning customers. One of the favorite spots was the top of the kerosene pump. It was a red squarish contraption with a flat top. Back then people would buy kerosene from the corner markets and, in many cases, the pump would be in the front of the store. Another likely location was on top of the soda machine. Soda machines were not like they are now, but more like a refrigerator on its back, which provided a flat, yet reachable surface. The whole point of the location for the bread boxes was that they had to be left high enough so that dogs wouldn't get at them. My job was to jump out of the truck or the back end of the station wagon, leave the box of bread, and jump back on for the ride to the next store.

What I liked most about working was spending time with Dad for the day. The morning always began with going out to breakfast for pancakes at this "art deco" style diner called The Highway Inn, with glass blocks lining the entry way. It was one of those places where you could smell what was on the menu. We always sat at the counter. Most of the work happened in the early hours before the sun came out. Other fringe benefits included having a soda at mid-morning and other snacks along the way. Getting a soda was an adventure of its own. After depositing a quarter, a customer would have to guide the soda bottle through maze-like channels to where the bottle could be pulled out.

All this happiness evaporated when my boy cousins visited from Houston. Before I was born, two of my cousins bonded with Dad, mainly because they were boys. So every time they came to visit, Dad took them to work with him and left me behind with my sisters and Mom. They become "sons" to my dad who had to wait until his fourth child to have a son. Back in those days, having sons meant you were macho, especially in the Latino culture. So Dad got a chance to pretend, while I seethed at home. When the first "change of life" came I couldn't pretend I was the boy Dad took to work.

The other and also important adventure that having a period curtailed was climbing trees. I still remember the trees I climbed, pretending they were airplanes and jumping out while yelling "Geronimo" as though we were parachuting. My sister fell out and hurt herself once so we were banned from tree-climbing until I convinced my parents that I shouldn't have to suffer for her clumsiness.

Shortly after I began "the change" our family had to move because Dad's bakery wasn't doing well financially. My favorite climbing trees stayed behind in Texas with my childhood while I went off to California with my family to start a new life. I pretty much stopped climbing trees, mainly because there weren't any nice climbing trees where we lived. I also stopped getting into fights with the boys in school. But I never really became a prissy young lady; tomboys rarely do.

I recently had the opportunity to visit south Texas again. The same trees are still there, but they seem much smaller. I didn't climb them though it would have been symbolic now that I'm on the verge of "changing" back. While visiting relatives I hadn't seen in years, my childhood came rushing back in torrents as I saw the house I lived in, the school and church I went to, and the trees I climbed.

In college I discovered a few things that made having periods somewhat easier: tampons and lemonade. Since I was a physical education major (no surprise), I spent much of my college years playing different sports. Leaving the game to deal with having my period wasn't something that I was going to let control me. Therefore double tampons helped me stay in the game. Lemonade was a discovery that one of my teachers (another jock) handed down. I used to drink lemonade on heavy days to stop or lessen the flow, depending on the amount of lemonade drunk. Our hiking trips usually included carrying lemonade in the water bottles.

Now that I am going through perimenopause, I asked Mom how going through menopause was for her. She went through it very quietly. Neither I nor any of my sisters really ever noticed that Mom was going through menopause. Mom's answer to my question was "just like I started, I stopped." Not wanting to believe this, I asked her various times, nonchalantly. Same answer always. I remember the stories Mom used to tell us about the change of life. They were usually about women family members who got in bad moods or had the experience of "gushing" while at public events. That was enough to scare me, but not enough to stop wishing my period to be gone.

One of my sisters recently mentioned having hot flashes and asked me if I was having them. We went through a bit of family sharing with Mom chiming in about wet nightgowns from the night sweats. Of course perimenopause is a new phenomenon, I certainly didn't hear about it from any source until recently talking to friends who are my age. Mom didn't have the luxury of perimenopause with doctors taking time to explain hormonal changes. My sister's doctor explained to her what was going on. I hear stories that many women still don't get respect from their doctors regarding symptoms of perimenopause or menopause for that matter. With those fears and fears of doctors in general I have not yet gone to a doctor about my symptoms. I find it difficult to go about finding a woman doctor who is okay with having lesbian clients. I do plan on looking for a doctor because I do feel it is important to decide about hormones. In the meantime, I take every opportunity to announce changes in temperature, usually by saying, "Is it hot or am I having a hot flash?" To which many women respond by saying, "You're too young to be going through that." Maybe it's time that menopause came out of the closet as a natural function and a milestone in our lives.

As I go through night sweats and hot flashes (or power surges as some out-of-the-closet women call them), I know that the time is getting closer for "changing back." I try to check in with my wife to make sure that mood swings don't affect our relationship. Being eleven years older has its drawbacks because the two of us aren't going through it together, but she is very understanding. She recently read about women experiencing menopause slowing down when it comes to sexual activity and said "I don't think that will happen to you." I'm hoping it won't. So far that aspect of our life isn't being affected. We are still very much in love (our seventh year anniversary is next month).

At a recent family get-together, I noticed my eleven-year-old niece, who is very much a tomboy, angrily beginning her "change of life." It took me back to the disruption it caused in my life. Thirty-two years and counting, I'm looking forward to "changing back."

"DON'T WORRY, DEAR, IT'S REALLY ALL IN YOUR GLANDS"
Sarah Dreher

Listen, I know what it is to be on the cutting edge. I mean, I got with the program back in the seventies, and I never left it. I dropped my patriarchal father-given name and took my mother's patriarchal father-given name. I can say "lesbian" without stuttering, never call myself a "gay woman." I know the names of the triune aspects of the Goddess, which to pray to for what during which phase of the moon, and which candles and oils to use to get my intentions up to the astral plane. I can run through the Wiccan holidays without thinking twice. I can even do it in Welsh. I can cook vegetarian, lacto-vegetarian, ovo-lacto-vegetarian, pisce-vegetarian, low-fat, sugar-free, or 1950's-style patio luau. I make a great barley casserole, and an even greater jello-mold-with-Dr. Pepper. I've dried my own herbs with and without food dehydrators. I know what chamomile can do for you, and how valerian would be the perfect sedative if it didn't attract rodents. I've traded services instead of fees, and have been known to enjoy an occasional recreational drug back in the good old days of decriminalization. I know all about "womyn," "wimmin," "womon," and "womoon," and which is singular and which is plural. I call myself Feminist, and I'm proud to be a Crone.

So don't tell me I don't know how to be cool about menopause, because I've been there, Sister. I've been there politically correct, and I've been there politically incorrect. I've been there and back. It's not the end of the world. I miss being a fertile woman about as much as I miss my wisdom teeth. It has never occurred to me to feel dismay over the passing of my youth. I'm just as much of a "real woman" now as I was fifteen years ago—except that now I'm a real woman who can't become pregnant. I was never really into breeding or bleeding. So menopause didn't bring any great loss to me, but it sure isn't any Goddess-given gift to sit around glorifying and beating drums about, either. Let me tell you how it was. I breezed through the period-stopping part, no problem. Made jokes about all the money I was saving on tampons, didn't know what all the fuss was about. It was a relief, especially the premenstrual part. I mean, who among us is going to miss the anxiety, the adolescent awkwardness, and the swollen breasts. Ah, yes, the swollen breasts. That had been a problem during my totally wasted child-bearing years. But when menopause began to signal its approach, "swollen breasts" became the understatement of the century. Imagine your worst premenstrual experience with water in the boobs, and multiply it by ten. We are talking *swollen*, kids. We are talking can't turn over in bed because they slide to the side and pull, and you think someone just stabbed you. We are talking thin-skinned grapefruits. We are talking water balloons with nerve endings. Like someone has a hose stuck in there, and they keep pushing water in, and you know they're going to pop any second, and DON'T TOUCH ME. As soon as the periods stopped, that stopped. (And, not to give away the dramatic ending, it hasn't returned.)

I had an occasional hot flash during and after my long, slow road to recovery from tampon-addiction. Only an occasional one. It was kind of amusing, really. It felt like blushing all over, starting at the knees and flowing up my body to the top of my head. Not a bad sensation. Sometimes it was even pleasant, once I grew accustomed to the fact that you could fry an egg on the back of my neck. They went away as quickly as they came on, and happened mostly at night or first thing in the morning, at times when I'd change my center of gravity. But when you live in New England, being able to warm a bed just by lying down in it is a definite asset. Sometimes women will even rent you for a night or two, which can be very… But I digress.

I decided early on that I wasn't going the nasty fake-hormone route, and I figured all my mother's moaning and groaning about "the Change" was just further evidence of her world-class neuroticism. She hit menopause and I hit puberty at just about the same time. It wasn't a pretty sight. There's a lot to be said for boarding school.

Anyway, I was doing fine, thank you. Except that the hot flashes started increasing. Maybe there was a month or two in there when nothing at all happened, but I don't remember it. To tell you the truth, I was beginning to have trouble remembering much at all.

Someone could say something to me—or I could say something—and ten minutes later it was as if the conversation had never taken place. I know, some women live their whole lives that way, but I hadn't. In fact, I'd been greatly envied for my memory. Especially during the '70s, when the F.B.I. was on the loose and we Lesbian Feminist therapists were burning our files like crazy. But that's another story. So it was strange to have these lapses and slippages, but at first it didn't bother me much. Everyone turns a little loose in the mind when they're trying to do a million things. That was early on. Later, it began to get frustrating, and then downright frightening. When you're half way through a sentence and can't remember what you were talking about back at the beginning, I figure it's time to ask yourself a few questions. If you can remember what they are.

After a while "hot flash" began to take on an entirely new meaning. They were coming at the rate of twenty to thirty a day, not just more frequent but more intense. No more maidenly blushing, this was like fire. I never got to the stage of having to change my clothes because I was sweating so much, but it was really taking a toll on me. These were not, I repeat, *not* Power Surges, so spare me the cute stuff. They were uncomfortable, unattractive, and enervating. I think I hit the absolute bottom on a visit to Disney World. It was November, usually a pretty good month to get out of New England. But they were having a heat wave. So was I. It was humid, as only Florida can be, and I was retaining water. I couldn't perspire, unless I was granted a hot flash. And those things were never coming when I needed them. Oh, no, they'd stopped being funny and convenient, and were showing their true nasty nature. I could feel the water in me, but it wouldn't come out. It was just there under the surface. I couldn't tell where I left off and the humidity began. My energy was drained. I learned three important things about Walt Disney World on that trip: there is no air, there are no available benches, and there are no accessible shade trees. Walt Disney World is no Magic Kingdom when you're menopausal.

There were other problems. Things I didn't immediately associate with plummeting levels of estrogen. My hair started thinning. Not enough to be alarming, but more than the usual bit of shedding we all do. My skin turned dry and papery, not just in the vaginal area, but over my entire body. I was tired all the time. It got so that I sometimes felt too tired and weak to cross the room. My joints hurt. After getting up in the morning, it would take me five minutes or more to walk the stiffness out of my ankles. Mornings are never a great deal of fun for me. This did not make them more attractive. In spite of being too tired and stiff to do it, I was having to get up five and six times a night to go to the bathroom. At that time, I couldn't just sleepwalk to take care of that bodily function the way most of us do, because I had an old dog with kidney trouble, and every time I got up it woke him up. Every time he woke up he had to go out, and sometimes he didn't make it to the door and then I really woke up. We were quite a pair. It does a number on your peace of mind to wake up five or six times a night, believe me. And that's not even counting the times the hot flashes would wake me, though I would usually have to get up then, too, just because I was awake, just like that old dog.

The bathroom problem wasn't just limited to night time, either. It could happen anywhere. I'd be driving along, not a care in the world, and suddenly HAVE TO GO. And I mean HAVE TO. No waiting until I got home, or until the next rest area. No thinking of something else and getting your mind off it. No crossing your legs in a ladylike manner to put yourself on "hold." No waiting until I'd walked from the car port to the house. I mean SUDDEN and AWFUL. Many moonlit lawns and forest clearings have been blessed by my holy water. At first, I didn't associate menopause with the "urinary urgency." That's what they call it, if you want to look it up or talk to a member of the medical establishment about it. "Urinary urgency." It's one of those medical euphemisms, like "you might experience a little discomfort for a few days," which really means you're going to be in screaming agony for two weeks. "Urinary urgency" is to panic peeing as "a little discomfort" is to major surgery without anesthesia.

And let's not forget the mood swings. We expect the mood swings. That's what we've all heard about menopause—hot flashes and mood swings. What they don't tell you is that you never swing up. You swing from despair to rage, with periods of nothing (no pun intended) in between. I'd find myself crying. Not "for no reason" as they try to make us believe. I had a very good reason for crying. I was crying because suddenly, without warning, I didn't know how

I was going to go on living. Everything was awful, and it would never get any better. Never. Sure, I told myself this was only raging (or collapsing) hormones. It didn't make any difference. I was more depressed than I'd ever dreamed of feeling, and I could talk myself blue in the face but that didn't make it GO AWAY. Knowing there was a cause, knowing what the cause was, knowing it wasn't my fault or the fault of anyone around me didn't change my feelings one iota, the way it does with normal feelings. This was chemical conviction.

Sometimes I'd be furious at the people I cared most about, convinced I'd been betrayed, neglected, double-crossed, you name it. Sure, we all feel that way sometimes, and sometimes it's true. But these were feelings and thoughts that would seem to fall into my head out of nowhere, and would go away for no reason. While they were around, there was nothing I could do to make them leave. Even though the rational part of me knew they were irrational, it didn't matter. I couldn't identify the triggers and avoid them, because there were no consistent triggers. Maybe no triggers at all, not out there anyway. The real triggers were little hormonal BBs carousing around inside my body. This craziness had a mind of its own.

The targets of my rages weren't limited to my nearest and dearest, either. You *really* didn't want to cut me off in traffic, or pull out in front of me, or have thirteen items in your shopping cart and stand in the "twelve-item only" check-out line. When the mood was on me, I was the crazed Vietnam vet, the flashing-back bad-tripper, the Incredible Hulk.

The best I could achieve, with all my hours of talking to myself, was to keep myself from acting on ideas I firmly believed were both absolutely untrue and absolutely true. "Wait a while" became my mantra.

One day I had an argument with a friend. I'm normally a pretty mild mannered person. It takes a lot to get me angry. To get me *really* angry, you have to do something Really Bad to me, and/or you have to do it over a long period of time. Arguments make me want to die. You can say whatever you want about fights being good for a relationship, but to me it's two egos clashing over a misunderstanding and I'd rather sort it out than slug it out. So "having an argument with a friend" is an event of major importance and trauma to me. I don't remember what it was all about (naturally, having no memory), but I remember that the anger I felt made every cell in my body hurt and I had to leave the house. Later, when I apologized, she said, perfectly normally, "It's all right. Everyone has little spats now and then."

"We're not talking about a 'little spat,' " I replied. "We're talking about one of us was going to be dead." I was glad the real extent of my fury hadn't come across. But it made me realize how far my emotions were from what was really going on, and how difficult it can be to make that real to someone who hasn't experienced it.

I have a rifle I keep for protection on trips to my cabin. I decided I'd better keep the rifle in one room and the ammunition in another.

So I finally got the message. This menopause business wasn't any rite of passage, or any "all-in-your-mind" kind of thing. It wasn't just some normal pothole along the Interstate of Life. It was an illness, and I had it, and I was in trouble.

I did the first thing any sane person does when faced with an illness—I went to the book store. There wasn't a whole lot of information (there's more now), and what there was seemed to fall into one of two camps:

1) The belief that hormone replacement therapy is terrible, dangerous, unnecessary, cancer-causing, and/or politically incorrect, or

2) The belief that hormone replacement therapy is the answer to every problem you ever had or ever anticipate having.

Both these approaches seemed a little unbalanced. The library wasn't much better. Time to make an appointment with the doctor.

He suggested we try homeopathic remedies first.

Okay, that seemed reasonable, and fit in with my need to do as little unnatural medicating as possible. Trouble was, it didn't work. After three months of going to his office and sticking out my tongue to receive some blessed drops, and feeling like a baby bird waiting for its dinner, I was still as miserable and sick and dangerous-feeling as before.

So we decided to try hormones. Or Hormone Replacement Therapy, "HRT," as we say in the in-group.

I had one really bad moment, when the doctor looked me straight in the eye and said, ominously, "Are you prepared to bleed?" It was sort of like joining a church, or taking the C.I.A. oath, or something. Like this was my last chance to get away. But I pulled myself up to my full five foot four inches and said, "Yes."

I know what you're expecting next. "Everything is fine and life is beautiful once more," or, "It was a total failure and the most useless experience of medico-patriarchal arrogance I've ever gone through."

You really think things are that simple?

First we had to find the correct level of estrogen and progesterone for my needs. This is done very scientifically—by trial and error. There are four different levels of estrogen available for the kind I took, and three levels of progesterone, and you really need to try it for two months to be sure of the effect. This gives us twelve different combinations. Guess how long it takes to do that? No cheating, and no pocket calculators allowed.

We started out at a high level of estrogen. I felt great. No more mood swings, no more sleepless nights. My energy level was rising, my skin was regaining some texture. Even the doctor noticed that I looked more alive—and you know how observant doctors are. If you haven't been weighed and had your blood pressure taken by the nurse, you could be choking to death and they wouldn't notice.

I was supposed to take the estrogen alone until the first of the month, then add progesterone for ten days, then I would get a period. Hah! Halfway through those ten days I started to bleed. And I do mean bleed. I bled as if it were the last thing I'd ever do. I'll spare you the gory details (no pun intended), but suffice it to say I didn't do anything for nearly a week except bleed and eat iron-rich food. So we had to stop cold-turkey and start over, and work our way up juggling this and that.

To make a long and boring story short, two *years* later we finally settled for the best deal we could get. Needless to say, during those two years, I was a real joy to be around. Life of the party.

The best deal falls a little short of the ideal. I still get an occasional hot flash in the morning or at night. I usually have to get up once during the night to hit the bathroom. Once in a while my emotions take a dip. My eyes tend to be dry and I get eyestrain easily (this is sometimes a side effect of estrogen). I bleed pretty heavily at times. Sometimes the way I bleed feels odd, not natural, kind of jerky. But wanting to kill myself and the people I love most in the world wasn't natural, either. I really don't miss that at all.

I don't forget things, and I can concentrate pretty well. My hair's not falling out any more and my skin's not drying up any more. I'm not back to my pre-menopausal self, but at least I can function, and there's no way I'd give up the gains I've made.

You can get almost every woman who's experiencing or about to experience menopause to talk about it. All you have to do is bring it up. We know we're the first generation that's willing to talk about it, and most of us feel an obligation to pass along what we know and what we don't know. We know where ignorance has gotten us—absolutely nowhere. We've come up with all kinds of other explanations for what's happening to us because we haven't had any information. I don't mean information out of books, or obscure medical terminology. I mean *real* information, the kind women share with each other, about the true things in life and what they're experiencing. Some of the answers we give ourselves out of ignorance are truly frightening.

I have a friend who had never heard of the memory loss that goes with menopause. She was convinced she had early Alzheimer's and was terrified.

Other women think they're coming down with an illness when they have the first tiny flashes of fever-like heat.

Some worry about things like cancer and bladder infections and their bodies deteriorating.

The fatigue can feel like Chronic Fatigue Syndrome or worse.

The joint stiffness is often mistaken for arthritis.

If we have a family history of anything, we're bound to start to worry about it. Most of us attribute our symptoms to aging, because that's what we've been taught.

Our real disease is ignorance. Ignorance added to the passion our media have for scaring us to death because fear sells advertising space, and most advertising is geared toward fear—fear of illness, fear of embarrassment, fear of being left out, fear of being laughed at, you name it.

The very first sign I had that things were starting to change happened one winter day when I went out to fill the bird feeder, carrying the feed in the usual coffee can. My fingers went numb. They'd never done that before, and it was disturbing, since I chalked it up to instant *karma* for my years of unhealthy living and debauchery, and was afraid it was some kind of brain damage. But that stopped, too, once I started taking estrogen, so I guess it wasn't my evil ways. Unless estrogen can cure us of the wages of sin. Interesting thought. I don't recall ever hearing that easy numbing of the extremities could be a symptom of menopause.

How many other women have been worried sick about memory problems, insomnia, bladder weakness and other strange symptoms? And what explanations do they give themselves? What kind of horror stories do they tell themselves?

The good news is, there really is help out there. Not only hormone replacement, but acupuncture, sunflower seeds and dong quai and all kinds of herbal remedies. All of them work for some women. For many women the hormone route wouldn't even be necessary. It was for me, and I'm glad it was available. Different women respond differently to HRT. Some can't tolerate it. Some are allergic to the estrogen. Some have political reservations about it. And some don't, and never will, need it. But for those who do need some help—or who think life is supposed to be more than merely bearable—there are a lot of things you can try. Herbs, diet, meditation (though I've never figured out how you can meditate when you can't even concentrate). I'm trying acupuncture to make up for the remaining annoyances the hormone replacement can't resolve. The acupuncturist says hot flashes are a matter of too much hot yang and not enough cooling yin. Whatever.

My mother became an alcoholic in the second half of her life. I'm convinced she was helped along by the emotional pain of menopause. They didn't have hormone replacement therapy in her day. Menopause was something to be ashamed of, not to talk about. Those were the days when cancer was called "The Big C" and spoken of in whispers. Women didn't share their worries or their solutions with one another. They didn't share anything with one another. So there was no peer support for her. If women complained of being depressed and "nervous," doctors patted them on the head and dismissed them. And the smart-ass psychologists, in all their male-identified arrogance, declared middle-aged women were grieving because they'd no longer be attractive sexual partners for men, no longer able to bear children, which is all women were really meant to do, anyway. It was the perfect no-win situation. "We can't help you, so we'll declare there's nothing wrong with you, it's all in your mind. You're just vain and neurotic." That was enough to shut anyone up.

My mother bought into the myths and prejudices of her day, and so did I. She judged herself, and I judged her, through that conventional lens. Now I often wonder what it would have been like for her if she'd had the help and support I've been lucky enough to have. And I wonder what she would have been like, and what we would have been like together. When I began to experience the symptoms of menopause, I understood so much of what she had gone through forty years ago. Maybe things would have been different.

Nowadays, I sometimes get the feeling women who choose hormone replacement therapy are looked down on in the lesbian community. It's as if we've sold out. This is unsettling, because for many of us HRT has kept us alive. I know women who can't use it, and their lives are hell. We're all different, and what works for one doesn't necessarily work for another. I could have eaten sunflower seeds until I was as round as an apple, and it wouldn't have given me enough estrogen. There are many, many women for whom menopause is no problem, and I really think they shouldn't mess with it. I also think those of us who do have a problem should do what we can about it. Lesbians are few in number, and precious. We have to help each other stay productive, self-respecting, and alive.

If I could come up with one golden sentence to summarize the most important thing I've learned during this life transition, it's this:

This is the real thing, it's no fun, and something can be done about it.

I'd like to pass along a few helpful hints for those women coming along:

1) The most comfortable sleeping clothes are V-necked tee-shirts (preferably old and roomy) and boxer shorts. (The truly femme can go with the tee-shirt alone. Or the boxer shorts alone.)

2) Don't panic, and don't believe the scare stories. If you have to take hormone replacement, find out everything you can about it. There are still a lot of negative myths floating around. Most of them are based on research that was done in the '70s. Check it out.

3) Remember, many women still have half their lives ahead of them once they reach menopause. Bleedless isn't the same as bloodless. The fun is just beginning.

4) If you find yourself feeling and acting like your mother (Goddess forbid!), don't forget that every other woman your age is probably feeling and acting much the same way you are, and is probably afraid she's turning into her mother, too. You're not.

5) Talk about it. Talk to any woman who'll listen, and listen to any woman who'll talk. We have to break the silence around this. Besides, it'll help those younger women, who are still so young they take everything personally and blame themselves for it, to understand your moods aren't something they did.

6) Use it. It really is a wonderful way to bond with other women. If you're over the age of forty and want to start a conversation with another woman over forty, start talking about menopause. Instant sisterhood. It cuts across race, class, and sexual orientation. It's part of our women's culture.

Boys have their war stories. We have our menopause stories. Maybe we should start clubs all over the country, "Veterans of Menopause," or "Menovets." (For those of you who are cringing over the use of Men...to describe it, let me suggest Womenopause or Womenovets or Fempause.) We could sit around in dark rooms where the boys aren't allowed and are afraid to go, what with all those women talking about *women* things and drink herbal teas and share our experiences and figure out ways to take over the world. We could form our own marching bands and call ourselves something like "Hecate's Amazons" and insist on marching in their parades. That would really upset them. We could even have our own parades and holidays, and not let them march, and make all the stores close, especially the liquor stores, and make it a no-hunting day, and not let them deliver the mail, and if they want to go to the bank, forget it!

Today I ran into a long-time friend in the local Super Stop and Shop, and we got to talking about the Pause. She said she started having the symptoms—the hot flashes, memory loss, etc.—ten years after her last period. Of course, she couldn't believe those symptoms were menopause-related because she'd stopped bleeding. The same thing had happened to me. I'd always thought you had those symptoms while you were stopping, and when you had your final period, all the rest of it stopped. My friend has MS, so when all the low-estrogen problems began out of the blue, she was truly terrified. She finally had the problems diagnosed properly, signed on for the hormone tour, and feels she got her life back.

As we talked we got into the inevitable "getting older isn't nearly as bad as they told us it would be" conversation. We agreed, all things considered, that middle age has a lot to recommend it. The most wonderful thing about it, to me, is that a lot of little things that used to make us nervous or anxious or self-conscious just don't any more. I don't know exactly when they go away; you just suddenly realize that you haven't been bothered by this or that in a while. You don't worry so much about how you say things, and you don't come home after an evening with friends and rerun every conversation to make sure you were okay. And you don't take so much crap from people. As she said, "If they're rude to me at the check-out, I just threaten to take my clothes off."

"I know what you mean," I replied. "It scares the shit out of the boys. Of course, half the time the young women just say, 'Gee, my mother gets like that.'"

"True," said my friend. "Well, gotta run." As she was wheeling her cart away, she turned back. "By the way, there's a special on Maxi-Pads in aisle eight."

HOT FLASH TO WARM GLOW
Jean Mountaingrove

I was shocked when the doctor casually said I was pre-menopausal. I was only forty-three. I wasn't thinking of growing old until some far distant time, and in my mind, menopause was definitely the gateway to "old." I was there for a PAP smear, not any gratuitous predictions about wrinkling, withering and shriveling up. "Well, you've been pre-menopausal since you were born," I joked to myself to cover my anger—and dismissed it.

In fact, he was correct. Four years later my hot flashes began. My periods were not as regular and menstrual pain was a little less than I had suffered previously. And I had changed. In those four years I had become a feminist and a lesbian and was considering the importance of menstruation for women's psychic development and wisdom.

So I watched menopause come upon me. From feminism I learned that all our life experiences are valuable. I knew I should keep a diary of my menopausal experiences, but I didn't do it. I did write a poem, "Aging Amazon."

How fortunate to "do" menopause with a mid-life woman partner, I congratulated myself. How odd and alone I would feel with a husband. No matter how "understanding" he was, how could he possibly understand as another menopausal woman could?

Our first hot flashes went unrecognized. We attributed them to the hot day, to the electric blanket, to the steep climb. Eventually we figured it out. You see, we were the first women in our social circle to reach menopause. It was at least three more years before an older woman arrived. She was still having hot flashes and sweats that woke her at night when she was fifty-five.

Now it is sixteen years later and I am still having hot flashes that wake me at night. When my lover visits, we laugh as we ask each other, "Is this your hot flash or mine?" And then we move a little apart until the heat passes.

With each hot flash I wonder if it will be my last one, or if they will go on forever. I'm sure I'll miss them if or when they ever end. Like breast feeding, they are an intense and often pleasurable sensation. And when the experience is over it will never return.

I have tried to describe my hot flashes to curious younger women. I considered using silver paint on canvas to convey the tingling sensation that often starts on my legs and flows upward, circling my thighs and then my arms, flushing my throat and face, moistening my upper lip. And each time a little different. Very wet hot flashes are recent for me. In the past when I began to feel hot, I would ask if others noticed it too (meaning, Is this room hot?). Then I realized I could just draw my finger above my upper lip. Damp? Hot flash.

Sometimes that gradual sensuous tingling doesn't occur. The first warning then is vague irritability. I don't like what's happening. I want to leave. But as soon as I'm aware of my impatience, the heat begins and I realize my discomfort is due to inner events, not outer ones, and the hot flash follows.

"And how frequent are they?" is a favorite question of my fortyish friends. From a few each day now to more than twenty a day in the beginning, I tell them. This is a guess because I didn't keep that diary. I hope others are. From sharing experiences with other old women, I believe we are as individual in menopause as we are in menstruation.

I am sweating now. I fan myself with my papers. I have pulled my shirt above my breasts. I wipe my face, throat and chest. When I have a hot flash and am alone, the urge to pull off my shirt is irresistible.

Now two minutes later, I am cold and dry.

When I was about fifty with very frequent and intense hot flashes, I sometimes had brief thoughts of suicide. And I mean brief. I would be writing and suddenly think, "It's no use. My life is meaningless. I can't go on." Just out of the blue I would feel utterly hopeless. I would put down my pen and tell my partner. By the time she could come across the room to comfort me I was all right, cheerful and ready to resume my writing. This happened perhaps once or twice a day for a few weeks. It convinced me that hormones affect my feelings powerfully.

Lowered levels of hormones also affect my energy. Mystified at first by sudden fatigue, I have gradually identified that "all gone" feeling unlike any other kind of tiredness as a hormone drop. I have to rest a while until my energy returns.

Hot flashes and tiredness sent me to the clinic. I was in fine health so the doctor offered estrogen replacement therapy. I accepted his prescription slip but couldn't bring myself to get the pills.

I am a skeptic about the latest medical miracle for our problems. I have witnessed the Salk vaccine; it gave polio to some of its users. I witnessed the birth control pills; they gave embolisms to some of their users. I witnessed the IUDs; they perforated many a uterus. I'll never know what life would be like for me if I had chosen to take the estrogen, offered to me with hints of eternal youth and never getting osteoporosis. I'll stick with nature's plan.

Medically, menopause is defined as having occurred when a woman has had no menstrual flow for one year. This is a tidy definition for statistics but difficult unless a woman keeps a careful calendar. Even when that year is over our hormones keep changing. The phrase women use, "going through the change," better describes my experience of a long transition. The obvious change that I ceased to bleed monthly was all that I was told to expect, but there are other significant changes.

I had heard of "the middle age spread" with the implication that women just let themselves get sloppy. I learned that estrogen is stored in fatty tissue, so the increased fat around my hips stored estrogen to ease the effects of my irregular and lowering estrogen production.

In response to my body's changes and the new sensations I experienced, I had to notice that some things were ending for me. I had to realize that even as my periods ended, someday my life would end. Far in the future, I hope, but closer than I thought during the years of my familiar monthly cycling. I looked for a new way to gauge my time and pace my aspirations.

This society dismisses these profound shifts in my body and consciousness as "post-menopausal." As if menses are what is truly significant in my life and after they end the next thirty to forty years are just a "post" script. But I asked myself, what are the potential benefits inherent in this natural unaltered process?

Menopause is not just a single event or ceremony, it is really a long transition, a change on all levels of a woman's inner life. Beyond the obvious changes in our bodies there are other profound changes in our interests, focus, direction, and aspirations.

FROM HOT FLASH TO WARM GLOW: FROM PASSION TO AFFECTION—TWENTY YEARS PAST MENOPAUSE

Twenty years without a period and I'm still having hot flashes at seventy: episodes of mild restlessness followed by increasing warmth which spreads over my body and then a pleasant tingling like effervescence gradually fades away. Hot flashes had decreased in frequency and intensity over the years until about six months ago when I had my first experience of night sweats. But now all of that has been replaced by a warm tingling glow. So long a part of my life, I think I may miss these sensations if they ever stop!

I have never taken hormone pills or shots. I believe that was and is the right choice for me. I have had no reproductive health problems or signs of osteoporosis.

For the past year I have taken a daily vinegar tincture of female toners (nettles, lemon balm, motherwort and raspberry leaves) along with hawthorne for angina symptoms. Perhaps these herbs have some effects on my hormone balance...and these continuing "glows".

The restlessness preceding the warmth wakes me several times a night. It stirs me to throw off the covers and get up to use the toilet. I usually go to sleep quickly, so don't mind. I joke that these nocturnal jaunts keep me limber enough to roll out of bed and pull on my socks in the morning even when my back is stiff with arthritis.

Another new experience for me in the past several years: four friends in their early fifties have broached this same question. "Will my sexual desire ever return?" And then, "I'm just not interested in sex anymore." Two others have volunteered "Sex is fine but it isn't the priority like it used to be."

For me, desire waned when closeness in my relationship went. Desire bloomed again at sixty when I fell in love, but energy and stamina for intense love-making and responding had diminished, alas!

I have been single and self-sexual for more than five years. I don't yearn for love-making or a lover. I appreciate the freedom and peace of my single life. The thrills, joys and delights of loving sex are precious memories. I celebrate them in women's lives. The pleasures of loving companionship would enrich my life, a life already full of loving friends and family and many satisfactions. If there will be no lover-companion in my future, I still feel blessed. Remember: just as there *is* life after menopause, there is delight after orgasm.

PRESCRIBING FOR MENOPAUSAL WOMEN
Barbara Bennett, MD

I've learned more about menopause from my friends than I did in medical school, but then that's true of a lot of things. At age forty-nine menopause is a part of the landscape of my life. As long as I don't think I'm hemorrhaging, I've learned to tolerate large variations in normal bleeding providing it's at least nineteen days from beginning to beginning. I thought I was buying my last menstrual supplies about five years ago, but now I'm back to buying large boxes again.

I think menopause waxes in the mid to late thirties for most women and wanes twenty years later. A fourth of all women stop menstruating before forty-two, half between forty-two and forty-eight, and only a fourth are still bleeding at almost fifty. I'll soon have bled for forty years, which reduces my risk of osteoporosis but raises my risk of breast cancer. I find it interesting that the same number of white women aged fifty to eighty-five die of breast cancer as die of hip fractures due to osteoporosis – 2.7 percent

I've learned my nipples can be as sore as they were in puberty and that I have most of my hot flashes while menstruating (when my estrogen levels are lowest). I've found herbal combinations from the health food store and homeopathic remedies that work really well for the flashes. They've also been effective for my partner, who would have had to be put to sleep if we hadn't done something.

I thought I would take hormone replacement, but I'm beginning to wonder. One study showed that if you start estrogen within three years of menstrual cessation, the bones build to almost what they would have been if you'd started immediately. As I get a lot of exercise and, at 140 pounds, am a lot heavier than I like, I think I want those three years to see what my change is like.

On the other hand, I watched both of my grandmothers shrink. One spent the last years of her life in constant pain from osteoporosis. This, plus the fact that I'm an ex-smoker, bore and nursed children and am recovering from anorexia, make me think I should start the hormones when I quit bleeding.

In my practice I strongly recommend estrogen to women who have significant risk factors for heart disease including smoking, diabetes, hypertension, surgical menopause, menopause before age thirty-seven and strong family history of heart disease. I also recommend it to women at risk for osteoporosis: smoking, family history, small frame, diabetes, medical problems that prevent physical activity and maybe thyroid disease.

I am backing off a little on recommending estrogen solely to prevent osteoporosis since we now have better tests for it, effective, fairly safe treatment and bone-building regimens. Of course I ride smokers about smoking, but if they are at risk for both problems, I really push the drugs. There is now some concern about how much benefit smokers get from estrogen, since nicotine interferes with its metabolism.

If a woman still has her uterus, I encourage adding progesterone. Since only six to seven women out of a thousand get cancer of the uterus on estrogen alone, I will prescribe only estrogen if they are willing to get endometrial biopsies periodically, and sometimes even if they aren't, but clearly understand the small risk of uterine cancer. I've had three endometrial biopsies myself, for bleeding too much and/or too often. Eventually I hope pelvic ultrasound for endometrial thickness will replace the biopsies, but the evidence is not in on that yet.

Progesterone has more negative side effects and less clear benefit. I give estrogen first, then after a month prescribe progesterone five mg. a day for two weeks. That gives the woman some idea how she feels on each drug. Natural progesterones made from yams are harder to get/take and more expensive, but have fewer side effects, and I think they are more beneficial.

There are some real differences in delivery forms of estrogens. Most women do fine with pills. Those who have nausea, breast tenderness and/or water retention often do better on patches or monthly injections. Vaginal creams absorb systemically and can give elderly women relief from bladder problems, prolapse, vaginal dryness and discomfort without side effects. I understand a ring placed in the vagina that will be effective for three months is going to be released soon.

I avoid conjugated estrogens made from 'pregnant mares urine' (bet ya'll can put that name together...) because I don't believe it can be collected in a safe, humane fashion. The drug companies discuss that subject with me on a regular basis

I do not believe estrogen increases cancer risk, and with progesterone it reduces uterine cancer risk.

If a woman is having breast tenderness, low energy, or lack of sex drive after two to three months, I add testosterone, usually as Estratest (or half dose Estratest HD). Testosterone can cause increased appetite, muscle mass, hair growth and even liver problems, but usually doesn't. Some women feel a lot better on it.

My preferred regimen is 0.5-1.0 mg. estrogen a day, and 2.5 mg. of progesterone. With this regimen the average woman who has just quit bleeding will do a lot of spotting, but without cramps or PMS, and quit bleeding within three months. Almost all women stop bleeding within six months. I don't need to explain how few average women there are. If they're still bleeding at six months, I get an endometrial biopsy and/or pelvic ultrasound for endometrial thickness. Many perimenopausal women prefer to cycle their progesterone, 10 mg. per day for ten days, or 5 mg. per day for fourteen days every one to two months. That way they know when they will bleed. Women who are years out from their last menses seldom see any blood on the continuous low dose regimen.

If a woman does not seem to be at risk for heart disease or osteoporosis, I discuss the issue of using any kind of treatment at all, and let her choose.

I do not believe that HRT affects depression, mid-life crisis, or arthritis. There is evidence that it may considerably reduce risk of Parkinson's disease and/or Alzheimer's. It certainly improves bladder function, reduces infections, vaginal dryness, nosebleeds, and lowers LDL, the bad cholesterol.

About half of menopausal women have hot flashes, some for the rest of their lives, though they usually diminish in intensity. An interesting association was identified with educational level—women with more education have fewer hot flashes. Also, women tend to do what their mothers did.

There are many treatments for hot flashes other than estrogen. I suspect some natural remedies work by stimulating or mimicking estrogen in the body. I would be suspicious of the ingredients in

Chinese medicines, some of which contain synthetic drugs. For women with little or no reason to take estrogen, or those who can't because of previous cancers, liver problems, or side effects, I try other drugs and encourage them to try health food store alternatives. Actually, I usually encourage women to try health food store alternatives, which I think are safer and I know are cheaper.

A doctor is a listener, a lifetime student and, with her patients, a problem-solver. My approaches to menopause are as varied as the women who experience it, myself included.

TWO OLD MAIDS
Judith E. Beckett and Paij Wadley-Bailey

Two old maids
Laying in the bed
One leaned over
The other one and said
"Hey, ol' maid,
Don't ya sleep so sound
Ya know what ya promised
When ya first lay down"
Let it roll, let it roll
All night long.[1]

Paij says that it comes down like rain, that it's warm and alive with electricity that she can feel all the way up her arm to her shoulder and then down the brown slope onto her breasts. She says, "You are juicy, you are lush." She says she loves the smell of my juices and they way I flow. The juices flow from the walls of my vagina, drip down like moisture seeping from the walls of a cave. They fill her cupped hand or her mouth or spill out onto the deep purple sheets we slept on when we first became lovers. "Your juices are nature," she says. They leave milk white patches on the purple sheet.

Paij and I are in bed together. I am reading aloud to her from an article in the June 26, 1995 issue of *Time* magazine: "Estrogen: Every Woman's Dilemma."

The natural waning of estrogen in the middle years often brings changes that can ruin a woman's pleasure in sex. The vagina...reverts to its prepubescent shape: narrower, shorter, dryer, less elastic, with thin walls that tear easily and are prone to infection. The libido may also dry up, if only because sex may become painful. While many women are spared these problems in their 50s, the odds are they will strike to some degree within a decade of menopause.

"What?" Paij shrieks, sitting bolt upright in bed. "Dry? Where do they get that from? Those women are drippin' honey. Their pants are all wet, non-stop wet, and they're sayin' they all dried up. They believe it cuz that's what they been told is gonna happen, but it ain't true!"

Paij is real good at using Black English to cut through the pompous self-assurance of the white male patriarchal medical establishment that tries to tell us who we are and just how we should feel.

We are very different Paij and I, and it's not only that she is Black and I am White. We're just about as different as a vagina and a pussy. Only Paij says "pusseh." Being a white woman and a nurse, I say "vagina." Believe me, lovin' and havin' a "pusseh" is oceans and continents away from loving and having a "vagina."

We differ in other ways too. For instance, when I'm having a hot flash I want to tear off all my clothes and run out into the street naked. I feel so irritable and angry that I'm afraid I'm losing my mind. My skin tingles and burns. Sometimes just one half of my body burns, the right half or the left. Or the hot flash might start on my chest and travel up to my face, steaming up my glasses. If I break out in a sweat, it helps some. It cools me down. I get a metallic taste in my mouth, too, that seems to come from under my tongue.

When Paij has a hot flash, she tells me "Hush! I want to enjoy this, to stay in the moment. I want to immerse myself in it. This is what it must feel like inside the womb. It's like immersing myself in a tub of warm bath water."

In fact, Paij has a wonderful bathtub. Porcelain with claw feet and shorter then most, it appears to squat on the old wooden floor of her cabin. Filled with steaming water on a cold winter morning, it is indeed like the womb of Dea Artio, the great Mother Bear.

In winter, Paij doesn't wear a coat no matter how cold it gets here in Vermont. "I have my own internal thermostat now," she tells me as she heads off on her snowshoes atop a mound of snow. I worry that she'll get frostbite; she doesn't feel the cold much anymore.

At night, when Paij kicks the covers off, they land on me.

"I like hot flashes!" she says. "They're spiritual."

My doctor tells me I should take estrogen because I have high blood pressure and a lousy cholesterol profile. She hands me a pamphlet that lists the risks and benefits.

The benefit are as follows: estrogen reduces the risk of heart disease by improving the cholesterol profile and increasing the resiliency of the blood vessels; prevents osteoporosis; reduces the risk of colon cancer; lessens mood swings and forgetfulness; and keeps the skin looking young.

On the other hand, estrogen may cause PMS-like symptoms, migraine headaches, weight gain, gallstones, and benign uterine tumors. Scarier still, estrogen can cause abnormal blood clots, increase the incidence of uterine cancer, and increase the rate of breast cancer.

I jokingly tell the doctor I'd rather die of a heart attack than from cancer. It's quicker. Then I throw away the pamphlet and find a new doctor.

My new doctor is a lesbian. She's located in the same building as the Planned Parenthood Clinic. Before I can see her a cop frisks me and runs a metal detector up and down my body.

This doctor looks like maybe she's menopausal herself. Peering at me over her bifocals, she tells me that very little research has been done on women so far.

"The drug companies are making billions of dollars every year selling fear and youthfulness to women in their forties and fifties."

Hey! I like this woman's politics; they're a lot like mine! I decide to trust her.

"Nevertheless," she says, "I think you should take estrogen."

So she hands me a prescription for Estrace and Progesterone which I'll need to ensure that my uterus sheds her lining once a month. This will lessen the likelihood of endometrial cancer.

I fill the prescription, but, soon after I take the pretty-and-oh-so-feminine pink and purple pills, I start to bleed. And I bleed and I bleed.

Paij says menstrual blood is "just baby food."

"You smell like copper," she says now when she is down between my legs. And when we make love, I imagine copper pennies tumbling from my vagina.

When I have cramps, Paij says, "C'mon, squat with me. It helps the blood to flow and relieves the cramps. Haven't you ever been inside a menstrual hut?"

She tells me that at the Michigan Women's Music Festival in 1980, menstruating women went into the hut to squat down on the Earth and let the blood and clots flow onto the soil.

"The menstrual hut smelled like copper, too," she says. "I liked going there, being in a women's space."

She tells me another story about menstrual blood:

"Once I had an apartment that had lots of tall, sun-filled windows where I hung a dozen or so spider plants. Every month when I menstruated, I'd wash out my cloth menstrual pads and pour the wash water into the soil in their pots. Those plants were so lush and luxurious. They burst out of their pots and hung almost to the floor." She laughs "My twin sister Patsy still talks about those plants. She would never have come to my apartment if she knew what I did."

Menstrual blood is powerful! Old women were once called wise women because they held their blood inside. Therefore, it was called "wise blood."

In January Paij turned fifty-six, the age when Saturn turns back for the second time in our natal charts. Our friend Dinny and I got together and planned a Croning Ceremony for Paij and another friend, Ellen. We would perform the ritual at Artemis Bow, Leslie and Dinny's home.

On the wall of Dinny's studio, I hung pictures of old women. Black women, White women, Native American, Asian and Latina women—*old* women looked down on us and the altar we were creating for the ritual. Women brought pictures of our foremothers, pieces of jewelry, candles, special stones, poems, bird feathers. Leslie contributed hair from her mare's tail. Later, each woman would talk about what she had brought.

During the long snowy afternoon, women made masks while others drummed, danced, and sang. Some relaxed in front of the blazing fireplace and read about crones and aging. Several women helped to make crowns for Paij and Ellen. All afternoon, and that evening, too, we feasted on the food women had prepared for the celebration.

Even though it was snowing that day and the creek behind the house was nearly frozen, it wasn't as cold as I wanted it to be. I wanted the wind to blow and whistle through the trees and the trees to creak and scratch against each other like dry bones. I wanted to walk through deep snow with crunching footsteps and to wear layers of warm clothes the way old women do: two hand-knitted sweaters and a shawl over long winter underwear; a warm woolen hat held on with a scarf; mittens (more than one pair if need be) and boots lined with sheep-skin. I wanted to know and to feel the power of that winter because Crones are powerful—strong and enduring. Isn't that why winter is the season of the Crone?

By the time Paij and Ellen arrived, it was late afternoon. We had made lanterns, put candles into Mason jars and glass bottles and then wound twine around the rims so we could carry them in procession. Thirty women or so—Crones, mother/warriors, maidens—we snaked our way out the back door of the farmhouse and up the snow-covered hill to the Spring.

In the dark, I heard Annie shout from a wheelchair to her lover, "Push harder! Push harder!" as they rushed past us through the snow to the top of the hill.

The two initiates had been told to discard something symbolic of their lives as maidens into the Spring. Paij had been carrying her beloved Swiss Army knife in her pocket all afternoon, touching it, wondering if she would be able to give it up when the time came.

First, Ellen let the music she had collected in Greece as a young woman slip silently from her hands into the water.

Then, "plop!" Paij let go of the knife!

Now the procession wove its way back down in the pine-scented grove at the bottom of the hill where some of the women had been waiting for us. Here Paij and Ellen would bury a symbol of themselves, as mother or warrior. Though Leslie had placed a shovel there, Paij crouched down on the earth and used her hands to dig a small hole through the snow into the dark soil beneath it. She stayed there for a long time, smelling the dying leaves and the winter loam beneath the trees. Then she carefully buried a crystal that her daughter had given her on her birthday many years before.

Now the two women were not allowed to return to the house. They were without an identity—no longer maiden or mother/warriors and not yet who they would become. Until the Croning Ceremony was completed, the other women could not talk to them or even look at them.

These are some of the names Paij and Ellen were given by the women as they re-entered the community:

She-Who-Is-The-Waning-Moon

She-Whose-Number-Is-Nine-Which-Is-Wholeness-And-
Culmination

She-Who-Has-Gained-Control-Of-The-Inner-Fire

She-Who-Converses-With-Spirits

She-Who-Controls-Life-And-Death

She-Who-Dwells-In-Caves

She-Who-It-Is-To-Assist-Those-No-Longer-Where-They-Were-
But-Not-Yet-Where-They-Hope-To-Go

She-Who-Teaches-Song-Story-And-Spindle

She-Who-Is-The-Force-That-Moves-The-Moon

Listen to the names. We know that the patriarchy would like us to believe that once we pass through menopause, we are "all dried up," that we are useless, that we have no function, no value to our community anymore. But these are the names of a woman who is powerful and vital, essential to her community and to the continuation of all life.

The Crones are given a mirror in which to study themselves and note the many changes that age and experience have brought to their faces. A maiden places a robe around the shoulders of each Crone. Then a bell is rung for each of them, counting the years of their lives, giving them the opportunity to reflect on all that they have seen and done before arriving at this place tonight. The two oldest women in the studio ask Paij and Ellen if they are willing to accept the responsibilities of Cronehood. Both say yes, and crowns are placed on their heads.

There is one final ritual. Because the Crones now have the ability to bring things to an end, we ask them to give us a gift. Red, black and white yarn had been knotted together to form one long piece. One end of it is passed around the circle from woman to woman. Each stretches a length of it between her two hands and meditates on something in her life that she would like to see come to an end. Then the two Crones walk around the circle and snip the yarn between each woman's hands, ending that for which they wished.

The evening comes to an end with gift-giving, drumming, singing and chanting.[2]

When I go back to my doctor, she tells me that an estrogen patch is what I need. That it will work better for me and stop my bleeding.

I put the patch on my hip or my stomach on Thursdays and Sundays. Paij makes a ritual sometimes of putting it on my buttock. It itches, but finally the bleeding stops.

Then my sister calls me. My sister who, when she visits, weeds my flower garden if I've neglected it or rescues an ivy tendril that is choking in a crowded pot.

"I can't stand to see a plant suffer," Gailann always says.

On the phone she asks me, "Do you know that estrogen is made from mares' urine? The mares are kept under even *worse* conditions than calves suffer before they're slaughtered for veal."

I never eat veal because I know about the calves. Now I can't stop thinking about the mares. I think, "Why should the mares suffer so that I can stay young? So that I won't have a heart attack?" I don't believe that my life is more important than the mares'.

I decide that I want to get old and to feel that happening to me. I want to hold my blood inside and become a Wise Woman... So I take off the patch.

But what about Paij?

"Hush," she says. "I'm having a hot flash."

1.*Let it Roll, Let it Roll*, Ernestine Allen for True-Sound, 1500x, 1961 with King Curtis, Paul Griffin, Al Casey, Chaincy Westbrauli, Jimmy Lewis and Belton Evans. Thanks to Catherine Green-Carlotti for this research.

2. Some of the rituals for the Croning were adapted from *Menopausal Years: The Wise Woman Way* by Susun S. Weed and *The Grandmother of Time* by Zsuzsanna E. Budapest.

WOMEN-O-PAUSE
change of life/in two voices
Laura Post

I was sitting on our bed, contemplating the softness of her smile in half-sleep, caressing her wrinkled hands, feeling the expansions of her deep breaths against my thighs.

"I have a writing assignment, and I need to talk to you," I whispered, hoping that she would waken but not realize that my voice had wakened her.

When she stirred, and squeezed my hand, I added, a bit more loudly, "It's about menopause." Her eyes briefly squinted open, her mouth closed, and she pulled the quilt more tightly around her.

"Judith," I called, then felt guilty. As a child, I had often awakened my parents in much the same way; by quiet persistence. Except that then I was five, and it was 6am on a Sunday; and now I am thirty-five, this is my lover, and it is eleven o'clock on an errand-Saturday.

I pressed my thumbs into the arch of Judith's right foot on the relief acupressure spots which my hands know so well and asked, as if we were in the middle of a conversation, "What do think about menopause?"

"Hmf," was her reply.

"I like your hot flashes," I ventured. "I remember they started soon after we got together." I chuckled out loud, recalling how beginning nearly seven years ago Judith would draw me close, claiming to be cold, then reflex-kick me to the other side of our king-sized waterbed a moment later, when the flushing internal heat came upon her.

We had both wondered, initially, whether she was feverish, since she was only forty-four, and her mother had not experienced menopause until her late fifties. After the sudden drenching sweats, flushing, and transient grouchiness at times other than pre-coffee mornings, we knew: menopause.

When I looked down at Judith again, she had shifted a few degrees further onto her left side, toward me, but nestled deeper under the covers.

"It means a lot to me to do this with you," I continued, kneading her left foot now. "It helps me prepare."

I turned as our dog, L.D. (Little Dog, Lesbian Dog, Laura's Dog) shook her toy bunny inquiringly at my knees, silently imploring me to throw it for her to fetch.

I let go of Judith's foot and leaned over to grab the spit-sticky stuffed animal, and felt Judith nudging my back.

"I didn't know you liked my hot flashes," she muttered, only half awake. "I thought they bugged you."

I leaned over Judith. "I feel close to you, knowing these things are happening to you and you share this stuff with me." I began massaging her left hand.

More alert, now, Judith hoisted herself into a sitting position and regarded me, her eyes narrowed. "Do you really want to talk about this?"

I explained that I had just heard of an anthology about menopause, and that, since we discussed the topic often enough, I thought we should contribute.

"Well," she began, rubbing her eyes and pulling the covers over her. "What I think about menopause is that I'm happy to not be staining any more!" She gave me a conspiratorial grin, knowing that I despised blood-wet sheets from the four-super-tampons-a-night heavy flows as much as she did.

"No more stained sheets, no more stained underpants," she continued when I didn't answer. "No more stained pants," she added, referring to those extra-heavy days when even the tampons, pads, and undies weren't enough of a barrier between her uterus and her trousers.

My mind flashed, briefly, to the continuing expense of my own tampons, and began its usual diatribe on the monopolies of the feminine hygiene industry. Had I said any of this out loud, my next topic would have been a secondary discussion about the offensive labeling of products for clean, healthy, normal menstrual blood as "sanitary," implying dirtiness in the process. Aware that this was my own stuff, and that Judith was more concerned with not awakening to find the dog happily licking a pool of clotted blood from between her legs, I was silent.

"What else?" she asked herself. "No more blood running down my legs during meetings at work. No more clients asking me whether I'm OK, in the middle of counseling sessions."

When Judith's whole-body flushing started, she would be instantly red-faced and dripping with sweat. She had reported to me that the people that she saw for therapy in her office would shift their attention away from their own issues and feelings and would focus, concerned, on her.

"My cramps aren't gone, though," she mused. "I can't wait for that to happen." She faced me, her voice pleading with her hope that I might be done with this topic: "Is that enough?"

"Can I ask you some specific questions?," I persisted.

Judith's voice was soft as L.D. "OK." Judith turned from me, momentarily, to stroke our pup, who, having tired of amusing herself, had completed several tight circles by the pillows and was settling quietly near us.

"Are you at all worried about physical changes that will come after menopause?" I was actually thinking about heart disease, the possibility and cost of supplemental estrogen, a lifetime of being dependent upon synthetic hormones, the risks of breast cancer, about Judith's mother's recent mastectomy remembering that Judith had given up smoking long before we met but Judith's thoughts took another turn.

"I'm not worried about osteoporosis!" Her laughter was deep and genuine; Judith is what k.d. lang would call a big-boned gal, and she knew that the fragile, bent stature of many older women would not likely be her fate.

But there was more. "What if my pussy hair turns all white, and I shrivel and dry up," she lamented. "My pussy has always been so nice and wet."

Judith pulled the bedclothes even further around herself. It was a warm spring day in northern California and I, a thin woman who will commonly put on a sweater when my friends are in T-shirts, was not the slightest bit cold. I smiled at the inadvertent display of Judith's post-hot-flash chill and waited.

"I'm afraid I'll get those nasty thick black chin hairs, and I'll seem old to you." Her tone intensified: "I worry you'll think I'm ugly, and that you'll have an affair with someone younger and leave me."

This is a familiar refrain, though usually the worry is that is that I'll get bored with Judith, or tired of her, or just find someone better. My usual response is that I love her, am happy, and have no plan to leave. Today, a twinge of fear passes through me; what if she doesn't want sex any more, or she goes through a late life crisis and has an affair, or suspects me of infidelity and has an affair.

I look at her face which is trusting me to love her, trusting me to tell her the truth. "I've never really thought about not loving you because of chin hair. You've given me something new to obsess about." She doesn't smile at my awkward kidding.

Involuntarily shifting my body closer to hers, I state: "I love you so much, I can't imagine that physical changes could drive me from you." Pausing to stroke her hair, I add, "Really."

She relaxes slightly. I'm about to say I feel anxious she'll perceive me as so much younger—that after all, seventeen years separate us and when she's passed through menopause, I'll seem like a child and she'll regret the folly of having gotten involved with me.

Her voice interrupts my anxiety. "Will you tell me if you're disgusted by my body?" Her voice holds an imploring note. "Please?"

"I love your body," I whisper. "I love these fat folds on your belly. I love your big soft boobles. I love your solid back and strong arms. I love your downy pussy hair, and I don't care if it's brown or grey or white." As I speak, my palms and fingertips stroke these areas. I kick off my shoes and slide next to her.

"I love your soft no-ass." It has long been her joke that people of Brit descent, which she is, have flat butts. I ease my fingers towards her asshole.

"Get out of there," she barks fondly. This is another joke between us.

"We do have lube. All kinds," I point out, reasonably, as I open the drawer of the nightstand. "Do you remember how this works?" I tease.

While I kiss her mouth, lick her lips, bite her cheeks, my hands are moving hard beneath her. For minutes we forget our discussion, then she cries out, arches, and pulls me close, drawing the covers over us both.

I hear, "What were we talking about?" as a warm draft tickles my ear.

"Whether we'll make it as a couple, whether menopause will drive us apart, whether I'll continue to love and want you, and whether you'll still love and want me..." I try to start a thought, but, my breath is coming in short bursts, and all I feel is love.

DESIRE PERFECTED: SEX AFTER FIFTY
Joan Nestle

Mabel Hampton, an African-American lesbian in her eighties, recently said to me, "Joan, there are some women I can't touch because the desire burns my hand like a blue flame, those women, those women!" We both laughed, but I was also humbled by the depth of Mabel's erotic feeling in the eighth decade of her life.

This knowledge of our own desires, perfected over many years of lesbian loving, can be one of our most enduring comrades in the later years of our lives. I say "can be" because I recognize that not all lesbians have been able to or have even wanted to fully explore their sexual selves. But for those who have been inspired by trust or need or opportunity to push at their sexual boundaries, the years after forty can provide a canvas for perfected pleasures.

I am not writing about sex as a sociologist or as a psychologist; I am speaking as a fifty-six-year-old woman who has been sexually active with women since I was ten. My own sexual journey began in 1950 when I became best friends with Roz, the butcher's daughter. We incorporated sex play into our relationship when I first shared with her the wonderful secret of masturbation. Then in weekly bouts of fantasy sex play, ensconced in her parents' double bed, we enacted such scenes as "The Sheik and His Harem," with Roz and me playing all the parts. In the year 1950, I put my head between her thighs to use my mouth to give her pleasure and I can still remember the softness of her skin against my cheeks. Our relationship changed in high school when Roz took commercial courses and I took the academic route; she married early and I found Greenwich Village.

Over the years, I have explored butch-femme sex, androgynous sex, intergenerational sex (where I lusted after much older women), S/M sex, group sex, back room sex, sex for money and, in a ten year relationship, domestic sex which included much of the above. I have made love when I was in love and when I was not, for many days and for one night. I do not mean this list to be flaunting, but when I came out in 1958, one of the most important freedoms I was choosing was to move my body into the world under my own control. In those days, the vice squad made sure that we never forgot we were obscenities, but their harassment and the general intolerant social atmosphere did not impede my erotic progress. I have used every day of my lesbian life to exercise this independence of desire. I think, in some way, many of us have made the same choice to be the guardians of our own bodies and the explorers of our own desire. This erotic self-possession is one of the gifts of our lives in exchange for the loss of societal privileges of heterosexual marriage, the domestic sphere and other "normal" protections of womanhood.

Having a lot of sex or being comfortable with sex does not mean that the body is always one's friend or that aging does not offer challenges that change the erotic terrain. Issues like physical well-being, body size, menopause and emotional fragility are always there, waiting to be incorporated into daily moments of intimacy. I have always been a big woman and now I am bigger. Sometimes I'm caught up in the old battle of hating my body for its fullness of flesh, that will show the effects of aging in a more dramatic way because there is more of me to show it. Menopause is a natural occurrence and so is the feeling of loss that can accompany it. I cry and yell more than I have ever done. When I see tampons in a friend's bathroom, I am looking at a cardboard and cotton bone, a relic from another time, another river bed. Because of a chronic illness, I often do not feel physically safe and I think a lot about death.

And yet, in the face of all these challenges, I have a comrade to strengthen me: my developed knowledge of what gives me pleasure in love-making and my willingness to put my body into play. Even when I am most at war with biology, I can find the life force to take all I have learned about loving and once again be the adventurer, the discoverer of new worlds, as I move down my lover's belly. To my old-time sense of sexual bravado have been added the woman-loving-woman insights of lesbian feminism that have helped me to value myself more as a woman, making aging an honored process.

We will all find different ways to keep our erotic identities alive as we change, different sources of inspiration and stimulation. I found mine in being open to what new generations of lesbians were doing with their bodies. I went to sex parties, talked to leather women and saw clearly what I could do and what I did not want to do. Then when I was forty-seven, fighting the depression of illness, I found the ground I could stand on. Gay Women's Alternative of New York asked me to read some of my erotic stories. I realized that I did not want to read about sexual desire in everyday clothes, that I wanted some way to mark the specialness of the language, so I decided to wear a black slip and black stockings for the reading. I wanted the audience to see a large older woman's body as I said the words of sex.

This wearing of the black slip publicly became my signature. I had found a way to transform perceived losses into newly acquired erotic territory. I wanted the public revelation of my aging larger body to be a statement for all older lesbians; I wanted to proclaim our image and with it, our knowledge. Sexual self-discovery and issues of self-presentation do not stop at any decade's door. The desire I experience as a fifty-six-year-old lesbian woman is not the same as the passion I pursued in earlier years; my desire has deepened and I experience it as a gift I bring to my lover. Stretched out on the bed, waiting for her, I sometimes feel as if I am bursting with sexual knowledge, that carried in the fullness of my breasts and hips is all the wisdom I have gleaned from pursuing the touch of women for half a century. I do not feel arrogant or invulnerable to rejection, but I do know the ground I am lying on. I have never traded sexual desire for security; I have no economic or legal monuments like a twenty-year marriage to mark the end of lust and the beginning of safety. I do have my own person, my own body, that has led me to a lifetime of new places, new resistances, new compassions.

This accumulated wealth of sexual self-knowledge that many of us have is not often discussed in our communities and, thus, we are still learning about the political and personal implications of our sexual wisdom. We need more discussion of our lesbian sexual vitality and explorations at all ages to stimulate our desires. Not a discussion that will make any lesbian woman feel inadequate because she did not "do that" or doesn't "want that," but discussions that allow each woman to put new value on the moments of desire she has experienced.

As I have come to enjoy my own middle-aged sexual wisdom, I

have also come to recognize it in other older women I see around me. Gray hair and textured hands are now erotic emblems I seek out. As I curiously explore the lines on my own chest running down to the valley between my breasts, I caress those same lines on the chest of my lover. I still want strong love-making, I still want to play and pretend and seduce. But a moment comes when all of me is stark naked in body and imagination and then I know all of who I am and who I am no longer and I rise to offer this honest older self to my lover.

As if to return the gift of acceptance, my body has rewarded me with new sexual responses. I now have multiple orgasms, a delightful occurrence that did not begin until my mid-forties; I have jettisoned leftover feelings of shame and some youthful reluctance to accept oral love-making. I allow myself much more time to look at my lover's body, to stroke her and caress her. Part of this tenderness comes from my sense of our combined years—almost ninety years of life between us—and thus even time becomes an erotic ally.

I have learned to incorporate safe sex techniques into my love-making in a way that preserves my desire and recognizes the agony of this time in our sexual history. I keep packets of condoms at the side of our bed along with a large tube of KY jelly, one for the dildo play we enjoy, the other for the occasional dryness that makes greater lubrication necessary. The first time I faced my lack of wetness and realized that my internal desire would no longer always have an external marker, I was deeply distressed. I had always loved the gush of wetness that was the body's own voice and, at first, I was ashamed at this change of language. I had to find the words to ask my lover to help me. As she anointed me, I felt a new sense of seriousness about love-making, similar to the sense of taking responsibility I feel when I am smoothing a condom down over our dildo. These conscious acts taken to allow for a spontaneous physical pleasure become spiritual moments of sexual reclamation.

While I have felt fear and change and loss, I have, even more, felt a glory in my love-making in my fifth decade. The glory comes from knowing I am using everything my fifty years of living as a lesbian has taught me, not just about our bodies, but about the wonder of our risk-takings, the strength of our autonomy, the courage of our choices.

THE SACRED M WORDS
Henri Bensussen

I'm fifty-eight this year, 1995. I've survived menopause, but it wasn't fun. I look back on it like I look back on adolescence, glad it's over. I used to jump into discussions about menopausal symptoms, but now I try to avoid that whole list of complaints: hot flashes (still have them), acne (ditto), sleep disruption. About the best one can say of this endless litany is that it certainly keeps the body from the slide into sluggishness it might otherwise fall into. To me, menopause is like being caught up in a vortex. You're sucked in without forewarning, whipped around a few years, and finally tossed out on an opposite shore, battered and relieved, a more sober and wiser person.

The good thing about menopause in the 1990s is that women can talk about it. In my mother's day, the early fifties, menopause was in the closet. Someone might whisper, "She's going through the change," when a woman acted unexpectedly emotional, did strange things like leave her husband or scream at her friends. Showing anger might result in her doctor prescribing tranquilizers, or putting her in an institution because of a "nervous breakdown."

Women didn't discuss menopause like we do now, they hid it. It was shameful, shameful as being caught in the act of menstruating by tell-tale bloodstains on a skirt. We menstruated in the fifties in secret, solving the problems of cramps, pad disposal, "accidents," as best we could on our own.

My aunt was in her forties when she met my uncle-to-be. They were both working in an airplane factory during the war. He was totally deaf, and the only one in the plant who could communicate with him, using sign language, was my aunt. She became partially deaf during childhood. It was her second marriage, and for a time they lived in my grandmother's house.

Our family was there for a visit once and an awful row was going on. I think my aunt and uncle, because of their deafness, did not realize how loud their fights were. My aunt was crying when she opened the door of their room and fell into my mother's arms, while Uncle stormed out by the opposite door where he was joined outside by the men. I made sure I was in the kitchen, being my usual quiet and unobtrusive self, when the women of the family came together there to soothe my aunt. The language wasn't direct, but I was able to piece together from various whisperings that my aunt had thought she was safe from pregnancy, had thought she would never have another menstrual period, and then she had had one. Somehow, by luck, she was not pregnant, but could have been! And now her husband wanted sex. It was his fault that she was in this state.

The Pill didn't appear until the late fifties. Birth control freed sex, but also continued the trend of medicalizing women's normal hormonal cycles. When I was going through menopause, with excessive bleeding, unbearable hot flashes that turned my insides into a furnace, and foot cramps at night, the doctors wanted me to get back on that pill, estrogen, that would make these upsetting symptoms disappear. When I refused, they tried to scare me about a future of osteoporosis, broken bones, collapsing spine. When that didn't work, they said the pills would protect me against heart disease. Now we have studies showing the risk of cancer as a result of taking estrogen.

I listen to my menopausal friends share information about more natural ways of treating their symptoms. I wonder what it would have been like if my friends and I had discussed menstruation in the same way. How liberating it would have been!

I remember the horrible awkwardness of adolescence and the problems and pains of menopause, but in the latter case I also retain some good effects: the increased energy that I seem to have, less need for sleep. Just as in my mother's time, anger comes to the surface, but now it is considered healthy to express it.

Both those important times of growth and great change are over, and as with adolescence I have gained an extra measure of confidence by surviving and learning from it. Now I am slowing down, accepting myself as I am. My hair is turning gray, my middle is expanding, and my cheeks are too red. My slim and fashionably-dressed aunt would not approve, but frankly, I no longer care. I don't have patience, or the hesitancy of the inexperienced woman, to accept a status quo that doesn't work for me, or situations that are not right for my soul. Willing to take risks, I reach out for what I need.

The world is filled with other women like me. We extend our arms and our fingers touch. We caress each other's textured bodies with compassion and appreciation as we trace the intricate tattoos formed by wrinkles and scars that tell the stories of our lives. We open our mouths and taste the sweetness of love stored like honey in a beehive, we eat the fruit that has been ripening to this perfect moment, the harvest season, before we need prepare for a winter soon to come.

CUM WITH ME LUCY
(excerpts from the novel)
Red Jordan Arobateau

The black-haired butch moved thru her apartment. Mickey was age forty-nine. The year, 1989.

This driving passion thru her had begun that summer.

Intensity that wouldn't find relief.

Went out romancing woman after woman.

Hot to lay down and fuck & make the woman enjoy; make her cum too.

Only after that did Mickey's soul feel free.

Didn't know where it came from—or where it was taking her.

Had a trip back through Chicago to New York in a few days & Mickey was going crazy. Was it hormones? Was she suddenly becoming a sex addict?

This had begun around six months ago—right before Marsha had their baby. Mickey had started going out.

"You spend all our money on other women! There's no room in this apartment now the baby's here! We'll never be able to buy a house!"

"I can't *help it*, Marsha! But you're Number One! You don't have to worry. I keep *telling* you! Our home is the most important thing! And the kids! I just got to go out! I don't know what's wrong with me!"

Mickey used the phone in private. Took it in a closet, spoke into it in a whisper, hand cupped the receiver. One of the calls on her sex mailbox.

Came back into the bedroom. "I've been rejected."

Marsha rolled around on the bed & laughed. "HA! HA! HA! HA! HA!" Merry as a child. The blond was genuinely happy. Jumped up and down on the bed and collapsed. "*HA!* SO HOW DID YOU GET REJECTED *THIS* TIME MICKEY!"

"........."

"Mickey! Who rejected you?"

"........."

"MICKEY! WHAT HAPPENED! WHAT DID SHE SAY?"

"She said, 'I'll see you around.'"

"HA! HA! HA! HA! HA! THAT'S *FUNNY*! WHY! BECAUSE YOU'RE TOO BUTCH! TOO DOMINANT! SHE DOESN'T WANT YOU COMING OUT TO HER HOUSE BECAUSE YOU'RE TOO OBVIOUS AND EVERYBODY'LL KNOW SHE'S GAY! *HA! HA! HA! WELL LET HER PUT UP WITH IT FOR A CHANGE! I'VE HAD TO GO THROUGH IT FOR 12 YEARS! HA HA HA!*"

"Shit."

"SO YOU'RE STILL NOT GETTING ANY SEX? *GOOD!*"

For the last six months of the twelve years they'd lived as a family, Mickey had opened up their relationship. It gave Mickey freedom to date & have sex with other women, while making home the priority. And Marsha could do the same if she cared to, which she didn't.

At age forty-nine, it was a time Mickey had doubts about her lesbian sexuality.

All the butch knew, it was a time when she hurt inside. Mickey had a good woman, a very good woman she slept beside, and loved and fucked nearly twelve years. The woman had her kid Joey already like a gift from heaven. Joey had become Mickey's own. And now they had baby Sonja together.

And she was still hurting.

Want caught in her throat, dry. Longing in her chest from the region of her heart, as a hot flash hit her. Her sex began to throb, and within a few minutes of waking, her mind had become a cage of driving need, pushing her to the verge of desperation.

She stood in front of the silvery glass of the bathroom mirror. The mirror reflected back despair. It was her face. Even Mickey noticed it. Stopped what she was doing. Ran a hand over her cheek. Dark eyes stared back out of the mirror, on the verge of tears. Rumpled clothes echoed into infinity inside the dreary cubical. Something about the reflection of the butchwoman shouted out from her very soul.

Marsha was often angry these days. Yet she stayed with Mickey for the kids' sakes and economic reasons. But also, hated to admit she loved her unfaithful butch. Felt confident, tho Mickey had to prowl and seek sex with other women, that she did put her, Marsha, first, with their home and the kids. And the money Mickey spent on going out and on other women was minor. Most of her paycheck went to their family and into the dream account for a home and maybe even one day to send the kids to college.

They loved each other and had a trust they didn't want to lose.

They had walked in the shadows, now they were moving out into the day!

The daylight of their lives!

Bed took up half the room. Nice quilt, drapes, rugs on the hardwood floor. Bed set & night stands were part of a matching set—stained with food spills. Shelf of the headboard held clean diapers and jars of baby food. The couple had enough money to furnish their place, but the baby and Joey & ravages of time had made their stuff look used, and the place was cluttered.

The house had order, but also an ever-present stink of dirty diapers. Food left out in the kitchen. A cat had thrown up on top of the TV set. This had been cleaned up, but left a smear down the screen and the women were too exhausted to clean it.

And they'd lie in bed asleep, arms still wrapped around each other. Love juice wet their faces, fingers & thighs.

Mickey would come home after a twelve hour shift sometimes — to get extra savings for their bank account, plus, recently, cash so she could throw a twenty-dollar bill around in a gay club on drinks and try to meet a girl for sex and still not interfere with the economics of their home and their future.

And Mickey was confused. Thought, "I have a woman waiting at home. I can do what I like with her for hours..."

What was it? A hunger greater and deeper than sex. Marsha lay next to her for the taking at night... The butch thought... "Why am I pursuing this? Because I found a grey hair in my head? Because I'm getting old and will lose my good looks? Is it the same feeling of inadequacy returning to me that I'm not a man? But men get worse. They're men, with all the privileges, but they go crazy over women, beat them, kill them... They're even worse than me... I'm still hand-some. I have a woman... She gave me a baby and named it after me. So what is this?" She had seldom felt this desperate, or as powerless before.

She felt like she'd been carrying a lot of pain around for a long time & didn't know where it came from.

Wind blew down the street from the night hills dotted with lights shining from homes.

Mickey felt like slugging something until the flesh across her knuckles got bloodied and the pain was greater than the pain with-in. To wipe that inner pain aside.

The feelings of a woman on the edge.

* * * *

Marsha's plan was to have a third child in a few more years and give it Mickey's last name as she had Sonja. She was mad about Mickey playing around. Confused, & didn't understand what was happening. Knew it was her Mickey came home to; knew her own sex drive wasn't that high—not like the butch's was. And even less since her pregnancy & now that she was breast-feeding. But she would still do what it took to make Mickey happy.

Mickey stood in the doorway, like the doorway of a passage of her life. Ran fingers through her jet-black hair. Kicked off her boots, peeled off her socks & threw them on the floor. Kids were asleep in their rooms behind them. A cat blinked its lucid eyes from atop the dresser. The dogs who had followed her inside stood waggling their tails and sniffing over the discarded boots, curious where she'd been. The stocky butch opened the door, shooed them out into the hall, and they went back to curl up on their beds and sleep. It was early morning—three-thirty am. The heat between Mickey's legs & longing in her chest had not been appeased. The butch had her needs. The growing circle of wet in the crotch of her boxer shorts proved that. She needed a lot of compassion from a woman. Very, very deep, deep love from a woman.

And a lot of sex. Nasty sex. Fuck sex. Whore sex. Slut sex.

The finer emotions and the hardcore rough stuff all mixed together.

* * * *

Just a week ago Mickey had to face the facts. She was forty-nine years of age. Birthday passed. She would never be a success. They would never have enough money, and having an extra kid would insure they would never own a house...

Marsha's silken blond hair was done in a bun. Sophisticated. Her blue eyes twinkle, peeved. "You're going off again tonight aren't you! To wander the streets of San Francisco aimlessly looking for some slut! To have sex!"

Mickey felt lonely, angry & hurt. About what, she didn't know. Marsha's love, and Joey & Sonja just took the edge off this—kept her from wanting to commit suicide. "My pants still aren't sewn, Marsha?" Mickey only responded, dully.

"WHAT DIFFERENCE DOES IT MAKE TO YOU IF I AM READING THE LOVELORN ADVICE COLUMN INSTEAD OF SEWING YOUR PANTS, MICKEY? I'M THINKING ABOUT LEAVING YOU! I LEFT YOU TWO OTHER TIMES, *REMEMBER!*"

"I told you, Marsha! I *need* to! I need to fuck another woman! It's stronger than the both of us! I can't help it! I've got no control over it! If I don't I'm blue & depressed & in a rage, and might as well be dead! After I fuck, I feel like a million dollars! And doing it with you helps, but it's not enough! I didn't plan this, Marsha!"

Mickey was tense. Distraught. Black hair mussed from running the fingers of her powerful hands through it. Strode around their bedroom. Wore boxer shorts, a fancy dress shirt and sox. Square body. Sturdy, from weight lifting. Medium-sized breasts pressed down by her teeshirt. She paced the floor waiting for her trousers to be sewn. Finally marched back across the width of their small bedroom to the closet & ripped down another pair of trousers from a clothes hanger.

Muscles in her back rippled under her fancy shirt as she bent over the side of the bed & pulled on her boots.

Marsha held the Advice to the Lovelorn column in the newspaper spread on the bed. "All of a sudden you try to change all the rules! We've been together twelve years, Mickey! I kind of counted on spending the rest of my life with you!"

"You will spend it with me! I'm not leaving! I'm just going out to play! If I didn't love you I would have lied and done it behind your back and you would have found out & it would have killed you!"

"It's killing me now, Mickey!"

The butch bent over & took her woman's shoulders in her hands. Face to face. Dark eyes peered at her. "Marsha! You sit up here and watch the Goddamn TV all day and night like a TV junkie! You watch straight people dancing around with each other. Femmes just like you, women who dress like you and act like you, but when I look at the Goddamn TV I don't see nothing that looks like me! Nothing that faintly resembles a butch!"

"So you have to go out and find some woman and take her to bed to prove who you are! I' m not good enough!" Marsha yelled, tossing her blonde hair back from her eyes & rocking tiny Sonja too vigorously, like a ship on a stormy sea.

"YEAH! I GUESS THAT'S WHAT I'M DOING! I don't even know what I'm doing! But I need it, I need too bad. Real bad, whatever it is!"

Tried to keep their voices down because of Joey & not wanting to upset him. Marsha turned the knob of the radio by the bed. Soon music drowned their words.

"YOU STARTED IT!"

"I can't help it! It just came over me!" Mickey's square hand ran over her face; black tousled hair; sincere expression. Veins stood out in her neck. Frantically gestured with her hands as she spoke. "If all of a sudden I developed cancer would you tell me, 'Mickey, what did you get cancer for? It's ruining our lives!' And blame me? It's like a disease whatever it is! If I had a heart attack would you ask me, 'Mickey, why did you go and have a heart attack?' And blame me?"

"BUT THIS IS DIFFERENT! IT'S IN YOUR CONTROL!"

Mickey looked at her reflection in the mirror again. Handsome, & growing lines of age. She felt time slip away, felt time was short. Needed to feel like she used to feel. Full of excitement, daring, courage; out in the world—not knowing what the future held. A butch on top, in power, on fire of sexuality. Engaged in a struggle to control her life.

If she was not in control of her life in society, & they denied her very being, at least Mickey could take control of her sex life.

So went the turmoil of their lives.

Marsha was furious. Being a mother of two kids & a lesbian

made life rough. There was no help at all from her own parents. Conservative, ultra religious, they had disowned her. People stared at them funny in the streets. This sex craze of her mate hurt. The single most important thing in Marsha's life was her relationship, she'd prided herself on that. And their commitment to being together. To love & raise their kids.

"Mickey, you've been *hurting* me! This going out and seeing other women! Even if you say they don't mean anything to you— you've been hurting me, Mickey! *I want you to stay home!*"

It had been a year since Marsha had worked a bookkeeping job in the Financial District. She had a bachelors degree from a good college, financed by her upperclass parents, was the product of a good, happy, stable home (even though they had now disowned her.). The taint of streetlife that Mickey was bringing into their marriage was unfamiliar & disturbing. The natural blonde sat, regal, moving her lithe body in its cotton dress, uneasily. Hair done up in a bun. Modest string of pearls. Buffed her fingernails as she waited in nervous anger. "How long is she going to keep doing this? I don't know if I can take much more. She's destroying our home." Applied dabs of yellow polish on her nails where it had begun to chip off from grueling mom-chores in her never-ending day of a housewife. Wiggled them, admiring; then her face frowned as she worried some more. When she had taken off time to have baby Sonja, Mickey had supported them, making up the difference from welfare that wasn't enough. And when it was time for the baby to be born Mickey saw that it was in a private hospital, she herself paying the bill where she felt mother and baby would have better care. So Marsha knew Mickey did love her.

* * * *

A few days after her conquest at a sexclub it began again. Streams of desire flowed through her body, low key, like a low burner, simmering; a wide erogenous zone—all over her body—not yet centered in her sex, but radiating out from it, slowly consuming her full being.

A few more days would pass, barely alleviated by lovemaking with her wife, the yearning becoming more intense, more paramount, even more important than life itself. Heavy laden in heat, the butch knew she'd take her love out to the streets.

It was a time when Mickey felt very inadequate about herself as a lesbian.

Time when she felt so low, sexually. Felt like she was nothing. Felt like killing herself—but she wouldn't.

Knew, from experience all-too-familiar in these last recent months, that the only thing that would take this mental pain & physical longing away was to go to a sexclub, or the bars, find a woman companion just for the night, have sex with her; and that compulsive feeling would die.

But as a wildfire, only to return.

And tho her marriage to Marsha was solid, and they performed sex five times a week, this felt like it was just a drop in the bucket of her needs.

Marsha had come to depend on Mickey, and to love her.

So she stayed.

Would not take the kids away from Mickey & leave, because of the infidelity. Not just for that.

Once in a blue moon the lovely blonde would get out and meet a woman and exchange phone numbers, but she never had an affair.

Marsha recognized Mickey's need; knew it was more than sex. Something mental that was bigger than the two of them, and let her go. After twelve years, all of it a monogamous relationship. The blond knew her butch would always come back and forever honor their home and kids.

* * * *

Now those days were over.

Not since she was a hungry kid had she felt such inner turmoil.

Night was black, but light from the street outside lit their living room. Sonja slept in her crib. Mickey lay down on the sofa, covering herself with a blue blanket.

Was it the weird hormonal changes she'd been going through these last six months that drove her to think so much about women that she must even fantasize women from her past; women who by now could be dead & buried…

And this gnawing of hormones; the change of season into Autumn, her self-doubt as a lesbian, whatever it was, only God The Mother or a psychiatrist could unlock. Mickey knew only, that twice a week, there she'd be, back at the lesbian bars, or the sexclub, or roaming the streets.

They too were drifting…

Mickey lay on the sofa in a teeshirt and red & blue striped boxers. Blue blanket over her lower body. Her strong torso, swarthy, black hair under the armpits. Mickey thought: "My hormones are raging, I'm going thru the butch menopause or change of life or something…" And she was mad and hurt and felt less than a woman… "And we have a bank account & I've worked as a janitor in the same place 16 years & we have our dream home all planned, & now I see…I want more."

Starlight, star bright. First star I see tonight…

* * * *

"Is this my good shirt?"

"Sonja threw up on it! So what! Are you going out again tonight?"

Mickey took the shirt, stalked angrily down the hall to the bathroom, threw the shirt in the sink, angrily turned on the faucet & added some bubbling pink detergent. Marsha hollered after her: "ALL YOU'RE WORRIED ABOUT IS YOUR DAMN SHIRT! YOU'RE NOT EVEN WORRIED ABOUT YOUR BABY! DON'T YOU WANT TO HEAR WHAT THE DOCTOR SAID?"

The dresser, cluttered with articles of their lives. Mirror wobbles as Marsha yelled, reflected back wearing a pink slip, yellow hair coming undone. "SPENDING ALL OUR MONEY! With $70 you could have paid your insurance! Mickey you're *killing* us!"

The butch turned away, fussed in a drawer for her sox and shorts.

"We might as well split up! seventy dollars for Sex Ads on our phone bill! YOU'RE NOT GOING OUT AGAIN TONIGHT! YOU'RE NOT GOING OUT SPENDING ALL OUR MONEY! YOU'RE GOING TO GET KILLED! YOU'RE GOING TO CATCH DISEASE!

"All right then, Mickey! Now go on and get out of here, hurry, so you can get to your sluts who I'm sure are waiting, and I can watch TV. My programs come on at eight-thirty." And her face frowned as she sank back into the bed.

Mickey had power.

A family. A woman who loved her.

Who had a baby for her and was her wife,

The butch had a job, sixteen years seniority with union benefits, cash in her pocket, a wardrobe of masculine clothes & men's cologne in a neat single file row on top of the dresser cluttered with Marsha's makeup & lotion & jars of face cream, and owned a car that ran. And had feeling & meaning in her life.

Mickey had power.

Yet she didn't know it.

All the inadequacies she'd ever felt, as a dyke, as a woman, and one who had lived poor for far too long; all these self-doubts kept her from loving herself. And from enjoying life to its full extent.

Tonight saw Mickey back at the sexclub.

Mickey was listening to her inner self. Her need. Looked down at her self. Satin shirt, trousers, man's sports coat, boots. Small in stature—barely five foot, six inches. Stared into her private mirror face to face. "I'm going on fifty years old. I have a wife and need another woman. A slut. A female in black lace & bare flesh. What is this driving me?"

Craving in her body, within her bones; bursting in her chest like a long delayed sunrise; flooding her entirely. Warm sex in her crotch in a knot from wanting so hard. Body longed to embrace some female she barely knew, to prove herself, to *live*! As if the act was life's breath. A woman who was hot and slutty in sex action. A bad girl. Needed to lose herself in a mini-vacation of sorts, into fantasy, on the plainsland of the sexual hunting ground in a night of hot sex.

"I don't know what's wrong with me. I should be at home, not here. I got a woman waiting. A good woman."

In some ways, Mickey had come to the crossroads of life. Mid-Life Crisis? If so, the butch had absolutely no intention of spending money on counseling to seek the answer, being unfamiliar with that process. Marsha at twenty-nine, twenty years her junior, was of no help, having never gone thru anything like it herself. Mickey fought on alone, with her family behind her to fall back on as an emotional pillow.

In some ways, having heard "NO" so much in her life—"*NO*"—no admittance to queers, not a chance. "NO!" from even her own mother's lips—so much she'd just given up on some levels—so sometimes…it was just easier to surrender herself to gravity. To walk on the edge, on the Wild Side. To fall with the gravity that pulled in the form of an alley cat girl beckoning her down to the streets again. To return to her old haunts, and style, like a sailor too long gone from the sea.

The butch would never be anything great or successful. So all there was was to screw, to show herself at least that she was a powerful lesbian butch. That, regardless of the lack of images like herself, drag-dressed women on every billboard, magazine cover or TV series, that she was something! And not a nothing. And standing in the clubs surrounded by younger women, a knowledge that she'd pull one out of the crowd and take her to bed, strip each other down; caress & touch each other's body, make her wet and fuck her hard; cum and make the woman cum—a lot, and all night long; seemed to take the edge off this low feeling.

Stars drifted outside the window & the late summer air of San Francisco was cool, waiting for change.

TESTING ONE, TWO, THREE
Julia Willis

Well, the test results came back from the lab today and, according to my hormones, I am NOT experiencing menopause. Of course when I got the call from Cindy, our friendly nurse-practitioner, who assured me I was still "going with the flow," I bit off the end of the receiver and spit it across the room. But no, apparently I'm not the least bit menopausal. Yeah, right. And Jesse Helms will actually go to Heaven when he finally dies and rots.

I frankly wonder if the medical community, in its fumbling empirical way, isn't administering the wrong test. While blood may tell, it seems a good deal more likely that a woman can draw her own conclusions in the matter according to the number and variety of symptoms she herself is experiencing. Thus from my vast personal experience I've compiled an uneven baker's dozen questions geared specifically for the transitionally-challenged woman. So put down that meat cleaver for a moment, and try answering them with a simple "God, yes" or "hell, no."

(1) Do you cry watching cat food commercials, especially the ones with the sappy songs, the crystal dishes, and the Lauren Bacall voice-overs?

(2) Does your clothing size, in anything from shirts to pants to socks, vary by the week from medium to extra large?

(3) In regard to those minor aches and pains, do you sometimes feel like you're recovering from yesterday's marathon when in fact you've only walked by the YWCA and picked up a brochure of low-impact aerobics classes on your way to the corner store for a pint of Ben and Jerry's?

(4) Is it hot in here to you? If so, have you tried convincing yourself that global warming is the only reason you haven't worn a sweater since January 1994?

(5) Have you ever awakened in the night doing the backstroke in your own sweat? Or have you sat bolt upright, your heart pound-

ing, wondering what that dream about Susan Sarandon could mean, so now you're blaming those frequent bouts of insomnia on Susan Sarandon?

(6) Have any of these thoughts relating to childbirth and/or nurturing crossed your mind recently? (a) "Well, it's too late to think about having my own children." (b) "Well, it's probably too late for my girlfriend to think about having children either." (c) "I wonder if all this lesbian baby business is the '90s fad, comparable to the '70s menstrual sponge fad and the '80s lipstick-and-garter-belt fad." (d) "You know, we could really use another cat/dog/bird/python around here."

(7) Are you experiencing short-term memory loss, becoming forgetful of things you read?

(8) Are you experiencing short-term memory loss, becoming forgetful of things you read?

(9) Can you honestly say you haven't had such wild mood swings, highs AND lows, since junior high school, when you fell madly in love with Cynthia Williams (oh joy, oh rapture!) and then panicked, realizing that must mean you were definitely queer (oh fear, oh misery!)?

(10) Have you begun carrying a cup in your car to pee in, and even if you haven't, does the idea seem a lot less gross than it used to? Besides, when you do pee, does it feel like you're peeing straight vinegar and water, a phenomenon now commonly referred to as "Summer's Eve Syndrome"?

(11) In the evening, is it just too damned much trouble to (a) do the dinner dishes, (b) put the clothes in the dryer, (c) walk the dog, (d) answer the phone, or (e) change channels with the remote?

(12) Has your sex drive actually diminished, or is it hard to tell since you've only lived with (a) cocker spaniels or (b) balding faggots for the past five years?

(13) Do you find that little things upset you more than they used to, and your initial response to these petty annoyances always involves elaborate, violent torture fantasies?

Finally, in spite of answering "God, yes" to at least three of these questions, and even though you'd obviously rather be napping, are you just about ready to go out and kick some serious butt?

Then congratulations are in order! Your "friend" is on its way out, and before you know it that much-anticipated menopausal zest will kick in. Soon a whole new world of possibilities for the uniquely pissed-off will unfold before you. So get yourself a nice hefty baseball bat and prepare to meet me, one Monday morning bright and early, on the steps of the Capitol building. Oh, what times we'll have, my dears, for the times they are indeed "a-changin'."

QUESTIONS
Mandy Carter
Adapted from taped narrative.

I am forty-six and going to be forty-seven November second of
1995, this year, and I'm not sure if I've gone through menopause or
not, so I have to just tell you what I know from my own experience.

I think menopause is something that doesn't really get talked
about a lot in our lesbian community. Maybe as more and more of us
from the baby boom generation after World War II, in our late forties
heading into our fifties start going through it it might be, but right
now it doesn't get talked about hardly at all. A lot of friends of mine
that are older talk about it one-on-one. But you don't hear about
menopause in general conversation like we talk about, let's say
S&M, or lesbians who have been victims of incest. It's also the same
with a number of women now having hysterectomies—that's more
and more becoming a topic of general conversation because so many
lesbians are having them.

Having run around in the circles I run around in, it's interesting
that I don't hear about menopause.

Menopause as I understand it means going through the change.
You start having hot flashes. You don't have your period. Whether
you have a hysterectomy or not, if you take hormones they're supposed to balance you out. I mean, this is some of the stuff I've heard;
I don't know how much is true and that's part of the problem. I'm
not sure people know what menopause really is, or even the symptoms and signs of it.

From the other end of it, when I started bleeding, I remember I
had no idea what was going on. One day I went to the bathroom and
I had my period. I didn't know what was going on and I didn't
know why I had it, how it started—it was a total mystery. I was staying in a foster home. The woman, when I told her I was bleeding,
never really gave me a full explanation. She just said you start needing to use some—not even tampons at that point—Kotex. I remem-

ber brushing my teeth that morning, going to the bathroom, starting my period and somehow associating brushing my teeth with blood, which is weird, but that's how little I knew. Maybe a lot of girls don't have their periods until later, maybe thirteen or fourteen, but I had mine at twelve. It was very weird and very uncomfortable and even to this day it's something I have a lot of problems or issues with just because of the way it never got dealt with when I was a kid. It was always very painful and I flowed very heavy.

The only reason I mention the heavy flow is that in the last two years I just stopped having my period altogether.

I had surgery about twelve years ago. I had a cyst on an ovary and one ovary was removed along with half of the other. I remember the doctor saying to me, "When you go to have this surgery you can, if you want, just go ahead and have a total hysterectomy." I said no. Now it seems very odd for him to say that. I mean, you should just take out the part that's not working and be done with it! I remember thinking no, I want to keep whatever I have left. So I kept the other half of the ovary and I still had my period, but it was no longer painful and it no longer flowed heavy like it did before.

Then as months and months went by, pretty soon the flow became less and less. Now, literally, I think I've had my period maybe once in two years. I don't know if that means that I'm in menopause or not. All I know is I'm not having my period and I'm worried about the other half of that ovary. What's going on with that—is there a cyst there?

I haven't really gone in and gotten a check-up and I should. That's another downfall, I think, for a lot of us in the lesbian and women's communities. We don't do our yearly checkups. I have never had a pap smear done and for all I know— I have no idea. I'm just hoping that I'm okay and my periods are over.

I think it is menopause that I'm going through. I have flashes once in a while and I start sweating a lot. Like, I'll just be sitting there and all of a sudden I get a huge heat thing and then I start sweating and then it will go away. I can't predict them; they just come and go. I'm not on any hormone stuff and hope I never have to take hormones. Yet I know that if a doctor told me I have to get this other ovary out and therefore should just have a hysterectomy I probably wouldn't be as scared about it now. I have some friends who've gone through it and it's not like it's some phenomenal thing for me.

In terms of racial issues, I probably have talked to more white women around the issue of menopause than I have black lesbians. Again, it's not something that seems to be talked about in general, but probably even less so in the black lesbian community. The one hope I have is that there are a number of lesbian and gay health services. I'm thinking of Whitman-Walker in particular in Washington D.C. Beverly Biddle, a black lesbian, heads up lesbian services. Whitman-Walker does focused workshops on menopause and also just around lesbian health issues. I think I should avail myself of those services and it would be great if more lesbians used them.

I always wonder about the differences between heterosexual women, bisexual women and lesbians in terms of health issues. Are there big differences? Does the lesbian lifestyle make a difference in how we handle menopause? Does it change how we deal with and think about hysterectomies?

Then there's the whole area of holistic health. A lot of lesbians don't want to do traditional health services or traditional medicine and are doing alternative medicine. I'm curious about alternative medicines and menopause and also about whether you can actually have a hysterectomy and never have to worry about taking the hormone pills that medical doctors prescribe. Those are questions I'd like to explore so I could make a decision about the change and whether I want to do the holistic route or just traditional medicine.

Whatever I decide to do, I feel great about getting older.

KOTEX, TAMPAX AND VITAMIN E
María

"This morning I noticed the skin on my throat, that thin layer just between one's chin and the space between the collar bones; it covers the adam's apple. Well, just since yesterday, that skin has softened. It's not quite wrinkled yet or really loosened, but I can tell it's softer and getting ready to wrinkle. I have few wrinkles so far on my face, not even the crows feet my mother's face has caused me to look forward to, just those little pads of fat giving me jowls like my mother's mother. Falling skin, shrinking eyes and receding lips invoking disapproval I don't feel, make me wish I'd smiled more. All this I watch with rapt attention and eager anticipation. The rose in full flower is as beautiful as the bud, but excitement lies in the unfolding of ripeness."

The entire process of aging has fascinated me ever since I began to notice that my own body had finished "growing up" and begun growing old. Menopause is the demarcation point our society places between youth and age. It is a convenient one for the dominant culture since it doesn't happen to them. This can cause us to confuse our passages. For most women menopause occurs long before old age. However, it is the point at which our lives cease to be useful to men, when we are no longer generative. And, when our bodies leave behind those marks men call beauty. Since we as lesbians need not concern ourselves with these things, all we have to do is rid ourselves of the internalized definitions of youth as beauty and age as ugly. That's all.

I wrote the above quotation for a contest in which I was challenged to describe my uniqueness in one hundred words or less. I felt compelled to illustrate aging as beautifying. With the words and concepts our society has given us this is not an easy task.

I do believe it is a task worth doing, because I believe our culture takes us a step further by acting as if menopause is a curable disease. We lesbians are in a unique position to change this. It matters not at all to us what men think is beautiful. We breed only when we choose, and are generative in many ways other than child-birth. We have no reason to defy or deny menopause or dread the aging process.

So, I continue to look for ways to describe my ripening body as she sags and folds toward Grandmother, loosens her tight bonds, stretches out...and stays there, as lovely. Then after I have found the words, I'll teach myself to believe them.

When I was ten, I bled (from "down there") for the first time. My mother took me aside and very seriously and sadly explained the painful lot of a woman's life that I must now begin to bear. I was given my first box of Kotex with one of those belts that cut into your crotch, and shown how to wrap the used pads so no one would have to look at or accidentally see something as disgusting as my blood.

Is it any wonder that each time I bled again I was also visited with severe cramping, vomiting, migraine headaches and fainting spells?

When I was thirty, my uterus prolapsed (after my seventh pregnancy). I had to wear a Tampax continuously to keep my womb inside my body. My doctor said the only solution was to remove it, but he would not discuss this until my husband told him it was OK. I didn't want my womb anymore! I didn't want to bleed, cramp, hurt, be vulnerable or pregnant again.

It was many more years before I realized why I had so much trouble feeling my second chakra. The sense of loss I felt as my daughters and younger friends came to womanhood and motherhood in positive female ways was profound. I was happy for them, sad for me.

When I was forty-three, I woke up one morning covered with sweat and a sense of excitement I wished I could have felt when I was ten. I was reminded of the day I first bled by the smell of my skin. I had been complaining, well, whining, that I wouldn't know when I started menopause because I hadn't bled in thirteen years. I was wrong. I knew! I called my best friend and we went out to dinner to celebrate. I think I called nearly everyone I knew that day.

I was determined to experience every nuance of every change my body created. And I have, mostly. Sometimes I discovered the connection with menopause after the fact from talking with other lesbians my age and older, and discussions in crone circles. It hasn't all been fun and roses, but I have been here, present and involved.

I have also been single and living alone for most of that time period, so no one else has had to try to sleep through drenched sheets or hourly trips to the toilet with me.

No one else has had to live through my spontaneous bottomless pit depressions that could last five minutes or five weeks without rhyme or reason. My roommate (me) insists I've never been cranky about the toothpaste cap or which way the T.P. should roll or annoyed that the dishes haven't been done, or done right.

It was just "interesting" to watch water drip off the end of my nose and feel it sliding down between my breasts to pool in my belly button during board meetings. I didn't know grown men in the '90s blushed at the mention of the word menopause.

Peppermint tea, ginseng, and vitamin E soothe or minimize most of my symptoms. Exercise in the form of Kung Fu classes and movement workshops finally exorcised most of the stiff joints my doctor and I had mistaken for osteoarthritis.

Since I haven't bled in twenty-four years, I also won't know for sure when I'm post-menopausal; won't know exactly when to have my crone ritual. I have had few symptoms in the last year or two, but it's probably not time yet. I've recently fallen in lust and hot flashes have returned...with that faint odor of my first bloods.

FREE! FREE! FREE!
Mariwynne and Lynn
Adapted from correspondence.

Menopause has been great for us! After thirty-seven years of pads and plugs and sometimes both at the same time because our flow was so heavy, we are free, free, free! We can make love whenever we feel like it and I no longer have the excruciating cramps that I endured for thirty-seven years. My partner and I are both white and neither one of has had children. I am fifty-three years old and Lynn, my companion of twenty-eight years, is fifty-two.

I have fibroid tumors in my uterus. Eight years ago, my gynecologist told me that I needed to have a hysterectomy. I told him that since I wasn't having any trouble (no more trouble than I have always had with my periods) I didn't see any reason to go through such invasive surgery. He argued with me for a while and finally gave me a booklet to read. Buried inside the booklet was the information that fibroids shrink with the onset of menopause. I was forty-five years old at the time and I knew that menopause had to be close. The next time I went to see the gynecologist, I told him that I thought I would wait for menopause and see if that didn't shrink the fibroids. He argued with me some more and finally told me that I would be sorry. He was very persuasive and I probably would have agreed to the surgery except for Lynn's support telling me that I was right and why fix something that wasn't broken. The last time I saw my gynecologist, he agreed that the fibroids had indeed shrunk in size and I knew that I had made the right decision.

For me there have been very few problems with menopause. I had one incident of flooding when the blood soaked through everything. I was unaware that anything was wrong until I stood up and saw a pool (I am not exaggerating) of blood on the seat of the plastic chair where I had been sitting.

Lynn, on the other hand, has suffered through three flooding incidents. Each time she was oblivious of the problem when it occurred. The worst time she had was four years ago when she bled copiously for two weeks. She spent most of her day tied to the bathroom. She would put in a Tampax and wander around five minutes and then she would have to go back and put in another one.

She almost died because of this. She became dehydrated and weak from loss of blood and I drove her to the hospital.

We live fifty minutes from the nearest hospital. Luckily, her profuse bleeding slowed on its own while we were enroute to the hospital because the emergency room doctor did nothing to help her. After she lay in the hospital emergency room for two hours, she drank a coke which helped the dehydration and she felt strong enough to sit up without fainting. She needed her strength because shortly thereafter they moved her to a regular room and the doctor wanted to run a series of tests and she wanted to go home. They argued for a long time until she finally picked up her clothes and told them she was going.

I have had a few mild hot flashes, but nothing that causes any problem.

Lynn suffered through horrible hot flashes and terrible night sweats. She doesn't believe in taking medicine unnecessarily and was willing to endure the hot flashes. She has a family history of osteoporosis and was concerned about loss of bone density so she decided to take hormones. Lynn started the hormones and the night sweats have stopped. She still has mild hot flashes, but she has them less often than before.

One interesting thing about our menopause is that four years ago our sex drive went off the scale. It was like when we first got together, except that now we are better at making love and we have much more variety to what we do. For a while we made love three or four times a day. Being old maid school teachers (Ha! Ha!) we had the summer free to indulge in our sexual exploits. Now four years later, we still can't keep our hands off each other. We make love every other day and sometimes more often in the summer. This part of menopause is fantastic!

LIFE WITH IRENE, THE MENOPAUSE AND THE PINK TABLETS
Beatriz Copello

LIFE BEFORE THE MENOPAUSE

This story is about two women who fell in love with each other and conflict arose, not in the shape of a villain third woman, but in the way of a physiological change: menopause.

We met, Irene and I, when in our early forties. I was living then with my two daughters from a marriage which was dissolved when the girls were very young. Growing up in a Latin American country didn't provide me with many sexual choices. I was born a woman and as such destined for marriage and motherhood. Yes, I was a woman but not the submissive type. I had rebelled: against the system, against matrimony, against patriarchy, and so on. When I realized that my "contra" actions didn't get me anywhere I migrated to Australia. Amidst the many things that Australia gave me, there are two that I value above everything. One, the chance of discovering my lesbianism and two, my feminism—both of which I discovered and learned from great Australian women.

When the passionate encounter took place between Irene and me, I had been a lesbian for longer than I had been heterosexual and my daughters were not girls but young women. Irene was a bit reluctant to get involved with a woman with a family, but I assured her that they knew about my sexuality and that they didn't mind; they had grown up amidst lesbian friends and lovers. It didn't take us long to decide that we were made for each other and we moved in together. It took a bit of time for Irene to adjust to the new life. She had been living on her own for a few years and moving into a household with three strong and temperamental women proved to be difficult for her.

Through screams, arguments, and menstrual cycles, through struggles for the right to choose the Sunday movie and an assortment of morning and evening dramas, the love between Irene and me grew stronger and stronger. It was not only love that flourished between us. We were also consumed by passion, a passion that saw outlets the minute the girls were out of the front door. It didn't matter where we were, whether the back veranda or the kitchen, the bathroom or the living room floor. We were made for each other. Such passion bred inspiration and I covered reams and reams of paper with "lesbian erotic poetry."

Time flew and three years went by without either of us realizing it. It was then that my menstruation started to go crazy. I would spend fifteen days with pre-menstrual symptoms and fifteen days with the period, sometimes longer. I consulted a few gynecologists who recommended that I have a hysterectomy. The fibroids in the womb were sending my periods haywire. Although I didn't intend to have any more children at this stage, I wasn't very happy about parting with one of my organs, even one as useless as my womb. Talking to other lesbians, I discovered that many of them had had hysterectomies, but as with menopause no one spoke openly about it.

In my search for knowledge I borrowed library books which discussed hysterectomies, but information therein was confusing and often contradictory. In the end I decided to follow the advice of my lesbian friends who said that it was a simple operation, that I was going to be tired for a long time, but that after a year or so I was never going to look back. They were right!

Irene was very supportive throughout this experience, so supportive in fact that my daughters decided that I didn't need them any more (I now had Irene to look after me!!!). They took off for London, to learn and grow in the old European capital. At the airport, my daughters and I cried buckets of tears and went through at least a box of tissues. Irene, controlled, calm and composed, had only two tiny tears stuck to her long eyelashes, two tiny tears that reflected the lights of the departing lounge.

The silence, the peace and quiet and the absence of arguments marked a new stage in our lesbian partnership. First we felt lost without the girls but soon, very soon, we learned to love our space and tranquillity. Time on our own allowed us to talk about many things. Amongst the many topics we discussed was the menopause and aging.

I was convinced that I was going to go through the menopause without even realizing it. As I no longer menstruated this event was going to pass unnoticed. I had never heard my mother or aunts talk about this so I assumed that in my family going through the menopause was a cinch. Irene, having left Scotland at the age of nineteen, knew nothing about the experiences of her mother and aunts.

We strongly agreed that the menopause was not going to affect our lives; we were not going to be bothered about two or three hot flushes. If our vaginas became dry we would use a lubricant. Aging together, losing our youth and reasonable good looks was a luxury and not the trauma the patriarchy wanted us to believe. We were convinced symptoms associated with the menopause were created by the multinationals in order to sell drugs to women. We made a firm commitment: No drugs for us!

Bliss and poetry, love-making on hot siestas, breakfasts with Mozart playing in the background, flowers for anniversaries, letters from the girls with hundreds of pictures from London, a new house, promotions…and life went on happier than we had ever been before.

LIFE DURING…

One morning, as we were finishing breakfast, the bomb dropped! Irene's white and translucent skin went bright red. Big drops of perspiration slid from her broad forehead. Swearing, she stripped to the waist. I watched all of this as in slow motion. What was happening to her? Had I poisoned her with the fried mushrooms? Was there a streak of madness in her that I hadn't noticed before? As I posed these questions in my mind, I observed her struggling to take off her clothes. After a minute or so she gave a deep breath and said, "I think I had a hot flush."

We left it at that and said nothing for a few weeks, until I noticed a hand towel in Irene's briefcase. "Why on earth are you carrying a hand towel in your briefcase? Has your Department gone to the pits so much that they don't provide you with paper towels?" I asked.

"Do you remember, a few weeks ago, when I had a hot flush?" Irene said.

"Yes, of course I remember," I said impatiently.

"Well, the same has been happening every morning in the train on the way to work. I can't strip, so I need the towel to dry my perspiration."

The hot flushes increased by the minute. They would come at the most inconvenient of moments: in the middle of interviewing a client, while talking to her boss, in the middle of an executive meeting, or when we were making love, in which case she would kick off the quilt and I would freeze. The funny thing about this was that it all happened in the peak of winter. On very cold winter mornings shivering fellow train riders, or cold office mates would look at Irene in surprise as she would suddenly go red and perspire as if in a sauna.

We discussed the inconvenience of the "hot flushes" and decided to search at the local health shop for a natural medicine. There we came across "Evening Primrose" oral capsules. They were quite expensive, but they promised to reduce the symptoms of menopause so we bought them. After a few weeks we realized that they were not much help.

In the meantime, something really weird happened to me. The Manager of the unit where I worked asked me for a report that I was supposed to have completed. Whilst I was explaining why I hadn't completed it, I went red and commenced to perspire. I had a hot flush! I haven't gone red since I was a shy teenager. I have a good relationship with my Manager, I was not lying, why then was I reacting like this? Later, after a few similar incidents I realized that my "hot flushes" were situational as opposed to Irene's which were more random. In my case, even a slightly anxiety-raising situation would bring the undesirable reaction.

Within two or three months of the hot flushes starting we went from making love nearly every day to perhaps once or twice a week. We became apologetic with each other. "Do you mind if...?" "I'm sorry, but—" "Do you still love me if we don't...?" "I'd love, but—" No, we didn't mind because we both were feeling quite the same. It was as if our minds wanted to make love, because they know that it's great, pleasurable, fantastic, but our bodies refused to respond.

Insecurities rose to the surface. "Do you still love me?" "Do you still find me attractive?" "Do I still turn you on?" We went to sleep most nights in each other's arms swearing that Yes, we loved each other the same! Yes, we were still attracted to each other! And yes, we were made for each other even if we didn't feel like making love.

I started to wake up at unusual hours, mainly to go to the toilet. The worst of it was that I could not go back to sleep. Even in times of anguish, depression or stress, never had I lost any sleep. The same happened to Irene. Between the two of us, every night we made at least six trips to the toilet to pass water. Snacks and tea in the middle of the night became our reward for not being able to sleep. It became a morning topic of conversation how many times we had visited the "dunny"(Australian for toilet) that night and at what time we finally went back to sleep.

It was about this time that I went to my mother for advice. How had she coped? My mother was a strong, no-nonsense woman, who took life as it came and never questioned her lot. When I told her that I was worried about the menopause symptoms she gave me a look of disgust. What was there to worry about? "A few hot flushes have never hurt any woman!" she said, dismissing the conversation. I had so many questions to ask but obviously my mother was not the person to talk to.

Through many years of reflection and introspection I had become a very positive and confident woman, but now, something inside me was destroying that "self" I so carefully had molded and nurtured with determination and gentleness. Why was I losing my confidence? Why was I doubting my professional judgment? Why was I doubting my value as a woman, as a lover, as a writer, and so on? Why quite suddenly had I become this woman who had to think twice before doing anything?

Irene had taken a different path. She had become vague, distracted and started to forget things. In a period of three months she fell over twice in the street and once at home, often locked the keys of the car inside, left her wallet at home and was faced with situations in shops and restaurants without money. She forgot her mother's birthday. Then came the day when she was run over by a car because she crossed the street without checking for oncoming traffic. Luckily, the car was going five miles per hour when she walked into it.

Mother died amidst all this confusion and I was confronted with my own mortality. No one needed me anymore: mother had died, my daughters had lives of their own, Irene was a strong dyke and could survive very well without me. Poetry seemed to have dried in my veins...was there any reason to live? Soon I was going to be old, decrepit and a burden to everyone. A heavy cloud had descended over my whole being. I was in a deep hole from where I could not emerge. Life was not worth living. Yet that positive little light in me was screaming: "It's not you it's the hormones!" I couldn't believe that all the unusual negative thoughts, all the insecurity, all the doubting of myself was the result of my body's withdrawal reaction to some chemical. As a feminist I couldn't accept that I was a chemically-driven being!

By now Irene and I had lost our patience with each other. We screamed and we nagged about the silliest things. "I don't like the way you hung my woolen jumpers!" I would snap. "Why do you always leave the taps running? There is a drought here in Sydney, you know!" she would say. "Why did you make two pieces of toast for me? You know I only eat one!" I screamed one morning. "Can't you see you nearly killed that pedestrian!" Irene accused. We went on and on and on. It annoyed me the way she set the table forgetting to put out the salt and the serviettes. It annoyed her when I said I wanted to die, that life was not worth living and we were just two old fogies. I got mad at her because she cuddled Pinie more than me (Pinie is one of our dogs). She got mad because I wanted to jump in the Wolli Creek and drown myself. (The creek is two feet deep.)

We both had become very emotional. The news on TV reduced us to tears and our bills for tissues tripled! Irene, who didn't cry easily, was now crying because Martina had won a match, a lost baby was returned to her mother, or a cat trapped on a roof was brought down to safety.

As well as my depression, our hot flushes and reduced libido, other symptoms emerged to be added to this repertoire. My bones started to ache, especially in my feet and legs. Just to get out of bed was a painful affair. Irene's skin became very dry and she tried various creams to relieve the itchiness. Instead of making love we spent many hours rubbing each other with creams for itchiness and muscle or bone pain.

"Enough is enough," Irene said one night. "We're going to see a feminist medical practitioner." I agreed. We smiled as we hadn't agreed to anything for a long time. We kissed good-night and declared our love for each other before falling asleep. The next day we saw Kath, a very supportive and understanding doctor. We explained that, as feminists we didn't believe in hormone replacement therapy. We wanted to age gracefully without having to pump our bodies full of drugs, designed only to make the drug companies richer. We also confided in her our many emotional, psychological and physical troubles.

Kath sighed and proceeded to explain to us that yes! all those weird things that were happening to us were the result of the menopause. No! There were not that many natural remedies to relieve all those symptoms, but hormone replacement therapy would. We arrived home deflated and disappointed, carrying a bundle of pamphlets about HRT. With embarrassment and trepidation, because we were acting against our principles, we reluctantly decided that maybe we should give it a go. "The quality of life is more important than principles." Kath's words reverberated in my head as I fell asleep.

LIFE AFTER THE PINK TABLETS

I was not at risk of getting cancer of the uterus because I had the hysterectomy, so I only took progesterone. Irene took one pink progesterone tablet and one blue oestrogen. After only one week I started to notice changes. How glorious to sleep a whole night without having to get up to go to the toilet! All my aches and pains disappeared. My depression faded and life became again the stimulating and exciting adventure that it always had been! Irene's well-being, memory and moods improved dramatically. Our sex life is poetry again and poems pour out of my mind and onto paper.

By the time my daughters decided to come back from London things were very much back to normal. Before coming they decided they were going to live on their own, a relief, as we had become used to a quieter life. At the airport we all cried, including Irene. "My god you have let yourselves go—you are both so fat!" they said in unison. I have given up trying to get feminist theory and practice inside my daughters' heads. Irene and I looked at each other and ignored their silly remarks. Yes we knew, we had put on weight, Irene on her boobs and belly and I on my hips. All thanks to the pink tablets, but for a good reason!

"It must have been sheer bliss, you two on your own and for so long?" the eldest asked as we were having dinner. Irene and I didn't say anything but we later agreed that we would eventually tell them. We are determined not to sweep menopause under the carpet as has been the case with other natural stages in a woman's life.

A few weeks ago an alarming study published in the *New England Journal of Medicine* was reported in the press. Women on HRT for more than five years increase their chances of developing breast cancer by a very high percentage. We panicked! It is now nearly five years since we started on HRT. With the newspaper clipping in Irene's hands we walked into Kath's consulting rooms. "Yes, I read it. Yes, it is very worrying because it is the first big scale study. Yes, I agree, it might be a good thing if you wean yourselves from the HRT. You should take a calcium supplement to prevent osteoporosis."

I am going cold turkey. I have thrown all my pink tablets in the rubbish bin. Irene is going to reduce the doses of HRT slowly. "Will the symptoms return?" I asked Kath. She doesn't know; they may, they may not.

I feel cheated, once again I have been used as a guinea pig. Many years ago in Argentina I was prescribed a contraceptive injection once a month, when in the rest of the civilized world the injections were not approved by health authorities. Why were we given HRT when its use was not totally safe? I don't blame Kath. She is obviously another victim of the system that uses and abuses women's bodies.

What should we have done when all our menopausal and related problems started? We needed support, understanding, knowledge of our bodies and ourselves. We didn't need drugs. HRT has helped us to get through a very difficult period, but at what cost! Kath has now suggested that we have a mammogram every year instead of the required two years!

Now it is too late to go back. Without our doses of pink and blue tablets the dreaded symptoms may return. We may get cancer. Perhaps neither will happen. Whatever the future holds for us it does not matter. We love and care for each other very much and whatever happens we will face it together.

LESBIAN MENOPAUSE
Mary Clare Powell

I burrow across our wide bed
and run my hands up your sides,
lift myself onto you, fixing
my breasts to lie amongst yours,
let my weight down slowly, and
kiss the end of your nose.
"I love you," you murmur
and we readjust arms,
always too many for lying together,
too few for making love. And
suddenly all of me that touches
you is wet, water rising
from you, sweet, and I
who was standing on firm ground
just looking around, begin to sink.
I roll off, you sweep the covers back,
lying dew filled and water heavy. Then
you rise out of bed
naked and vertical,
lovely thick water lily
rooted in mud. Porous
stem, weeping leaves,
and extraordinary white
flower on top.

OUT OF THE SADDLE AT TWENTY-SIX
Meredith More

Full consciousness returned slowly. First I became aware that I was in my hospital room, alone, lying flat on my back. Then I saw the IV tube taped to the back of my left hand. After this I heard a machine humming somewhere beneath me to my right. Turning my head toward the sound, I saw two other tubes, apparently attached to my body, disappearing over the side of the bed. I did not yet know where they were connected to me (one at my upper right armpit, the other at my upper right side) nor why they were there (to drain fluid).

Wondering if the lump had been benign, but fearing it had not, I felt for my right breast. The entire right chest area was numb. It was also covered by a large, thick bandage. I could not tell whether or not my small breast was beneath this.

Then I remembered my surgeon's words five days earlier: " If the lump's malignant, we'll have to remove the entire breast and take skin from your thigh for a skin graft." I slid my right hand down to my right thigh. Feeling the bandage there, I knew.

It was early June of 1964. I was twenty-six years old. And I had just had a radical mastectomy.

I had also just had my ovaries removed as part of this procedure. "If we don't take the ovaries too," my surgeon had explained, "in all probability you will develop a malignancy in the other breast within a few years." There was, he said, a connection between the ovaries and malignant lumps in breasts (he never said the word cancer to me).

My radical mastectomy in 1964 was truly radical. In addition to losing my ovaries and all of my right breast, I also lost all of my lymph nodes under my right armpit, as well as a lot of upper arm muscle tissue. I was told this was done "to be sure the malignancy had not spread." The fact that virtually all of these lymph nodes were malignant was kept from me for many years, as were all the grim predictions about my survival. But as the seventeenth century

British poet Thomas Gray wrote, "Where ignorance is bliss, 'Tis folly to be wise." I was young, naturally optimistic, in otherwise excellent health (ironically), so it never occurred to me that I might die.

It was the second or third day after the surgery that I was, as I used to say to my mother in my teen years, "back in the saddle again." This old cowboy song was my metaphor for menstruation. I had two younger brothers and an even younger little sister, and in the 1950s most of us teenage girls would sooner die than let our younger siblings know about that reality sometimes called "the curse." The subject itself was virtually taboo both within the home (except between mothers and daughters) and outside it (except between best friends or sisters).

I felt somewhat strange on that June afternoon in 1964, knowing that this would be the last time I'd menstruate, yet not quite believing it. The ugly red, four-inch-long wound from my navel down to my semi-shaved pubic area proved I would not be "back in the saddle again," but the fact that I was currently "in the saddle" made me doubt that I would ever really be free of it.

The unbandaged incision was so irritated by the elastic sanitary belt that I finally resorted to stuffing a wash cloth between the belt and the wound. It was as if the sanitary belt were saying, "You will keep having these periods," while the incision was saying, "You won't."

I felt strange also that day in another way, one that truly surprised me. Even as a small child I had known, on some level, that I was a lesbian. Since junior high school, during which my many secret crushes on movie stars and female classmates had begun, I had known that I would never get married and I would never have children. In my teens and early twenties I dated males because I was "supposed to"; I broke up with them as soon as they wanted to do more than give me a tongueless good-night kiss. Shortly before moving to Virginia at age twenty-five to teach college English, I had decided to stop playing this stupid dating game, no matter what the pressures from peers and relatives.

I had felt no more sadness about giving up motherhood than I felt about giving up marriage. I had about as much maternal instinct as did my brothers, with whom as a child I shared a strong dislike of baby dolls and a strong attraction to cowboy games, sandlot baseball, tree houses, jeans, bare feet and sailor hats.

And yet, on that June morning in the hospital, when I began my final menstrual period, I was surprised by an unexpected emotion that I felt realizing then that I could not have any children. Being unable to have them was not the same as choosing not to have them. I felt some part of my being, as well as vital parts of my body, had been taken out of my control forever. A strange melancholy swept over me, but it did not last very long.

That afternoon my parents arrived from North Carolina. My mother was angry at me for not telling anyone except my two house-mates that I was having this surgery. (I had not wanted my parents to worry.) When she found out that I had lost my perfectly healthy ovaries, I think she was more upset over that fact than over the loss of my breast. She was still under the delusion that I would one day marry and make her a grandmother (which my three siblings would do during the next two decades).

One good thing that came from this loss of my ovaries was that my mother stopped mentioning marriage and children to me.

It was about this time that I complained to my surgeon about the climate control system in the hospital. "One minute it's too hot in this room," I said, "and the next minute it's too cold. Can't they do something to fix that?"

"You're undergoing surgical menopause," he said.

I had never heard of this term before. "You mean it's not the air conditioning system, it's me?" I asked, remembering the hot and cold flashes that my mother had had before her hysterectomy.

"Yes," he replied. "You are having a premature menopause."

"How long will this last?" I asked, somewhat uneasily.

"Oh, not long, another week or so." He then told me that I would not be given hormone therapy to replace the estrogen pro-duced by the ovaries. He explained that other glands in my body would produce whatever estrogen I needed. If he gave me addition-al estrogen, he added, that would defeat the whole purpose of removing my ovaries and I would be in great danger of developing a malignancy in my remaining breast.

To this day I have not had estrogen replacement therapy. I have not grown a beard, my voice has not deepened, nor have I developed any other masculine traits. I have not lost interest in sex, either. Nor have I experienced problems such as vaginal drying that sometimes happen during menopause. Maybe I'm just lucky.

Compared with everything else I was undergoing related to my radical mastectomy, the hot flashes and chills I experienced that month were a minor inconvenience. By the middle of the second week of my hospitalization, my menopausal experience was basically over, as was my final period.

Near the end of the second week of my hospitalization, my doctor came into my room to remove the stitches from my chest. I discovered then that, ironically enough, in another way, I was still "in the saddle." Along with the gauze, tape, scissors and other things on the tray the nurse sat beside my bed were two sanitary napkins. Curious, I asked my surgeon what they were for.

"Part of the dressing," he answered as he began removing the bandage that had been there since the operation. "They help to protect the skin graft," he explained. A moment later he lifted from my chest two sanitary napkins I had unknowingly been wearing since the surgery. They were stained with dark dried blood.

I continued to be "in the saddle" in this respect for over a month after I left the hospital, having several more bandage changes that included protective sanitary napkins.

But when "that time of the month" came, and then went, in July, and nothing happened, I knew that it was really true: I was "out of the saddle" for good. And I was overjoyed, absolutely elated! From that time to this, I have never for one second regretted my surgical menopause at twenty-six. "Out of evil, good," as John Milton wrote. The one good thing that resulted from the loss of my breast was that I was freed from what to me was always an unwanted and pointless monthly burden.

This meant also a new freedom in my love life, which did resume again the following summer. No longer did any woman with whom I was romantically involved and I have to contend with two of us "in the saddle" every month.

My personal experiences from that time forward have also reinforced what I had always believed about women in general and lesbians in particular: we care more about people than bodies.

I have watched various friends and relatives go through natural menopause, occasionally involving hysterectomies. Some of them, knowing about my surgical menopause, have actually said to me at times that they envy me that experience (but not the cancer). They say it jokingly of course, but to some degree I think they really mean it.

I am now at (or maybe beyond) what would otherwise have been my normal menopausal age. I am having no menopausal symptoms. I feel not particularly different, physically or spiritually, than I have in the last five plus years. I have finally found the woman I was meant to share the rest of my life with, the waterfront home I've always dreamed of, and the almost perfect dog (though male).

My menopausal experience was a part of my cancer experience, since both happened at the same time. However, as time passed the two became increasingly separate from each other. I very quickly adjusted to the loss of my ovaries. The loss of my breast, however, was a deeper cut, not only literally (the physical recuperation took many months) but also emotionally. But that is another story.

THE PERIOD: A SEQUEL
Marilyn Murphy

I had my first menstrual period toward the end of my twelfth year, and I remember it well. My mother had prepared me for the coming of blood "down there." No one had prepared her for her period, when she was a child, so she wanted the experience to be less traumatic for me. I was in the bathroom at home when it happened. Mother was home, too, so she went to the store for the small size Kotex pads and the "sanitary" belt I needed, postponing, for me, the embarrassment of carrying the tell-tale Kotex box past the neighborhood boys hanging out in front of the drugstore. That humiliation was still ahead of me.

When the cramps struck, I was surprised and dismayed. Mother had talked to me about my womb practicing for the time I was old enough to make a baby, just like the Blessed Virgin Mary made Jesus in her womb. She forgot to tell me about cramps. No one was there to tell me that masturbation eased the pain of cramps, either. Not that the information would have done me any good. I didn't know there was an activity, engaged in by females, called "masturbation" until I read Doctor Spock's baby book as a new mother. I hated having cramps, except as an excuse to stay home from school or to be excused from my chores. These abstentions happened rarely—Mother didn't believe in sickness or pain—so that I was reduced to persuading my sister Jeanne into doing my after school chores for me. She seldom helped me out until, a year and a half later, she got her period.

I continued to have crampy periods until I became pregnant at nineteen. They weren't terrible cramps, and they didn't last long. I found the experiences that surround having a period harder to live with than the period itself. The pads cost money, and we were poor. We were a family of girls who emptied the Kotex box faster than we could get the money to refill it. Then there were the boys and their jokes, and the blood stains discovered on the skirt after returning home from school or church or the grocery store. Oh, no! Cramps were the least of my menstrual problems.

When my period returned after the birth of the first of my four children, I no longer suffered from menstrual cramps. I was grateful, of course, but not as grateful as I would have been if the periods themselves had ended. Still, I was damn lucky to have cramp-free periods, regular ones at that, for the fifteen to twenty menstrual years ahead.

My menopause wasn't terrible, either. My period began to decrease its flow, in quantity and duration, when I was in my early forties. By forty-five, my period was quite irregular, lasted two or three days and was a scant flow, when it did show up. By fifty, my period was gone.

I don't mean to imply that menopause was a snap. I had my share of hot flashes, ten years of them, in fact. I would start warming up slowly, reaching a peak where I thought I'd burn to death if the flash didn't start cooling down *this very minute*. However, the flashes weren't constant, didn't wake me at night and didn't drench me in sweat. So, I can't really complain, especially since my beloved companion, Irene Weiss, was suffering all of the above, more often and with greater intensity.

Menopause caused my disposition to take a turn for the worse, but that wasn't *all* bad. I was a member of a feminist collective at that time, and had a lot of trouble confronting the middle-class members. AH! When I was having a cranky spell, I was great. I'd speak my mind. I'd call them on their wishy-washiness, on their ability to avoid doing the work of the collective. (It warms my heart to remember those days. I only wish I had kept that skill.)

I loved being post-menopausal, loved having no periods, no hot flashes, no mood swings. For more than ten years, I lived in a "sanitary napkin"-free, tampon-free home. I always meant to keep those products in the house, for the convenience of our neighbors and guests, but I never got around to doing it. Often, women would ask if we had any to spare. I'd say, "I'm sorry I can't help you out, but this is a period-free household."

Those days are gone now. One year ago this month, my doctor told me I should be taking estrogen and progesterone. It seems that estrogen replacement therapy is supposed to significantly lessen post-menopausal women's chances for developing cardiovascular disease and osteoporosis. I had managed to avoid that step since my first hot flash, but was more or less persuaded to give it a try. "Oh, by the way," said the doctor, "you will have a fifty-fifty chance of getting your period back." I started to get all bent out of shape, but recalled my menstrual history, filled with lucky breaks, and picked up the prescription. " I'll take my chances," I said, tempting fate.

Twenty-five days later, I was attending a Center meeting at the Pagoda with fourteen other Lesbians. I was not feeling well, and was even more cranky than I usually am at a Center meeting. I realized I was feeling squishy "down there." I went to the bathroom and became awash with terror at the sight of the blood in the toilet and on my clothes and body. Several long, scary minutes passed before I realized my period was back. I was furious. Not only was my period back, but I had no tampons or pads to deal with it. I had to ask the women for assistance. The meeting turned rowdy and was recessed while my friends and neighbors laughed and teased and carried on about my predicament. Claudia was the only one to commiserate. She started estrogen replacement late, also. She only had one period, she told me, and she had a friend who had two. I shouldn't worry.

Claudia was wrong. I haven't missed a month since I got my period back. The flow isn't terrible, but it lasts about a week. And I can't use a tampon any more. When tampons came on the market around 1956, I thought they were one of Mother Nature's gifts to women. Now, I can't get them to stay in. I have had some miserable experiences with traveling tampons, experiences akin to those I had as a girl, when the Kotex pad would work its way off that little metal tab that was supposed to secure it to the "sanitary" belt. I must admit the new kind of napkin, that adheres to the crotch of my underpants, is an important advance.

I must be in denial about the return of my period because I cannot remember that it is back. As a result, I am as messy during it as I was at twelve. I'm just not as embarrassed about the mess. I have cramps too, like I had when I was a kid, growling cramps that last for days. Since I forget I have my period back, I spend a few premenstrual days of hypochondriac concern, wondering which of a variety of disease or conditions I am suffering from. When I see the blood "down there" again, and remember my period has returned, I groan and complain. Then I smile and open my copy of Betty Dodson's book *Liberating Masturbation*.

LEARNING TO LIVE WITH MY BODY
Julia Penelope

What we call 'menopause' is not a single isolated event in our lives. It is interwoven with how we perceive ourselves, in particular how we feel about our bodies and our sex. The shutting down of our reproductive systems is a process that takes five to ten years, and it signals the end of another decades-long process, menstruation. The two are impossible to separate from our understanding of what it means to be a 'woman.' In a society run by and for men, who do not menstruate, our monthly bleeding makes us different from them. It makes us Other. Menstruation signals our physical readiness to reproduce the species, to participate in heterosexual coupling, and we become the prey of men. According to male mythmakers, women welcome menstruation because bearing children is our 'purpose' for living, and dread menopause, because it ends what men consider to be the 'useful' years of our lives. Male descriptions of what being 'a woman' means are the basis for most of the information the medical 'experts' sell us, and most of that is the dung of cattle. For me, and for millions of other women, menopause is a much-anticipated event. It is the beginning of the freedom unique to the second half of our lives. To understand how I felt about menopause, you need to know how I felt about being female and menstruating.

Born in 1941, a teenager during the 1950s (the years of Joseph McCarthy and Ike), my feelings about 'being a woman' have been ambivalent, at best, downright negative at worst. Intuitively, I knew that being female was a 'bad' thing. I never wanted to be female. When I was about four, I announced to my mother that god had 'made a mistake:' I was meant to be a boy but had somehow been erroneously stuck in a girl's body. Apparently, I was so convincing that she took me to a doctor. After a thorough physical examination, he assured her that I was 'perfectly normal,' and that my conviction that I was a boy was 'all in my head.' So it was, but I didn't abandon my hypothesis. Although I held to this belief well into my adolescence, I am not, nor have I ever been, a 'transgendered person.' I consider my belief that I was a male 'trapped' in a female body as one among many theories I constructed to account for the fact that I, a female, wanted to love only other females. Being told repeatedly that only boys could love girls, I concluded, falsely, that I had to be a boy. That deduction took the logical form of a syllogism:

Only men can love women.

I love women.

Therefore I am a man.

Since I wasn't 'really' a woman, what possible reason could there be for me to menstruate? I didn't believe I was going to menstruate, especially after my mother (avant-garde for the time) had carefully explained menstruation and hetsex to me when I was nine. She'd even casually left *The Stork Didn't Bring You* lying out where I couldn't fail to notice it and pick it up. She knew her Gemini baby's insatiable curiosity. Oh yeah. I read the book, examined the diagrams, carefully noted what went where. I was not excited. I was appalled and disgusted.

My mother, unaware that she was the bearer of bad news, had even shown me the 'feminine hygiene' equipment available in those days: an elastic belt with metal hooks dangling in front and back, and a box of pads. These were not the days of bleeding 'liberated' by Procter & Gamble and Kimberly-Clark, giants in the billion-dollar industry built on making women believe we are 'unclean' because we menstruate. We had no Carefree, New Freedom, Stayfree mini- or maxi-pads. There was only Kotex and Modess (sic!), only those bulky things we called 'mattresses' that bunched up between our legs and sagged into the crotches of our panties so that the blood flowed over either side of them, staining underpants, slips, skirts and, especially, white shorts. And there was Tampax (which my mother failed to mention), but those, well, *those* were for married women! Being a good mother, she even took me to the drugstore and bought me my very own belt and pads so I'd be ready when 'that time' came. I was not grateful, and I didn't feel 'special,' and I certainly didn't want to marry a man and have babies. I was sure of *that*. Oh yeah, I knew what 'womanhood' was: a life sentence!

Of course, my mother was right. Sure enough, in 1952, when I was eleven, the 'impossible' happened: I awoke to find my sheets soaked with blood. I was horror-stricken. Every twenty-one days for the next thirty-three and a half years, I bled for three days: 17.4 times a year, a total of 582.9 periods. I hated menstruating, hated the pads and the Tampax later (a lover showed me how to use them). The elastic belts and the hooks that held the pads cut deep welts into my flesh (as did bras and girdles). We didn't have Playtex tampons with their 'gentle glide applicator' (no toxic shock syndrome either), no maxi- or ultra-thins, with or without 'wings.' Being female *hurt*. And it cost money! All I could do was wait for menopause. Like so many other women, I looked forward to the freedom menopause would bring.

Since before I can remember, I've been at war with my body. I do not choose that metaphor carelessly. I was born struggling with a body that constantly betrayed me, born upside-down, with the umbilical cord tied around my neck, an 'RH baby' who required a complete transfusion of blood from my father in order to live. I was a sickly child, going from one illness to another: whooping cough, impetigo, pneumonia, chicken pox, and measles (five times!). Of the first and second grades, I remember mostly being home in bed where sulfur was daily inserted into my sinus cavities until I finally had my tonsils and adenoids surgically removed. While in the hospital, I got 'pink eye' from a washcloth!

I've been a sickly adult. Merrill Mushroom, also middle-aged, tells me, "The whole time I've known you, your body has been falling apart." Her simple statement brings me up short. She's known me since 1958. She knows my life story as well as anyone, better and in more detail than most. Pneumonia: five, six, seven times? I can't remember. Pleurisy: three times. My body is scarred by the knives so favored by U.S. 'healers.' I count my surgeries: nine, not counting having my tonsils removed. Two of those were operations to remove ovarian cysts, but the surgeons refused to remove my reproductive organs. 'Just in case,' they said, 'you decide you want to have children.' I assured them I did not want to have children, ever. Our desires, even when asserted, do not 'count.'

My life is the story of the war between my mind and my body. My body has always betrayed my mind, demanding sleep, requiring attention I haven't wanted to give. I didn't 'have time.' For years, I lived in my mind. I 'forgot' that I had a body. I pushed at the limits of what it would endure, driving for days without sleep, dancing and drinking night after night until the bars closed at dawn, twice addicted to speed because then I didn't 'need' sleep, making my body function according to the dictates of my will. Menstruation was the BIG message my body sent me, telling me that it wasn't merely the vehicle of my mind. I wasn't listening, yet.

I anticipated the onset of my climacteric (what most of us erroneously call 'menopause,' which refers only to our final menstrual period) with the same intensity that I dreaded menstruation. I've never been one of those women who proudly wears a smudge of her menstrual blood in the middle of her forehead. I breezed through menstruation without ever having cramps, 'bad' days, or PMS. Always athletic, my period was never a reason to skip gym class, and it never kept me off the court or playing field. Because I didn't have cramps, I believed that girls who complained of them were lying, using their period as an excuse not to 'dress out.' And I know for a fact that some of them were lying; sports weren't 'ladylike.' Using one's period as an excuse not to play volleyball or basketball was the ultimate declaration of one's delicacy, one's femininity. I despised them.

When I was thirty-eight, my body had a pleasant surprise for me. My periods, which had always been regular, became erratic, and I bled between periods a couple of times. Thinking this might be the beginning of the end of 'the curse,' I asked a couple of lesbians who'd been through it if I might be starting menopause. Full of superior wisdom, they assured me I was 'too young.' I knew better. I went to my doctor, who said, "It's either menopause or cervical cancer." She did a Pap test. It was negative. I'd entered the climacteric; the door to freedom had swung open at last, and 'early!' It was now only a 'matter of time' before I could throw away the tampons, the pads, the menstrual sponges. The end was in sight. I happily calculated the money I'd save.

As I got into my early forties, more distressing things began to happen. I lost five or six teeth to gum disease; I had to get my first pair of bifocals and learn to compensate for the distortion they introduced when I walked. As arthritic pain (in the form of gout) set in, the athleticism I'd always taken for granted faded and became memories of things I *used* to do. I had to give up sports like softball, volleyball, and tennis. I found that walking or driving at night was now dangerous. All of these unpleasant changes I attributed to 'aging.' Without realizing it, I'd bought into every myth about aging, including the idea that pain and aging are inseparable.

More alarmingly, something was terribly wrong with my mind, which I'd always counted on. I'd begun to have uncontrollable rages and fits of hysteria ('suffering in the womb') for no apparent reason. I couldn't control these feelings and I'd suddenly lash out at my lover and then burst into tears. She never knew what she would come home to. I thought I was going crazy. I felt guilty: she deserved better. I thought my fits were caused by menopause. I believed the stereotype; my hormones were 'out of control.' (Only my lover noticed that my emotional outbursts occurred when I had forgotten to eat.) And I couldn't think clearly. When I tried to concentrate on a project, I felt as though I was trying to make my way through quicksand or a dense fog.

My body was also behaving in alarming ways. I only had one hot flash a year, but it was a doozie. The first time it happened, I thought I'd had a spiritual revelation. The rush started at my carnal chakra, sped right up my spine and through the top of my skull, leaving me exhausted, and drenched as though I'd been caught in a thunderstorm. It felt a lot like the initial rush I got when LSD hit my bloodstream. I had night sweats. I had to urinate frequently, often every half hour, and, if I was away from home and couldn't find a public bathroom, I suffered the humiliation of incontinence. (I told no one about this.)

And once, only once, I had cramps. It was enough to change my attitude completely. I had cramps so bad that I (then a Separatist) prayed to die, prayed to get out of my body. I thought I was dying. I wanted to die. Anything to end the pain. I finally knew something of what my partner went through during the first day of her period every month. I'd not been very sympathetic, never having experienced cramps myself. I'd been attentive, fetching her a heating pad, drawing a hot bath for her, bringing aspirin, but not sympathetic. I never again secretly suspected that it was 'all in her head.'

I attributed all of my emotional and physical extremes to menopause. Seeking reassurance for my hypothesis, I got out my copy of *Our Bodies, Our Selves* and read what was then a very small discussion of menopause and its side effects. Sure enough, emotional extremes, night sweats, and frequent urination were associated with menopause. I relaxed.

I shouldn't have. I discovered that accepting the stereotype of menopausal symptoms was a big mistake when I was diagnosed as having diabetes in 1988. As I read the literature about the disease, I found out that losing control of one's emotions, frequent urination, and (yes) incontinence, night sweats—in short, most of the symptoms I'd attributed to menopause—had, in fact, been signs that my body was no longer able to use glucose. It wasn't clear from the beginning whether I had Type I or Type II diabetes. Type I diabetes usually occurs in children and teenagers, who must start taking insulin immediately. Type II is a different disease and usually occurs when people hit their forties, and can often be controlled by changing one's diet and exercising.

Initially, my doctor treated me as though I had Type II diabetes, but she warned me that I'd probably end up on insulin. She couldn't predict when this might happen two months, two years, or twenty years. My diabetes had grown more and more serious as the years passed. By the time I was diagnosed, it was already too late for me to control my glucose levels with diet and exercise alone, and I immediately started taking the maximum dosage of oral medication. In addition, I was already experiencing neuropathies, extremely painful areas of the body caused by nerve damage; such complications usually begin to occur ten to fifteen years after diagnosis.

I'd had diabetes for several years before I finally saw a doctor, and I wouldn't have gone then if I hadn't been in extreme pain. Because the warning signs for diabetes are so similar to the stereotyped physical and emotional side effects of menopause, because the onset of Type II diabetes occurs during exactly the same period of time as menopause—middle age—I thought I knew what was happening to me and failed to seek medical help when I should have. In July, 1994, I became an insulin-dependent diabetic.

Menopause. Oh yes. As I progressed into my forties, my bleeding slowed, became intermittent, and finally stopped in 1987, when I was forty-six. Friends of mine are only now entering their climacterics, just recognizing the beginnings of the years-long processes that lead to menopause. Like me, they are overjoyed. Like me, they are also angry because their bodies hurt and require constant monitoring; we laugh among ourselves as we compare our aches and pains and share the ways we've found to deal with our unexpected pain. Yeah, I've read all the 'happy' stories about how middle age is wonderful, about how aging doesn't 'have' to mean the end of health, the end of strenuous physical activity, the end of passion and they only piss me off.

I miss the physical mobility I used to take for granted. I am bitter about all the things I now have to do, *every* morning and *every* night, in order to minimize my discomfort, in order to manage my losses. Spontaneity is a virtual impossibility in my life. I must have my insulin at just this hour and just so long before I eat; I must have these pills at just this time to manage my cholesterol, to suppress my neuropathies, to ease the pain in my arthritic joints. I'm now paying big-time for my dissolute and heedless youth.

Of all the heralded 'gifts of age,' only menopause has delivered its promise of freedom. Yet even that hasn't been an unqualified blessing for me. But I have, finally, learned that my body is important, that I cannot ignore its messages, that pain is not 'normal,' that it's a signal from my body I must attend to. I know, for sure, that if I don't care for my body, I'm also neglecting my mind, a lesson I've learned the hard way.

MY LIFE AS A VOLCANO
Merrill Mushroom

Today is a perfect morning to start writing this piece on menopause. I feel haggard (a word I never felt like until recently). Today, ha, ha, I am a hag and not a crone. Last night was another sleepless one, a night of raging hot flashes, wide eyes, aching bones. I had one of those stirring premonitions of the impending situation before I went to bed, so I turned on the air-conditioner. That turned out to be a mistake. Every half hour throughout the night, I woke to the "aura" of an approaching heat wave which burst over me with cascades of boiling perspiration. As each surge subsided, the sweat chilled in air-conditioning, and my damp bedclothes became cold and clammy.

It seems like just the other day I was a sassy teenage butch in the '50s; but suddenly, we're in the '90s, and I'm in my *own* '50s, and the theme is menopause. In typical arrogant '50s butch fashion, I expected to breeze through menopause just as I'd breezed through menstruation. I was very healthy. My periods had always been regular and easy. I generally maintained a smooth temperament and optimistic outlook. I'd always eaten properly, supplemented my diet with vitamins and herbs, gotten plenty of regular exercise. I'd done everything right.

I wasn't affected by media hype around menopause, because when I was young there wasn't any. Menopause was known only as "the end of a woman's child-bearing years," and since, as a dyke, I was not involved in child-bearing, I knew that this couldn't possibly apply to me. Occasionally, at our frequent family gatherings, I'd witnessed a red-faced aunt fanning herself while her sisters joked about hot flashes, but I knew, as I grew older, that this wouldn't happen to me. After all, I drank herb teas and swallowed vitamin E and evening primrose oil and ginseng. I had a lot of information and made good use of it. What I didn't count on was the strength of my foremothers and the genetic heritage they passed on to me, the patterns and messages in my DNA.

* * *

Sometime during my forty-ninth year, I wake in the night to feel a line of fire creeping up from my midsection, over my chest, and into my face. *Aha!* I think. *This must be a hot flash.* I find that recognition somehow satisfying. The next night I have another, and another one again the night after that. I really get into the experience, feel as though it's a rite of passage of sorts. Then the hot flashes stop. *That wasn't so bad,* I think smugly. That month my period, which I can usually predict down to the second, is two weeks late, and I bleed for fifteen days after that.

Three weeks later, I awaken again in the middle of the night to the familiar heat rising up my body and exploding in volcanic fury from my face and chest. *Here comes another hot flash,* I think with the satisfaction of familiarity. I have three more hot flashes that night and four the next night and four or five every night for the next three weeks. Having them starts to get very VERY old. I do not start bleeding on time, and then I begin to experience sudden, intense heat rushes during the day, too. Nothing I do helps.

I call my mother on the telephone long distance. "Mom," I say when she answers, "what's our family heredity on hot flashes?"

"Terrible!" responds my mom. "Your grandma had them until the day she died, and I still have two or three a week myself." Mom is seventy-three.

"Oh, great," I mumble. "Thanks, Mom. I love you."

The women I work with on my job follow me around, closing the windows I've opened as they get too cold, turning off the air-conditioning when they can't stand it any longer. They are very patient with my needs. After six weeks of non-stop hot flashes, they subside, and I bleed heavily and with lots of cramps for the next two weeks.

* * *

I sit on the commode while blood and clots pour out of my body. Seems as though I am giving birth to an army of amazons, chunk by chunk, into the bowl. I wonder if I could pass out from loss of blood this way, wonder if I have cancer or simply am experiencing one of the results of changing hormone levels. Who knows, maybe I'm even passing my fibroids. Maybe I'm passing my entire uterus.

I remember how my periods always used to be light, predictable, easy. Then, sometime in my late thirties, my cycle shortened. I began to experience cramps which were NOT fun. My flow became erratic, sometimes very heavy or very light. Now I'm almost fifty, and lately, some really weird stuff has come out of my cunt from time to time.

* * *

I yank at the bed covers that are twisted around my body and between my legs. My eyes stare wide into the darkness of my bedroom. I throw my body over, straighten out, toss over again, seeking a cool place on the sheets, fighting the urge to hurl my body against the wall. I sigh, reach for the clock, look at it. The time is two a.m. Normally I sleep well, fall into a hard zonk as soon as I hit the mattress and barely stir until morning. Now I am slow to slumber, wake easily and cannot get back to sleep, sometimes cannot fall asleep at all. I am frustrated, exhausted, furious. I despair of ever being able to sleep through the night again; not that it would matter even if I could, since lately I am also up two, three, four times a night to pee.

* * *

I feel exhausted! I snap at friends, scream at children, cry easily. I fly off the handle with little provocation, wallow in dejection, experience the throes of PMS hell for the first time. Whenever I am enough in control, I warn everyone within range of an impending hormone attack. Fortunately, I am able to remind myself that nothing in my life has changed, that these ordinary events would not affect me so strongly were my hormones not swinging me around. Maybe the real problem is that I'm just *so* tired from not enough sleep… I am thankful to the goddesses that these extremes don't happen very often and that the duration is brief.

* * *

My breasts are swollen, tender, burning. They haven't felt like this—like boils coming to a head—since they first started to bud. My sex organs feel like hot weights hanging from the bottom of my body—twenty-seven pound womb, thirty-four pound ovaries, fifty-six pound cunt. I do not like the way my body feels.

And where, oh where, has my libido gone? I've always liked sex, always been able to do it at a moment's notice. Now nothing could be farther from my thoughts. The idea of sex is an alien notion, and I really do not want to be touched in any way at all, not just sexually, but for *sure* not sexually. Except that sometimes, suddenly, unexpectedly, I might get an immediate, hard, horny feeling, usually at an entirely inappropriate moment; but if I *do* get turned on, even just a little, my cunt clenches, and it hurts. My general energy is good, but my parts are killing me. I do not like this at all.

My lover bemoans my lack of interest in sex. She is the only woman I know of who went entirely through menopause and never missed a libidinal beat.

Friends tell funny stories about their own experiences of being somewhat out-of-step sexually with their lovers and assure me that this, too, shall pass.

* * *

The weird thing now is that my *scalp* hurts! Each hair feels like a hot wire penetrating my scalp, just the scalp, not the whole skull, not anywhere near the bone or the brain. I used to love having my head rubbed, loved any kind of petting or stroking. Now I can't bear a touch at all on my head, my hair, my skin.

* * *

I look in the mirror. My parts hang, fold, bulge, shrink, crease, drop. Parts are wearing out, getting stiff, tiring more easily lately. My body is changing very quickly now, it seems. My cunt is pulling up, looking more like it did when I was a little girl, while my breasts have become wide and flat, like those of my old tantes. I'm losing hair all over, losing teeth, too, and my arches are falling. I look like a much older person than I feel like. Inside I'm still the same, the me I've always been. I don't feel very different inside at all—except when I reflect on this, I really do, too, at the same time that I don't.

* * *

I am having dizzy spells, episodes of muscle cramps and numbness, heart palpitations. Finally I see physicians. My body checks out just fine. I know what I'm experiencing is really a chain-reaction response within my organism to this change in activity of my endocrine system.

I wonder what I'd do if I have one of these spells that's so severe I couldn't keep on my feet while I'm in a store or on the street, and there's no place to sit down or even pass out. I imagine passers-by rushing to my rescue. What would I say? "Oh, thanks, I'm really perfectly all right, just having a menopausal episode—" Do I really think I could maintain my cool in the face of public embarrassment? I think about being embarrassed in public, remember a story my mother told me about the time she dropped a clot on the floor of the Louvre Museum, and I laugh to myself.

* * *

Sometimes it's difficult for me to know what is *really* happening, or why. I wonder, for instance, if my see-saw emotions are a sign of a new dissatisfaction with my life, a symptom of midlife crisis, a result of changing hormone levels, or just a matter of not getting enough sleep. Is this unusually heavy bleeding a symptom of a serious medical problem or an indication of changing hormone levels? Are these leg cramps and spells of fatigue a sign of aging, a symptom of allergy or illness, or a reaction to changing hormone levels?

There's not very much information about menopause, and most of the best of what there is comes out of our own sharing of personal experiences. The little medical information we get is colored by the male members of the medical establishment. "Not much is known," a physician may say, "because women have only recently been living long enough to go through menopause." This is supposed to excuse the historic lack of interest in women's health.

Those of us older dykes who are now in or past our own menopausal years often had to buck the system for much of our lives in order to survive as lesbians in a hostile world. As women who often were also involved with early feminism, we try in our own ways to circumvent the male manner of defining the universe in their linear fashion. We work also to overcome the lack of attention paid to interrelatedness and the limited definitions of function and purpose. Lesbians have always been outside the mainstream, and we are usually the leading edge of small revolutions. We tend to be more aware of our social conditioning and want to break free from the dependency it encourages. We try not to listen to men who tell us how we should think and what we should feel—the doctors, the therapists, the advertising boys—in their attempts to control us and take our money and energy and prove that they are smarter than we are. We lend our strength and support to each other in these efforts.

We dykes talk about our bodies. We talk about other women's bodies. We are familiar with women's bodies. We discuss the changes we are experiencing. Where older lesbians gather, we also usually make space to talk about menopause. We get and share information. We learn that much of what we are experiencing seems to be typical—or not. When we have the support of our sisters, we don't have to be bound by a need to be told how we are feeling. We consider information we get from the traditional medical doctor, but we also learn about different approaches to dealing with stress and difficult changes that may be associated with menopause. We discuss what "studies show." We try to be supportive of one another and respectful of individual choices. We try not to make judgements or do put-downs or trips on one another about being guilty or politically incorrect or functionally out of control around our choices, whether they be to do ERT or herbs or meditation or Prozac or nothing. We maintain our own integrity.

* * *

Okay. That's enough. I'm tired of working on this lousy essay. My dogs are barking at something in the field, and they won't shut up, and my temper and temperature both are rising hard and fast, and if I make one more typo I will hurl this machine through the window, and anyhow I really have to pee again …

the menopause cocoon
zana

as i travel through menopause i feel many of the same things i've felt during my bloods: moodiness, need for quiet solitude. instead of a menstrual hut, i have a menopausal hammock! it's a two-person type with no spreaders, so one person is pretty well lost in it. the soft folds of woven cotton come up over me, completely enclosing my head and body like a cocoon. i lie there in my hideaway soothed by the feeling of weightlessness and sometimes rocking gently. there's nothing to look at but the fabric, and soon i am more aware of sounds—mostly birdsounds here where i live in the country. very peaceful and unstimulating balm—to my often raw nerves. lying there for hours i lose track of time and the necessity of planning, doing. i am being. thoughts drift in and out, feelings come and go. my cocoon-time is precious at this phase of life when so much is changing inside of me. these transition years are a cocoon, too, and some day i'll emerge in my new butterfly form!

TOWARD A NEW UNDERSTANDING OF THE IMPORTANCE OF EATING WEEDS
Lauren Crux

On my way to Spanish class, I look down at my notebook and see a lavender "sticky" that says, "Hormones." I don't remember writing this note, but it is my handwriting. HORMONES. These days they occupy my thinking disproportionately. I want to be thinking of other things: the fact that spring is early this year and the plum and apple trees down the road have already pushed into blossom; that the day-glow color of wild mustard would offend me in a sweatshirt, but thrills me in the fields. Or when I ask my Spanish teacher for permission to photograph her wearing the adorably butch man's hat and jacket she keeps stuffed in her file cabinet for role-plays, should I use the polite command form with the subjunctive, or the informal command, and where do I stick the reflexive ending? And what is the pluperfect of the verb to dress? And for that matter, what is the pluperfect? These are questions truly worthy of the menopausal lesbian, along with where are my car keys? how do I continue to subvert the dominant order? and what do I want to do with my life now that I have grown up?

This morning I am grinding flax seeds to sprinkle on my breakfast cereal, while I imagine others are grinding their coffee beans. This makes me a little crabby. Oh well. Flax seeds are a good source of natural estrogen and taste infinitely better to me ground up than in oil form. And then there are the greens. "I have one piece of advice for menopausal woman," the herbalist said. "Eat weeds. They are high in calcium, magnesium, high in estrogen." I eat bunches of kale, mustard greens, collard greens (alas, my favorite, chard, as well as spinach is not estrogenic). Estrogenic—the magic word. Seems that many women in other countries, those I hear about who are having so little trouble with menopause, usually have diets high in naturally estrogenic foods. I walk down my street examining the weeds with new enthusiasm and interest.

I have learned that I can easily identify estrogen/progesterone cycles in my body. When I start crying in my morning Spanish class for no reason at all, I think, *hormones out of whack*. When my breasts get sore, *oops too much estrogen*. When stress incontinence shows up, or I sleep poorly, *oops too little estrogen*. When I get raggedy and edgy and too anxious, *oops time for a little progesterone*. I enjoy knowing this about my body. I like knowing which herbs to take, which vitamins, how to care for myself well without intrusive medicines. Menopause with its often bewildering symptoms and changes has invited me into a more focused listening, noticing, caring for myself when I am not just plain pissed off, of course. Which brings to mind...

My memory. Despite the homeopathic remedy I am taking, or the Chinese herbs I was taking, or the greens I eat, the flax seed, the primrose oil, the vitamin E, the calcium, magnesium, despite all the yoga to strengthen, focus and calm, my memory continues to lead a life of its own. Mostly it wanders away from home. Yesterday I spent a couple of hours chasing down my favorite jacket which I left somewhere between Santa Cruz and Berkeley. Today I opened a kitchen drawer looking for scissors and found the cat food that is supposed to live in the refrigerator. My friends and I forget words more easily. To compensate we have it down to: "It's an M' word," or, "Begins with a K." Usually one of us, using context and imagination, can figure it out and supply the missing word "marzipan,"or "kryptonite." My doctor assured me that memory lapses are normal for menopausal women and I am reassured. But I will never feel complacent; my mother died of complications from Alzheimer's disease. There is a horror that lurks.

And what is a discussion of menopause without talking about hot flushes? Someone once wrote me that she and her lover had to coordinate their love-making around their hot flashes. The letter was written in good humor and at the time I did not recognize the painful undertones. My lover and I, both in menopause, can't hold each other longer than thirty seconds before she breaks into a violent sweat and unfortunately not from lust. I miss holding her throughout the night.

Despite enthusiastic reports from some women about hot flashes as 'power surges' and the like, my lover's flashes do not feel powerful or sexy to her. They feel uncomfortable and she is sleep deprived and exhausted. All the remedies she has tried have not yet worked to alleviate her symptoms. I like hot sweaty dirty sex. So does she. But the hot sweat that takes over her body during a flash does not feel sexy to her. This does not make for good sex. I am not exactly a hot biscuit myself these days. The skin on my lower legs is drying out so severely I now have eczema and scratch a lot. My libido is so low an ant couldn't crawl under it. And what about feeling tired all the time? *Que va!* Power surges, indeed! Fatigue surges is more like it. One of my reactions to this loss of plenty of hot sex seems to be that I have decided that the sweet stuff, of which I am usually quite fond, the tender nibbling, the long slow fascination with an ear lobe, the roaming around a body with no particular goal, is no longer enjoyable. Diminished sex-drive perhaps. Mind on other things could be; we girls do seem busier than ever. Don't like her any more—not true; so far we're still enthusiastic about each other. I think in all honesty part of the problem is that the sweet stuff at this point signals to me the end of the hot and dirty stuff, the lusty, knock-over-the-lamps, fall-off-the-bed, do-it-in-the-kitchen-up-against-the-wall-with-your-hand-coated-in-olive-oil-sex. So, unwilling to give up that, I protest and deny it all.

I never realized I was such a brat. Or so scared.

When I die I want to be cremated and my ashes buried in a duck casket. A ruddy duck with a blue beak and rust-colored wings. I want my friends to have a wake with lots of good food, music, dance, celebration and encouragement for me to pass over easy. I want Sweet Honey in the Rock, or a reasonable facsimile, to sing "They Are Falling All Around Me."

What do duck caskets have to do with menopause you may ask? Well you see, a good friend of mine who is only in her forties may have colon cancer. Another has breast cancer. My lover's best friend just died at age forty-five of lymphoma. They are indeed "falling all around me." I am nose to nose with mortality, full force into menopause and full force into my lesbian life. Weavings and braidings. Like puberty, like coming out, menopause is incontrovertible CHANGE. In many ways a welcome change—I like ripening—but I cannot pretend any longer that I am not going to die. Don't misunderstand, I don't feel morbid, but rather juicy and plump with reflection.

How can I not think about these things at menopause? How can I not wonder whether my life has been meaningful, if I am happy, what else I would like to do with all the time I have left, as little as that might be? How do I negotiate body pain without complaining too much, without depression? How can I best pass on what I have learned—my knowledge, my wisdom? Have I loved my friends well enough?

A good friend and I are talking on the phone: she has just seen her doctor and learned that she doesn't have colon cancer after all; her symptoms were created by stress. We are both immensely relieved. We discuss all our latest aches and pains, commiserate enthusiastically. We joke that now, experience has taught us that aging is more interesting in theory than in practice. She has a new job that she loves; I am closing down my twenty-year-old psychotherapy practice and returning to graduate school in studio arts. It is a dream unfulfilled and I am chasing it down.

And so it goes, permutation after permutation. I experience the joys of increasing wisdom, the terrors of deterioration, and the power that comes from having been around long enough to figure some things out. And always, always, always, a delicious and vital curiosity. What next?

FLOSSIE'S FLASHES
Sally Miller Gearhart

Flossie Yoroba woke for the third time that night with the tingling at her hairline skipping around to the nape of her neck. "Here she comes!" she thought, opening herself to the gathering explosion of pleasure. She grinned in the dark. "It's from the bones tonight."

Always it was one of two sources. She called the first "Volcano." In an increasingly urgent rhythm it would rise from the spot directly behind her navel, erupting in bursts upward to her arms and head, downward to her legs and feet. It moved patiently, irrevocably, relentlessly, inevitably, over muscle and bone, nerve and tendon, capturing layer after layer of forgiving flesh under its flow of molten energy. Then, in its surges toward freedom, it would strike the wall of skin and burst free of its encapsulation through welcoming pores, transforming itself always at that last second into ten thousand rivulets of pure sweat that sang and danced their way up and down her body. Or across and under it, depending on whatever position that body occupied at the moment. Her toes and fingers always got it last, just about the time the sweat on her back was beginning to cool.

The other kind, and the ones she was waking with tonight, rose from a different place, from the geometric center of each part of her body, simultaneously from thigh, elbow, backbone, phalanges, the middle of her head. This kind she called "Hot Seep," oozing as it did from the marrow of each bone outward toward the skin, not in waves but at most in small eddies, all pacing themselves according to the thickness of the flesh they sought to conquer, all carefully timing their emergence from the body to be a synchronized drench, all at once and altogether, over her whole being, top to bottom, back to front, spilling out at precisely the same instant from her big toes and her nipples, her shoulder blades and her waistline, the palms of her hands and the caverns of her ears.

This Seep was seconds short of emergence. She reached for her clitoris, carefully avoiding its tender, aggressive tip. She pressed it gently side-to-side, then up-from-under. Once. Twice. Then with a whoop of joy she flung off the quilt and arched her back into a long stretch of denouement, collapsing at last into inert flesh, drenched and dazzled in the frost-filled air.

A high wind was outflanking the protective eaves of her cabin. It drove a deluge of snow through her window and onto her naked skin. Sweat met flake in a mighty clash of elements. Flake melted. But flake won, cooling the sweat in an embrace both familiar and triumphant.

Flossie whooped again. She stretched wide another time and urged more of her undaunted wetness into its stark encounter with the cold. She smiled and shuddered as she sucked a raging winter into her lungs. She felt the air transfer itself from lungs to bones, there to entrap the heat and follow its path, moving on it from behind until now her skin felt downright crisp, crisp and encased in what she knew must be a thin sheath of ice. She whooped a third time and catapulted to the window, drawing it tight against the storm.

Back under her quilt she subsided, giving thanks to Whoever Was that Daaana had decided not to stay over with her tonight. She preferred not to share a bed these days, much less spoon, what with this waking up four and five times a night to sizzle and freeze, sizzle and freeze.

Though as for that, she thought, marveling at the completeness with which the quilt encased her, cuddled her—though as for that, Daaana was a great bedpartner for flashes. She actually envied Flossie, and advertised her in public to be better than Solar Central, hottest woman in the Grand Matrix, north-south-east-or-west.

Even from the depths of an early-dawn spoon Daaana could sometimes feel the moment coming before Flossie knew it herself. Then she would chuckle and cling to Flossie, holding her close in anticipation of the explosion of heat. Flossie, torn between the loving clasp of a good woman and her desire to leap to cold freedom, would throw the covers at least from her own burning flesh and lie only tokenly connected to Daaana by finger or kneecap. That, of course, threatened to deprive Daaana of one of her greatest pleasures: the slick sensuousness of their undulating sweat-bathed bodies. It led, usually, to loud laments as Daaana protected herself from the window's blast and Flossie, naked as a jay to the churlish chiding of the wintry wind, inhaled there like a card-carrying health freak. Sometimes it all led to a tussle that ended in shouts and uncontrolled laughter.

Flossie loved her nights with Daaana and sometimes missed the dreamwalking that spooning could bring. But right now, these months, these years, she was exhilarated with her changes and often sacrificed the adventures of spooned sleep for a night of solitary encounter with the elements. Since childhood she had loved the run from the sweat tent to the waterfall, the smell of hard-worked body dripping in pungent clothes and the subsequent dunk into an icy mountain stream. She craved the contrasts, the sudden changes, the jig that her feet danced and the thanks that her heart sang every time she gifted them with those extremes.

Under the cover now she stroked her ample body, drawing her knees to her chest and lying spoon with a phantom self as she cozed back into sleep. Not only did she get these wild free swings of heat and cold, but several times a night now she got to fall asleep again. Falling asleep, she thought. Sheer contentment, always, even with another spooned body. But, she mused, there's a special balm to doing it in a wide bed all alone, with the margins of your body quite unbounded...

Alien androids were attacking the cabin, rattling the windows and whipping the roof with giant rubber hoses. They were calling her name. "Flossie! Flossie, open up!!" She clamped her legs together. She heaved her extra pillow over her head, dug deeper into the tired old foam that supported her. "Stick it where the sun don't shine," she mumbled, trying for her gentle drop back into dreamland.

"Flossie! Get the bar off this door! I gotta talk to you!" More beating on the non-offending cabin. Flossie turned her face to the foam and smothered her breath. She willed the androids back to their planet of sterile basalt. She held her breath.

"Floss, dammit, it's me, City Lights! I'm freezing my butt off out here! Flossieeeeee!!"

Flossie breathed. No fun to wake up this way, she thought. She hauled her bare feet to the floor, feeling for her nightgown. Where had she left it? More banging. "I'm comin', I'm comin'!" she croaked. The banging stopped. Fighting her way into the warm flannel she reached the door and drew back the bar.

City Lights, No Bigger Than A Minute And Twice As Frail, stomped into the room and kicked the door back into place. She dumped a large patch of snow onto the floor with her jacket and laughed a greeting. Then she made for Flossie's stove. "You still got fire," she warbled. "How about a lamp?"

"City, I'm a gin day short of lacing you good. What you want?" Flossie cut the damper and opened her stove door. She lit a candle from a twig.

City shook possible spiders from some kindling and forced the wood under the smoldering logs. She looked over her shoulder at the flannel-clad figure, its arms akimbo, and got to the point.

"We got to spoon, Flossie. You and me."

"You and me? City, your peanut butter's slippin' off of your bread. Last we spooned was five years ago. . . ."

"We can do it." The younger woman sank to a stool in front of the fire and held out her hand to Flossie. "I'm not proposin' wild abandoned sex. Only a sweet gentle little spoon..."

"You proposin'—!"

"Not that I wouldn't love it, Floss. In fact...."

Flossie let out her breath. "Wait till I get my socks." She threw the quilt from her bed around City's shoulders. Then on her knees she strained to rescue one wool sock from under her bed, another from her boot. She sat on a straight chair by City. "Coldest night in a universe and you got to come knockin' your way into my sleep ."

She felt a reassurance, a satisfaction, as the sock stretched itself around her leg. When nothin' else helps, she reminded herself, pull up your socks. It always worked. She cut her eyes toward City. The tiny woman was intent on moving a log to catch the center of a volunteer flame. Still pretty, Flossie thought, the girl's still pretty, else the fire's makin' a lie of her face. Flossie pulled up her second sock and resigned herself to a conversation.

"City, I'm bound to tell you I won't try that flyin' again if that's how come you want to spoon."

City wove her hand up though folds of quilt and held it out to

Flossie a second time. "No," she urged, "I just need to dreamwalk. All the demons been visitin' me lately. Like when I go to the lake where Eleea died. You know?"

Flossie knew. She wanted to reach for her pipe, light it up and stay safe behind a cloud of smoke. Instead she took City's hand. "Umm-hmmm," she said.

"I just need you to hold me, Floss. You always been the best for walkin' together with me and findin' healin' waters. I can do a new incantation I made up for right after the master chant. It'll take us so deep, so easy." City Lights, No Bigger Than A Minute And Twice As Frail, raised the soft brown openness of her eyes to the soft brown openness of Flossie's. "Will you spoon with me, Floss?"

There was never any brittleness to be found anywhere in Flossie Yoroba, and at this moment, she was sure, there wasn't even a piece of solid bone or cartilage. She harumphed her way toward a response. "Well, we might be ridin' a lame donkey," she growled. "It's not for certain I can stay down long enough to dreamwalk anywhere."

She was about to say more but at that moment her forehead began no tingle, just around her hairline. Her eyes grew a millimeter bigger. She stood up and wiped her brow. "City," she said, "City, come here to me." She pulled the small woman to her feet. "How come you got on so many clothes?" She turned toward the door, heaving the quilt onto the bed as she slid the bar closed.

City Lights knew when she'd been blessed. Move, girl! she admonished herself. Don't let your coattail touch the ground! She began peeling off her clothes, struggling all the while to meet the swell of primordial earthpower that was emanating from Flossie's body. She was just working her way out of her last pant leg when Flossie flung off the flannel nightgown and stood before her, wet and shiny in the candlelight, exuding wave after wave of unquenched fire.

First it was the warmth, then it was Flossie's arms that encompassed her. As she sank onto the bed, City Lights, No Bigger Than A Minute And Twice As Frail, heard the big woman say, "They's good spoonin' tonight, girl. But first you got to let me show you what a hot woman is all about."

The candle, outdone in both heat and light, guttered, and then courteously extinguished itself.

LEARNING TO LISTEN TO MYSELF
Pearlie McNeill

My mother had little need of friends. Close contact with her many sisters and brothers provided a sense of community. They were a wild, raucous bunch, thirsty for excitement, ready to create their own at a moment's notice. Emphatic about family loyalty, particularly when it suited their needs, they lived their lives tempestuously, quick to take offense, picking fights, taking sides, embroiling all who came near in the latest feud. Periods of chastened harmony followed these rows till the next eruption took them by storm.

We, the next generation of daughters, lived on the edge of all this fuss and bother, children seen and not heard, but oh, how intently we listened to the swirl of conversation above our heads. Alert to sudden shifts of mood—lowered voices, hushed tones, the signal that something dramatic or dreadful had happened to someone. We knew how to behave, casting our attention to the floor even as we drew closer, eager to know the latest family gossip. And so I learned of the precarious nature of women's lives. Birth, death and insanity were a grim and bloody mix in the back streets of Sydney during the 1940s and '50s.

Like my mother, my aunts all had big families. These women approached childbirth as a death-defying feat. Their mother had died giving birth to her tenth child so how could they be sure that next pregnancy was not an omen announcing their own deaths?

When Aunt Jessie was admitted to an asylum and given shock treatment, her sisters conferred in huddles around the kitchen table. That she'd buried a baby the previous year and endured Uncle Tom's illness since the war was enough to drive anyone round the twist they agreed. My mother had been allowed to visit and reported that Jessie's hair had gone green and now small handfuls were falling out. Beneath the table we kids sat in stunned silence. Green hair? Handfuls falling out? What had caused this terrible state of affairs? The change of life my mother called it.

My aunt was never the same afterwards and frankly, neither

was I. Watchful and wary, I latched onto other rumors with a compulsive, scary fascination. My aunts reported instances where women in this change of life situation either went frigid or threw themselves at every man in sight. The dictionary at the local lending library helped me to understand what frigid meant, but no matter how intently I looked at women in the street, I never did see any throwing themselves at men.

My fears were heightened when, about this time, my sister started her periods. She spent days in bed doubled over with pain and I walked into our bedroom one morning in time to see my mother doing something odd with safety pins, my sister's pants and a small towel the like I'd never seen before.

My mother's brief explanation, that my sister had growing pains because her bones were stretching, left me with a ghastly image of girls' bodies pulled taut on some medieval rack. Later, I asked Lizzie if she thought this was what was meant by the term change of life? Did women's bodies grow and stretch in some inexplicable way? Was that what happened to our aunt? Had the pain driven her mad?

Many years later, about to be wheeled into an operating theatre, I remembered how frightened I'd been. Growing older seemed cruel, unfair. Now I was facing some of those fears head-on. Would I become frigid? Sex-mad? Unable to control myself? The surgeon stood alongside my trolley, his bedside manner an attempt to assure me everything would be all right. I felt woozy but determined to ask my question.

"What about my ovaries, Doctor?" I spoke softly, embarrassed to be having this conversation in such a public place.

"We'll see what we can do, but never you mind, I'll do everything I can."

I wonder if he did. Much later a nurse explained I'd had an oophorectomy as well as the expected hysterectomy. Both ovaries had gone.

It is hard to explain fully how this operation, and the circumstances before and afterwards, acted as a threshold experience. In one direction lay the familiarity of the past, my life as a heterosexual woman. I was not yet strong enough to imagine the future but I could feel the pull of it, knew it would be different. I was slowly, ever so slowly, coming to terms with the knowledge that I was a lesbian. I savored that word in my mouth, whispering it softly last thing at night. I was a lesbian. I am a lesbian.

I'd been married for twelve years. In that time I'd had five miscarriages, given birth to my two sons and been laid low by a terrible depression that sucked away my vitality and robbed me of any wish to stay alive. Treatment to alleviate the symptoms included lengthy spells in psychiatric hospitals, numerous and often dangerous drugs, and a series of shock treatments.

The psychiatrist had ordered six shock treatments but I'd had eleven before I managed to persuade him that enough was enough. My recovery began months later, the night I heard my older brother had committed suicide. Call it shock or a catalyst, either way his death had an incredible effect. I was in a psychiatric hospital, it was to be my last time, when I heard the news. I attended the funeral in a drug-foggy state.

Getting out of the car was an ordeal. Using both hands I had to lift one knee onto the footpath, then the other. Struggling to stand up, I heard my mother and aunts whispering about my appearance.

"She'll be next," I heard my mother say. I didn't have the strength to look her in the eye, but on the way back to the hospital I laughed hysterically with my companion, another patient, a Catholic brother whom my mother had mistakenly thought was a member of staff.

Anger surged through me a few days later. Invigorated and swept along by its power, I imagined myself walking inches above the ground. I wasn't mad, I was angry, so angry I had to get myself out of there and fast.

My brother's death taught me that to take my own life and leave that legacy for my children was to continue the cycle of destruction. It was as though, unwittingly, he had given up his seat on a bus so that I could travel a much longer distance. I was, I am, immeasurably grateful to him.

When I left that hospital I promised myself two things. I would never take another mind-numbing drug nor would I bend over, ever again, for one of those bloody Largactil or Anitensal injections. I didn't tell anyone of my decision; the strength of it lay in acting for myself. I didn't want an argument, I just wanted to get well.

Withdrawal was surprisingly easy. At the first possible opportunity, I collected every last bottle of tablets from the medicine cabinet in the bathroom, including Librium, Lithium, Serepax and Valium in different strengths. In my fury I repeated the names over and over. Librium. Lithium. Serepax. Valium. They sounded like some mystical chant. Back in the kitchen I took a large saucepan, filled it with water and whilst waiting for the water to boil, I uncapped each bottle and emptied the contents into the saucepan, stirring the lot with a wooden spoon. Finally, I flushed the vile foul-smelling mess down the toilet. In the days and weeks that followed there were no moments of regret nor was I bothered by a single adverse reaction. Was I lucky? Or did the anger act to protect me in some way?

No one came after me; no calls from the doctor, no letters from the hospital, nothing. The depression didn't lift straight away but in working to accept it as a fact of my life, I was astonished when it lifted almost immediately. At first there was only an hour's respite, sometimes two, but before another month had passed, I was experiencing six or eight hours' freedom every day. My relief was immense. I began getting up early to watch the sun rise and I strived to be on the back step when it set behind distant mountains. Many times there were tears in my eyes, I couldn't believe how good it felt to watch something so beautiful, to feel a part of everything once again.

Reclaiming my mind, feeling once again that I could work things out for myself, was remarkable, exhilarating, but the process was uneven—two steps forward, one step back. Often I felt overwhelmed. I'd become a problem-solver, but the problems kept coming at me, hard and fast.

Sitting in the doctor's surgery faced with a medical report stating there were fibrous growths in my uterus, and the advice that a hysterectomy operation was called for, as a matter of some urgency, I was in no state to protest or to enquire about other courses of action. The doctor was single-minded in his attitude. For him, there was no other alternative.

The pill became available in Australia in 1962, the year I got married. Like many of my friends I was relieved. This method of contraception would be safer, simpler, no fuss, no mess. I put on weight in those early months and twice the local doctor thought I was pregnant. No one suggested it might be beneficial to consider other methods of contraception in order to have a break. In my hospital bed, recovering from the operation, I thought about this a lot.

I perceived a link between the deterioration of my uterus and taking the pill for so long. I wondered what implications there would be in having had both ovaries removed? The answer came when one of the nurses explained I'd have limited natural hormone production. My irritation was apparent when next the surgeon made his rounds. Ignoring his glowing comments about Estrogen Replacement Therapy I was immediately cautious, insistent that I would make *no* decision until I could find out more about possible implications one way *and* the other.

During the next three months I made numerous phone calls to doctors, a few journalists, to research laboratories and gynecological departments in many Australian hospitals. I concluded that ERT in 1976, like the pill in 1962, was unproven despite obvious initial benefits to women. Due largely to my experience as an ex-psychiatric patient, I was now anti-drug in my attitude. No way was I going to trust yet another drug that seemed more like a problem to be dealt with at a later date. I've not ever regretted that decision, but I would defend every woman's right to make up her own mind about such matters.

The next two years were difficult. The hysterectomy operation became, in effect, a surgically induced menopause. My symptoms included hot flushes, night sweats, feelings of suffocation, brief moments of disorientation. The most severe symptom was painful stiffness in the joints. It began in the feet but spread, affecting my knees, hands, neck and spine, but usually only one area at a time.

Much later, I suffered with cystitis and various forms of dryness, vaginismus, painfully sore eyes and breasts. I remember arguing with a lover about vaginismus. She insisted it wasn't possible for sexually experienced women to have this problem. In her opinion only women who feared sex, say after rape, or were terrified virgins, could be affected in this way. It was like hearing my mother, my aunts, all over again. Did she think I was lying when I described penetration as painful? A woman doctor confirmed my symptoms and explained that vaginismus was more common in menopausal women, surgically induced or not, than many people realized.

A good friend suggested acupuncture. She'd heard it was helpful after surgery and went with me for the first few sessions. Encouraged by the (almost) immediate lessening of some of my symptoms, particularly the night sweats and the hot flushes, she tried it for a troubling neck injury that had occurred some years before. When the pain in her neck miraculously disappeared after two sessions she couldn't believe it. Startled, laughing nervously at her daring, I watched her climb trees then jump to the ground. So great was her suspicion she had to prove to herself that this treatment had really worked.

Before the operation, I had joined a Pre-Menstrual Tension (PMT) group. Roche Laboratories agreed to our request to do vitamin assay tests (from blood samples) for each woman in the group. When the reports came back, two of us had very low Vitamin B12 readings. Mine carried a note saying this was the lowest reading they had ever recorded and suggested a course of Vitamin B12 injections (because B12 is difficult to absorb through food).

An article I'd read in a medical journal at that time made a link between Vitamin B12 deficiency and schizophrenia. The label given to me as a psychiatric patient had been Paranoid Schizophrenic but later, a different psychiatrist had changed that label—to Manic-Depressive. I had the Vitamin B12 injections, as suggested, but hadn't noticed any perceptible difference. Some months after the operation, when I felt myself sliding towards depression, I had another course. The difference was astonishing. The depression lifted slowly, like a bad headache. Could it be that simple, I wondered? I began to think about what I was eating. My diet consisted of meat, potatoes, pumpkin, a few other vegetables (no fruit other than an occasional orange), lots of bread, sugar, processed cheese (Kraft), packaged cakes, the type you poured into a bowl from the packet and added an egg to, lollies and soft drink. Many drugs, like Lithium for example (often used in the treatment of manic-depression) cause a terrible thirst. I had drunk bottles and bottles of soft drink in a matter of hours when taking Lithium.

My health improved slowly but the most important thing was how my attitude changed. I was, in some strange way, looking backwards and forwards at the same time. I had, suddenly, irrevocably, a different perspective on my life, on the lives of my mother and my aunts. Realization, as I experienced it, was a continuous display of fireworks exploding in my head leaving brilliant sparks of clarity in their wake. I was changing at a cracking pace. My future would be different, of that I was certain. My recovery from breakdown was complicated and worsened by also having to recover from a surgically induced menopause. It was hard knowing there was no map, no blueprint, no feminist sister up ahead leaving marked signposts for me to follow. No one could advise me, there was no published material that spoke to my experience. I was committed to my path, but felt the isolation keenly. I'd have to make my own mistakes and learn from them. But I was getting stronger. The way I thought about allopathic medicine now was with a great deal of skepticism.

Flickering in my mind constantly was the memory of a time, years ago, when I'd got a job in a tobacco factory. In the building where I worked, a long concrete trough ran along the back wall. Taps fitted onto a copper pipe jutted out over this trough. Before the machines were switched on each morning, women congregated here to swallow analgesic tablets or Bex powders. Bex powders, like Vincent's A.P.C. (Aspirin, Phenacetin and Caffeine) powders, were sold in flat paper packets that opened up to reveal a small pile of pain-killing powder. Production and sale of these powders was forbidden by law in the early 1970s after a number of deaths. I remember how deeply shocked I felt that so many women needed this kind of help to get through the day. That memory has greatly affected my thinking. We have been taught to rely on drugs in so many ways. To resist the quick-fix, to do something different, less harmful, for our own well-being, is a radical act and needs to be recognized as such.

It's almost twenty years later and as I approach my fifty-sixth birthday, I sometimes wish I could tell my mother that lesbian sex is a wonderful thing, that the feel of an older woman's skin, so soft and silky, just cannot be described adequately with words. My mother will never meet my lover but I see that as her loss rather than ours. As we all know, some mothers do accept their lesbian daughters, others do not. I'm happy to live with my choices and the consequences.

I'm fit and well and active. I ride a bike, swim all year round, take long walks and recently achieved a long-time wish to do a deep sea diving course. Five years ago I took up weight-lifting, more for the value of the stretching exercises than the heaviness of the weights. Although I sometimes wonder who designs these machines, there's no doubt in my mind that they work. Reflecting on my experience of menopause I see it as a particularly difficult time, but if I had to go through it all again, I would follow the same path. Learning to listen to myself was what it was all about.

"A DISEASE OF HOUSEWIVES"
Valerie Taylor
Adapted from correspondence.

It has rained all day and all night here in Tucson, and this morning (a little after nine) the sky is still heavy and the air chilly. The farmers need the rain, but I can't help thinking about all the homeless people; the shelters take in only a small percentage.

I can't offer much information on my menopause thirty years ago. It was remarkably easy, late starting, the periods gradually diminishing and then stopping, no hot flashes or nervous problems.

My doctor, a wonderful tough old dyke who had pushed her way through med school before that was as easy for women, said it was supposed to be that way. My fellow workers were taking pills for being menopausal. My doctor laughed when I asked about them. "What for? Menopause is a disease of housewives. Women with jobs don't have time for it."

In some places it is called "the American sickness."

Also, I never had menstrual cramps or pre-menstrual depression (they hadn't invented that one yet), nor morning sickness during my pregnancies. How un-American. How lower class of me!

Perhaps not taking pills had something to do with it. I wonder if pill-taking has some effect on the bodily functions, as it almost surely has on every aspect of health. Americans are subjected to all kinds of medication, now almost from birth. (Or before it). I suspect that the inoculations our children get from babyhood on influence every aspect of their physical development and performance. It seems reasonable that all this tampering with the immune system leads to permanent damage. It may even account for the terrifying rapidity with which the AIDS epidemic is spreading. But then I am not a doctor, just an observer of life and the way people handle it.

Back then, my own biological complaints, which now seem as remote as the dinosaurs, may or may not have been typical. I have always thought I got off easier than most women, but how does one know? How can you tell what patterns are typical of lesbians and which ones are common to women generally? That is, are there differences? How can you sort out emotional from biological factors? Age? Racial or ethnic groups? How to determine which experiences are socially explicable?

I suspect that 'female complaints' are commonest among women who have internalized male ideals, or maybe among those whose mothers and other social influences have led them to be frightened or ashamed of their own femaleness.

My first information about sex came from a schoolmate, poor white trash, and when I hastened to my mother in a state of panic she said yes, she had been meaning to tell me all about that but didn't know how. The Kotex people used to put out a little facts-of-life booklet called *Margie-May's Twelfth Birthday*, which was written in such ladylike language that if you didn't already know, you would never guess what it was about. In high school (1926-1930), I learned that Catholic girls and others who equated sex with sin were always getting excused from gym because of cramps and that they stayed home on physical examination days. Any connection? Who knows? My sister and I often walked four or five miles at a clip; does exercise make a difference? Does nutrition? Overt and unconscious factors seem to be all jumbled together in these matters.

My granddaughters couldn't wait to begin menstruation. It seems to be a prestige factor at junior high school level and they seem to get involved with sex (hetero) at a very early age. One has now had her first child and she had an easy pregnancy, but a very difficult birth. Maybe it's all random.

Early starters are late stoppers. Okay, I had my first period at twelve and a half, my last somewhere in my fifties; they dwindled off. A vague period of time I barely noticed.

Once, in 1970, at about age sixty-one, I was taken by surprise after a heavily traumatic experience—my son's trial for draft refusal. A couple of hours after the Defense Department threw out the case and set him free, I began having very heavy cramps followed by a lava flow of dark dusty-looking blood full of clots. Then came the usual female reaction, oh my God, I have cancer.

I called Dr. Isaacs at home and she said it was probably nothing much (my last period had been two or three years before), but she hustled me into the hospital and got someone to do a D and C under general anaesthesia the next day. Nothing. Not a thing. The cramps and clots stopped before I was out of the recovery room and I have never had a recurrence. Being a poet, I assumed that the uterus which had hatched that kid twenty-eight years earlier had been involved in all these happenings of his. A little humiliating as I had tried never to be a silver-cord mother. But how do I know?

I might add, though it probably isn't relevant, that I was technically a virgin when I married at twenty-five, that I expected first intercourse to be painful and it wasn't, that I taught country school the first five months of my pregnancy and no one suspected what was under that school-teachery smock. That I fully expected to die when a kid was born, but didn't, and that two years later the twins took four hours from first pang to second baby. They wouldn't let me nurse the twins, but I could have if they sneakily hadn't dried up my milk during the ten days of that (routine) hospital stay. Are lavish menstruators also lavish lactators? Who knows?

The mention of femme-butch in this context makes me chuckle. I knew tough butches who would almost rather have died than admitted they menstruated. But then, they would rather have died than let their partners make love to them. Must have been a shock to some when they discovered that straight women often make love to their husbands. Not only were straight couples our only role models, we didn't know much about them. Then the sexual revolution came along and the hetero patterns were shot all to hell, and we were left with nobody to imitate. Good clue to make up something for our own selves.

Another question: little girls seem to be arriving at menarche earlier than they used to, eleven or twelve instead of fourteen or fifteen. Does this mean that menopause starts earlier?

Last week a woman sent me a check. Her letter said she hoped I no longer urgently needed money and could spend this on daffodils. That makes me feel justified in keeping it, though it will give me six months of Douglas and Douglas is no daffodil. He is a tall, homely man of fifty or so with more allergies than I can list on one page. He does my shopping and cleaning among other things.

I am doing pretty well, took eight steps on the quad cane without holding to the rail, and can get down and up the three steps at the end of the porch with cane and railing to hang on to. I don't know what the limits of recovery are at my age, but am still progressing slowly but consistently. Of course it was easier to get around when I was a young thing of sixty!

One bit of gratuitous information I will add. Unless you have a relationship after seventy, all the fuss about menopause seems to become irrelevant, and that's rather a relief. Gives you more time to worry about things like colitis and glaucoma and working hard to be able to walk to the mailbox and back.

TRAPPED IN JELLO
Mattie Fast
Adapted from correspondence.

About ten years before I stopped flowing, I began having hot flashes. My body would get very hot, but my face never flushed. It was not a real nuisance. I mean, it was, but it just meant taking off a sweater, putting it back on. I didn't break out in sweats. I once timed the hot flashes at once an hour. My periods became irregular.

Someone recommended bee pollen, which you can buy in pills in health food stores, for the hot flashes. I took it and it worked beautifully. For about a year I had no flashes, then it stopped working. Then some time in my fifties I stopped flowing.

A doctor persuaded me I'd get osteoporosis if I didn't take estrogen, so I did. I've already got a touch of osteoporosis, I know, because I've shrunk from 5'3" to 5'2". However, I have fallen a couple of times in the past two years, on ice, without breaking anything.

Another doctor persuaded me to take progestin twelve days a month to break down the bloody lining which the estrogen causes to grow every month. Supposedly if you take estrogen without progestin you end up with cancer of the uterus. The first time I took one of those pills it was as if the (bloody) dam had burst. I thought I'd never stop flowing. Which persuaded me he was right. So now I have periods again, although they usually are not so heavy as when I was menstruating on my own.

Imagine this bloody comedy of errors: the heroine has just gone home with a gorgeous woman to an isolated country home where she just can't up and leave, because it's too far from civilization. Heroine spies a trail of drops of blood on the floor and is afraid Gorgeous, who is too old to be menstruating, has murdered someone. Gorgeous turns pale with embarrassment, not wanting Heroine to know she still has periods from taking pills…

One thing that keeps me on the estrogen is the fact that when I began it, my hair grew in thicker. It had thinned out considerably. Now a bone scan indicates that my bones are ninety-three percent of a woman in her twenties, so I guess it works!

It's so hard to know whether to trust doctors or not.

My roommate, also a lesbian although we are not lovers, is trying to persuade me to drop the progestin. She gets along fine with the patches (which I use too) of estrogen only, and will not take progestin. The progestin puts me in a bad mood, you see. Depression, anger, all the PMS stuff. However, she had her uterus removed years ago, so can't get cancer.

I was managing to handle the depression, knowing it was merely chemical. I hate pills! I don't like tinkering with my interior. I really believe if I had a woman to love and a job I enjoyed, I wouldn't suffer from depression. But sometimes I can't function as well as I'd like too. Generally, I've been in a state of inertia, what I think of as being trapped in Jello.

I went to an MSW at my medical plan. She's okay, my age, but probably grew up in cotton wool. Then I had to talk to a real psychiatrist, who is also nice enough but he would not understand when I told him I am not happy but I am cheerful. That's exactly what Beverly Sills said in an interview and I realized that's my position too. The psychiatrist said it was impossible. Screw him. Beverly Sills and I know it isn't.

I tried an antidepressant, Zoloft. A week before the Zoloft the psychiatrist had started me on a tranquilizer, Lorazepam, I think it was. These names! They love Zs, don't they! Zoloft sounds like a blind date: "Marvin Zoloft is here to see you…"

The tranquilizers were okay, but he wanted me to take both. I got a bad reaction from the Zoloft, dizziness and a feeling of being about to explode, so I dropped it and the tranquilizers.

I'm sure I've had physical changes. I used tampons all my life, now can't get them in. Even the thinnest ones hurt, so I must have shrunk or am so dry they won't slide in.

As far as sex is concerned, I don't think I've had any change. I'm not so sexual as I was in my teens and twenties, but that has nothing to do with the menopause. It's hard to know how I really feel about it. If I had a lover, I'd probably be having sex once or twice a week. If I were not working, it might be more.

I don't become passionate about anyone any more. That might just be experience. A child looking into a bakery store window might lust after every pastry she sees, but someone who has tasted them all would be more discriminating, not to say cynical.

Especially someone trapped in Jello. I may have spent fifteen years working out the change, and I'm not sure I'm finished yet!

THOUGHTS ON *KONENKI*—MENOPAUSE
Naeko Wakabayashi
Translated by Barbara Summerhawk

I was born in 1947 and now am a forty-seven-year-old Japanese lesbian. Since last fall, I've been thinking more and more about menopause because I haven't been feeling up to par mentally or physically.

In Japanese, the term *konenki* is used for the English word menopause. *Konen* means "a new time" or "changing years." We can interpret this as a time in which one's body and mind enter a new stage of life. I think of it as a very good word. Nonetheless, although my condition has improved somewhat since last fall, it looks as though I'm facing menopause and trial and error is the rule on how to deal with it.

If we get down to specifics, last fall I was suddenly very constipated. I couldn't move my bowels, although I tried and tried. I felt so bad I even considered calling an ambulance. Instead, I called an acquaintance who is a moxa and acupuncture healer. She instructed me in a method for loosening my bowels and finally I was able to find relief. During this time, I also noted that spotting would continue for several days after my periods. With all of this, I decided to start acupuncture treatment.

My healer, an acquaintance for more than twenty years, explained that my body had lost its balance and so my condition worsened. After I began treatment, fortunately the spotting stopped and the constipation didn't return.

There were several reasons for my condition worsening, I believe. One was that I suffered a severe mental shock when a relationship with a good friend suddenly changed last summer. Further, last summer saw many continuous hot days. I was exhausted. Although I was able to recover my strength and vitality later, it was too much at the time. Then, some time near the beginning of last year, I could feel a bulge on the lower part of my pelvic region.

162

Perhaps I have a fibroid tumor, I thought. From about six years ago, I experienced flooding on the second or third day of my period; I became anemic and was quite exhausted. When I read a book on menopause, I became aware that I might have a fibroid tumor.

Eastern or Western medicine? For more than twenty years I have rejected the idea of immediately jumping into surgery or taking antibiotics popular in Western medicine, and favor a more holistic approach. When I was a year old, I contracted polio which affected my right arm. If I was just a little weak or my condition was not good, I would be rushed to a hospital specializing in Western medicine.

When I was twenty-three, however, I participated in the Women's Liberation Movement and began a diet of brown rice and vegetables. Soon, the allergies I once had disappeared. I grew in health and self-confidence and for thirteen years have been operating my own natural foods store. The thirty-four year old me then and the forty-seven year old me now differ totally in stamina and strength. With the influence of the recession, making ends meet became more difficult and the stress has become enormous. I don't suffer under an awful boss because I'm my own boss, but I have no replacement for myself, so I always have to look after the store and have little time to relax.

Because I reject Western style medical exams, I haven't had a gynecological check-up since I was forty. I would like to know what my condition is now, so in the near future I intend to consult a feminist gynecologist.

Aging. My thoughts on menopause also bring up the difficulties of facing the aging process. My white hair is increasing, my glasses are no longer strong enough. It's difficult to accept that I am growing older.

The other day when I was on the train, I observed an interesting thing. Among the women who looked in their mid-forties or older, all had dyed their hair; two were wearing black hair wigs. When I checked the men of the same age group, not one had dyed his hair. People living in Japan are generally dark-haired and when we reach our forties, white hair begins to appear in most of us. Many women use harmful dyes to color their white hair black. It shows that this society doesn't accept the changing, or aging of women's bodies.

Japan is a male-supremacist, sexist society. The lesbian movement is only twenty-years-old, but in that time, we have created little by little a nation-wide lesbian network. However, the prejudice and contempt for lesbians still being so strong in this society, it takes courage for a woman to come out.

Recently, at a lesbian gathering, I did a workshop on "Are you passing though menopause?" As we listened to all our various experiences, our interest and courage deepened. I want to ripen menopause into a fruitful period, so I am looking forward to hearing from other lesbians and sharing our experiences.

HALF OF A MAP
Sandy Boucher

Party. Kitchen. I'm sitting up against a high counter behind a collection of Calistoga and wine bottles, looking out into a room where women, dykes like me, stand talking. Two of them have sat down on the floor to compare shoes. One wears those soft brightly-colored laced shoes that are fashionable this year. The other arches her foot to show off a pair of brown and white Spaulding saddles that she found in a secondhand store. Immediately I recall how absolutely crucial it had been, when I was a high school student in the early fifties, to wear Spauldings. And I realize I am the only woman in the room over thirty. Usually I don't notice ages, but now as I look around I see the firm cheeks, the slim or if not slim, resilient bodies, the clear eyes and particular freshness of very young women.

They examine the laces in the shoes, thick ropes of pink and gray. And I find myself talking, my words astonishing me. "When I was young," I say, "the boys wore charcoal gray flannel suits with pink shirts."

The women in the kitchen barely glance at me. There is a small jerky pause, and then the woman with the Spauldings says, "Oh yeah, charcoal gray, I could get into that. I could see it and a pink shirt, hey I bet that'd look hot."

When I was young... I am numb, sitting there staring at a wide-hipped greenish bottle of Chablis. I can't remember ever uttering that phrase before. It has pointed to a chasm that I never imagined to exist: between that presumably distant and unreachable time *when I was young*, and now. Now... what?! Now, according to the logic of the phrase, I am *not young*. Then am I old?

I look around the room. Any woman here under the age, say, of twenty-seven, is young enough to be my daughter. That spiffy dyke over there with the crewcut and the three earrings in a little row up the curve of her ear: I imagine her as my daughter. What an arresting thought. As it is, I am free to enjoy her loud laugh and the swagger of her thrust-forward leg, her tanned arms crossed over her silky shirt. How differently would I feel about her if she had suckled at my breast, had tested me with the demands of her growing up, had given me the delight of her developing mind and body, had loved me and then rebelled against me and finally condescended to me or maybe become my friend?

But she *could be* my daughter, and this fact stuns me. She has only heard and read of the Second World War, whereas my childhood took place under its shadow; the fifties exist for her as "Happy Days" on TV, while I lived that complicated decade as a high school and college student; there is so much that formed me that she knows nothing of.

Another woman, lounging near the doorway, draws my eye. She wears shorts, and her legs are flawlessly smooth. I am reminded of the picnic in 1979 where I first noticed the changes in my own legs. I happened to glance down at my thigh beneath the hem of my shorts, and saw a little swelling under the skin What is this? I wondered. And then I noticed on the inside of my calf a lumpy snake of bluish vein crawling toward my knee. Once I saw it, it began to ache. Later I remembered my father's legs, on the rare occasions when he wore a bathing suit, his calves clutched by the bluish crooked fingers of varicose veins. So the hereditary weakness arrived. Having lurked outside the door like a shy friend, now, noticing my body's (only beginning) loss of resilience, it came furtively in to bestow its gift.

In 1982 the letters on the page of the book I was reading began to blur if I read by anything but intense sunlight. If I moved the book away—ah, there, it's better—I could find just the narrow range in which my eyes could focus. Soon my arm was not long enough to manage this. One of my students who was near my age told me I could buy magnifying glasses at the Emporium for twelve dollars. I did so, and use them now when I must.

Yet my picture of myself lags behind the actuality. For many years I thought of myself as a big rangy girl, an Irish-setter-type person, long-limbed and supple, flopping about good-naturedly. That image had little to do with the constricted ladylike creature I most certainly appeared to be through my teens and twenties. I came closer to it in my thirties after I became a lesbian, with all the freedom that choice brings to be oneself. Still, people tell me I was often remote and intimidating when threatened. Now sometimes I sense a person's conception of me when she looks at me, and if I am seen as an "older woman," someone weighty with years, dignified, to be deferred to, I feel like snorting raucously at the deception. No, no, I want to say, you're not *seeing me*. I'm as vital, as "experimental with my life" as you. Then if I am tired or in a position where I need to get something done, I use the deception. The deference becomes a lever to get what I want, the deception works in my favor and I let it, while knowing that this erodes me morally.

But I am only forty-eight years old, at the very beginning of this journey. When I think of my Aunt Helen, who is eighty-three, who can barely see or hear, who walks with two canes and is so twisted by age that to cook a meal in her kitchen is a slow, torturous and even dangerous endeavor that requires tremendous energy and inventive skill—when I think of Aunt Helen still insisting on cooking meals for my mother and me, I experience the vacuum of my knowledge about age. Standing at the stove, Helen shakes her head and says with the brevity that has always characterized her utterances, "Don't get old."

But my body has begun speaking to me differently than ever before, and so I am brought to these thoughts, this investigation that Helen has been engaged in for thirty years or so. I'll know more when I'm eighty, but that's no reason to keep my mouth shut now.

* * *

In the summer of 1982 I was driving across the Midwest doing a promotional tour for my book *Heartwomen*. Alone in the car, I would drive for six, eight, ten hours, arrive at a town, be interviewed by the newspaper and the radio station and that evening give a reading and slide show at a university women's center or a women's coffeehouse or bookstore. Then I would sleep over at someone's house, get up the next morning and drive six, eight, ten hours to the next specified town. Perhaps because this schedule was so strenuous, my period was delayed, and for weeks I endured the swollen breasts and belly, the irritability, the increased emotionality that precedes my period. In Iowa City, I happened to examine my breasts and found several distinct lumps, and even though I knew that before my period my breasts always show such changes, I decided that cancer had finally struck. The next morning, my birthday, I awoke in a strange bed in an empty house, with a thunderstorm raging outside, and my first thought was, "I'm forty-six, I'm over the hill." That noon I went to lunch with a young woman from the Iowa City Women's Press, who, noting my depression, asked delicately, "Are you tired?" I glanced up at her, gauging whether I could lay this burden on her, but she appeared so dewy with youth that I felt the way I did in the kitchen at the party when I noticed how young everyone was. Lonely. And not able to speak of what bothered me, because I would have to start at zero and so it might take all day and even then she might not understand. "Yes," I said, "I'm tired."

Here I am reminded of an encounter with Elsa Gidlow. Several other younger women and I drove Elsa, who is in her seventies, home from a poetry reading. As Elsa is a lesbian poet of a time so remote from our own, we were eager to talk with her, and asked her many questions. Elsa responded with tart half-sentences or mono-syllables, her strong lined face set in an expression of restraint, until finally we gave up and drove in silence. When she had left the car, my friends wondered whether Elsa had not been feeling well or if something in our questions had been particularly annoying to her. But when I thought of it, it seemed to me that perhaps Elsa simply despaired of communicating to us a reality so different from our own, of doing this in one short automobile ride, with women she did not know and might never see again. Remembering her in the front seat, small and sinewy and elegant, her gray hair bound with a pur-ple headband, her narrow shoulders swathed in plum-colored suede, her back resolutely straight under the barrage of questions, now I feel her loneliness.

On my return to Oakland from my promotional tour, I discov-ered that the cancer scare had been a false alarm this time. But a week later my period arrived with a violence I had never experi-enced. I was not bleeding, I was hemorrhaging. All strength left my body, and a great heat entered to take its place. I lay in bed, my flesh burning. When I did manage to get up, I was shaky and sweating, and poised on the edge of tears. I had never felt so vulnerable. All my life I had experienced regular periods with little pain. I had looked forward to my periods as a time of folding in, of taking care of myself and listening to myself. Now what I heard when I listened was a rampage. Odd how predictability brings the illusion of control, for obviously my periods had never been under my direction, and yet because I knew what to expect from them, I experienced that order that feels like control. Now my body was running riot. I had read about hot flashes, of course, but nobody had said that one's body might burn with a deep heat from one's very center for two days without relief. In this condition I craved the comfort of my lover's understanding and acceptance. Although she is much younger than I, she could sense how unprotected, how at the mercy of my body I felt. She tucked me into bed, brought me ice cream, stroked my head. I welcomed this special treatment. And as I lay in bed I understood something I hadn't before: that the deference paid to old people comes, when it is most genuinely offered, not just from respect for their years of experience but from the recognition of their vulnerability. They are not so insulated as we by our strong bodies and sharp sensory capacities. They become more and more fragile, prey to accident, to disease, to emotional distress.

I think of the photographer Imogen Cunningham, who had just turned ninety when I met her. My lover at the time was shooting a film about Imogen, so she spent whole days with her and often went out to dinner with her. Now and then I came along. On one occasion we were all to go out to a Chinese restaurant in North Beach, but when we arrived we found Imogen in her bathrobe, and she told us she was experiencing the vertigo that sometimes came on her and said she couldn't go with us this time. Her hair hung in a long white swath down her back, her tiny body in the flowered robe trembled as she went to get back into bed. Sitting against the pillows, she was like a gnome, her eyes blinking at us snappishly, as she shot questions at us, always in a tone of annoyance that was meant to be, and was, provocative. Her flame burned brightly, but it was a small flame, her presence light. It was her skin that struck me most, for it was so delicate as to seem transparent, in places ash white, with here and there a faint blush of rose, so delicately dry-seeming that it looked as if it would tear at the touch. So little protection between Imogen and the world: no wonder she felt the need to hold people at a distance with the scourge of her wit.

* * *

It was June, 1983 in the makeshift camp next to the freeway which was being used as a jail to house the three hundred women anti-nuclear protesters arrested at the gates of Lawrence Livermore Laboratories. On my first day of imprisonment there, seated on the ground at a meeting in the tent, suddenly I experienced the worst pain I had ever felt. A dagger plunged deep in my jaw. Stumbling outside the tent to hold onto a guy rope, I bent forward under this agony, tears in hot rivulets down my cheeks. Three days before I had gone through the first procedure for a root canal in one of my molars. The dentist had prescribed codeine for the pain he said might come, but there had been no pain at all, and so I had not even tried to sneak the codeine into jail with me. Now, clutching the tent rope, I longed for some relief. Mercifully, the pain lessened and disappeared after a short while. But it was to return each day for the first five days of our incarceration, and impale me for some minutes. After each bout, I was exhausted and could barely function for a period of time.

In the warehouse I sat on my cot for the meeting of our "cluster," the Cosmic Elders. This grouping had come about because of Sarah, a seventy-year-old indefatigable member of our affinity group who decided if she were going to jail she wanted more "white heads" with her. Here they were, in their sixties and seventies, the eldest eighty-two. I felt privileged to be included in Cosmic Elders after a few of these meetings, for there was such accumulated political experience and wisdom in the elders that our group generally dealt with problems more efficiently than the groups of younger women. While they struggled to understand the significance of a particular move by the sheriff or happening in the camp, our veterans quickly put the event in a political context developed over years in the labor and peace movements. The elders knew what things meant and what our alternatives were.

I soon noticed, though, that it was not easy for them to be in jail with us. Conditions were harsh for everyone, with inadequate beds and blankets, constant wind and sun, wretched food, fumes and noise from the freeway, and the subtle harassment of the guards, but the elders brought with them additional hardships. Rose suffers from arthritis; I would watch her get up with great difficulty from her seat on the straw littered ground. Marion has skin cancer; she wore a hat and rubbed sun-screen on her face and hands. Helen apparently has some form of neurological disease, for she often tottered and bumped into things, and her hands shook. Goldie's high blood pressure showed in her flushed cheeks and her dizzy groping for support when she got up quickly. Sitting with these women in our meetings, I rarely thought of these infirmities, for such steadfast energy came from each woman, but when I did notice something—a hesitation in speech, a shifting of stiff limbs, or attempt to shield the face from the relentless sun—I knew that my five minutes of excruciating pain each day were nothing next to this constant management of a problem, this continual dealing with discomfort or incapacity.

The elders probably did not understand before their arrests what their presence might mean to the rest of us in jail, but on the third day of our eleven long days there a crisis occurred that prompted us to call upon them, and it become clear that their contribution was essential for the cohesion of the whole group. On that day certain women made a decision, independent of the larger group, to go for arraignment. The three hundred of us had previously pledged to refuse arraignment in protest against the punitive sentences being meted out by a prejudiced judge. When these women acted against the interests of the whole group, my heart dropped; along with most other people, I felt betrayed and panic hit us. Suddenly we were in trouble; women who had been resolute and cheerful the day before becoming angry, confused and depressed. The feel of defeat was in the air.

Then someone thought to ask the elders if they would speak to us that evening. After supper, we gathered, women of all ages and backgrounds and political experience, in a giant circus tent. When everyone was there, a mob of bodies sitting, squatting, standing along the walls and at the back, four or five old women came to the front of the tent. From my place against the canvas drape of the side wall, I felt the waiting silence gather, its presence so intense that the roar of the freeway fell away.

Soon the voice of a white-haired woman in a red t-shirt and jeans filled that silence. She spoke of early labor movement struggles and how, often, just before success was to come, the strikers would feel most dejected. "We must never give in to that," she cautioned.

Another woman told of how she had not engaged politically with others until a few years ago, had been a staunch Republican individualist, but this threat of nuclear holocaust had brought her here with us, and she felt honored to be among us. Two more old women stood before the group, simply, unselfconsciously, to tell of the political battles of their lives and how they had managed to keep going when all seemed lost.

As they talked I could feel the mood in the tent and in my self changing. I was encouraged by these old women, I would be them one day, and if I could be as honest as they, as generous of myself as they were, then I could be proud to be old. A warmth, a cheerfulness began to grow in the tent. We trusted these women, we loved them for coming here with us and in so doing, we trusted each other again, began to believe once again in our collective strength.

I guess it was when I was about forty that I noticed that life is a long time. Most women over forty have lived several lives—the growing up and becoming a woman, the twenties and thirties of marriage, child raising, professional growth, searching, establishing one's lesbian identity, whatever occupied and fed us then, and the life that began when that earlier existence fell apart or drastically changed. Looking back, I see that with the end of each period and beginning of the next, I knew more, could dare more, and opened myself more trustingly to life.

Now at this new juncture, I feel tremendous possibility. And I know that the progress of each of our lives is not really as linear as we sometimes imagine. Elsa and Imogen, my Aunt Helen, the Cosmic Elders, the spiffy dyke with her crewcut and earrings, my thirty-two-year-old lover, my teenage friend who has just started college—we stand not in a line reaching from the womb to the grave but in a casual group, like women at a picnic, lounging, resting after hard work, playing together, sharing our minds and bodies, living the present with all the joy and attention we can call up in ourselves.

MENOPAUSE WALTZ
Sue O'Sullivan

It wasn't as if she woke up one day and it was gone. Not at all. There were literally years of taking leave, and it was never straightforward. Even now, at fifty-one, when she hadn't seen a drop of red on her knickers for three or four years, its effects lingered: a hot flush here and there; a low down ache in her gut which took her by surprise before she remembered it wouldn't come again. Over thirty years of bleeding, and then the wind-down and final dribble. She realized there was no way to tell a menopausal tale without a menstrual story.

She had never been one of those women who loved their periods. As a child, and she had been only nine when it started, initially excited, rushing into her parents' bedroom in the early morning of its first appearance, her mother's spontaneous reaction dampened things considerably. "Oh dear, I am sorry. You're so young." Still, looking back, she was pretty sure that even if her mother had swept her up in pride, gushing, "Now you are a woman," she would have seen the truth before long.

When her periods started coming regularly, from about the age of ten, she experienced a monthly cycle which often included at least one day of heavy, hot, aching cramps, and a week of bleeding into bulky disposable towels which had to be saved in paper bags in her closet and then taken out to the incinerator and burned. She meticulously tied up each used towel and wrapped it in miles of toilet paper. These tight, bloody knots took hours to burn, her cross to bear. What fun was it, and how could she be pleased about the fact that every month she inevitably bled through, at least once, on to her knickers, and had to soak them in cold water, rub salt onto them, scrub them, and still have light tan stains left in the crotch? In her teen years, on her heaviest days, she was known to stuff two or, in desperation, even three Kotex down her knickers, or into the special rubber-crotched pants her mother bought her.

173

Sometimes the cramps were agony. Her mother was of the get-up-and-go school. She rarely communicated any sisterly commiseration, which possibly meant she didn't experience the kind of pain her daughter did. She had a little green-and-white-striped terrycloth-covered electric pad which the girl would go to bed with, holding it to her tummy, fantasizing about a long wooden spoon, wrapped round with cool, wet cotton, which dipped into her and scooped out the dark pool of clotty liquid that lay like poison in her belly. When something was planned by her parents, and she had already spent a half-hour or so curled up with the hot pad, her mother would call her, telling her to get ready to go out, claiming that if she would just get up and start to do something it would feel better. As a result, more than once she lay in misery, brutish and rolling rhythmically, in the back of the station wagon while her parents and brothers swam or picnicked.

No, she knew it was not a good thing, although she quickly understood it was the way of things. Her mother was modern in the 1950s sense of the word. She never suggested that there was anything about menstruation to be proud of, but then she never called it the curse either. No, it was something to get used to, to try to ignore as much as possible. Keep busy. Be active. That would take your mind off any little discomfort.

Somewhere along the line, the girl became obsessively concerned that her father or her brothers—or any man—for that matter, might guess that she had her period. Nothing was to be said by her mother. But she could never quite trust her to guard this secret. She wanted her mother to understand without having to tell her. But her mother was careless about her feelings and often seemed oblivious to her distress as she dropped hints that the girl was acting oddly because she had her period. Agonies of burning shame and embarrassment. In high school she worried every single month about bleeding through onto the back of her skirt. She worried about smelling. She worried about starting somewhere without access to a Kotex. All these things happened.

The truth was that after so many years of bleeding every month, she did get used to it. Life went on. She was generally a happy girl, with lots of friends and a good sense of humour. She was blessed with a good 1950s American-style diet, a lot of fresh country air, plenty of exercise, and an urge towards nonconformity. Fucking didn't happen until she was eighteen, so for most of her teenage years she kissed and petted and rolled around with boys fully, or at least partially, dressed. No worries about contraception then, or waiting with bated breath for a period to arrive, but what did you do about a boy feeling the heavy wedge of Kotex as you pressed your clothed bodies together?

Fucking brought new menstrual worries, more concerned with how you told someone you had your period when they wanted to root around down there than with the possibility of getting pregnant. One time she didn't say anything, and he, an older man, removed her pants and her Kotex, and proceeded to fuck her without realizing that she still had a tampon in. She never said a word, but it was hard getting hold of it after it had been banged up inside. Tampons had become possible only after experiencing intercourse. Before that she hadn't been able to get one in, practically fainting in the toilet stall at school with the effort of unsuccessfully poking and pushing about.

Somewhere along the way, she picked up that her period pains would improve after she got married. Then, as she got older, she understood that meant after she had a baby. Fortunately, periods did not play a role in her decision to get married or have babies, although she did end up doing both. She fell in love with a British boy and became an American living abroad. She also spent six years on the Pill, which got rid of cramps, got rid of heavy bleeding, prevented conception, but made her feel bloated and strange.

After two babies, living in London, she threw away the Pill for good, tried the coil, which created blood baths from hell, and finally got sterilized. Pregnancy had brought the first disruption of her regular periods. As she settled back to normal, it was clear that her cycle was changing, as was the world. Women's liberation arrived in the late 1960s, hot from its American successes. She was captivated, enchanted, transfixed. She was in the midst of her drudge years, all lank long hair, sleepless baby-filled nights and identity crisis. Now, with other women, she discussed many things, including women's bloody cycles. She could see clearly how menstruation's meaning, and even some of the ways it was experienced, arose from what they began to call conditioning. It fascinated her; menstrual stories revealed so much about how girls became women, about fear and loathing, about the female body, about sexuality, about difference.

But she could never make the existential leap into totally accepting and adoring her periods. Embarrassment and shame might be the result of conditioning, but bleeding would happen, happy or sad. She cringed at the new matriarchists who wanted to reclaim menstruation, celebrate it and even—oh my God—dabble in it, adorn their faces with it, drip it across city pavements and country fields. Symbolic or literal, either way, it didn't sit well, it didn't strike a note of recognition. It was ridiculous. Menstrual blood was sticky on the thighs if it flowed unplugged. It smelled. Sorry, but it did if it was left on a pad in the warmth. Of course she wanted to change attitudes to menstruation, the attitude of girls who would bleed, her own, men's, and society's. But she wanted nothing to do with locating women's possibilities and powers so firmly in their biology.

She fell in love with a woman, and with lesbian sex. So besotted with making love to women was she that even their blood didn't stand in her way. Now, all these years later, she took her mother's advice and plunged in, keeping busy, letting passion transcend any worry, licking and tasting, and finding it not at all displeasing. To think that the man in her life had told her for so long that it didn't matter to him if she was bleeding and she never really believed him, and certainly never talked about her periods with him.

Periods became a small part of her woman-oriented life. Lovers shared the intimacies of bodies and wondered if, by living together, their cycles were synchronizing, like nuns' did. Fucking with a bleeding lover was one thing; sharing all these details made her go queasy. She might be compelled by her own bloody discharge, but that didn't mean she felt the same way about her girlfriend's. Why did lesbians have to talk about bleeding all the time? It seemed that every time you got together someone was menstruating, feeling premenstrual, having period pains, or suffering from something related to it. Every serious lover she had had terrible period problems, and she was expected (and fully expected herself) to be commiserating and sympathetic. In fact she was much better at telling and listening to menstrual stories than at coping with blood clots themselves.

In her late thirties her cycles were changing again. This time, after about six months, she realized something different was beginning: her period was more irregular, and the cycle was getting shorter and shorter. She wondered to herself if this was part of a changing pattern leading to menopause. Could it be? Wasn't it kind of early? No one else her age brought up the subject. The more she read about the menstrual cycle, the more she realized that there was no clearly defined thing called menopause. It seemed rare for anyone to be pre-menopausal one moment and post-menopausal the next. The fact was that this process might take years and years to complete.

In the early 1980s she attended an international women's health conference in Switzerland. She went to a workshop on menopause run by one of the original American *Our Bodies Ourselves* collective members, who eloquently approached the subject with a fan in her hand. She came away from that workshop imagining legions of hot flushing women, willing to whip out their fans in offices, parks, on the streets, in cinemas, recklessly declaring to the world their bloody crisis, perhaps even delighting in it. She fantasized herself as such a woman, and found pleasure in it. But it still felt a long way off.

By the time she was forty-three, she began to experience the odd hot flush. What a peculiar sensation! The first time it happened was in public on her own. She felt like a little girl, dying to tell someone, turn to the next person she saw and say, "My God, you know what's happening to me?" The sweat poured down between her breasts, and her face blushed steamily. And then it was gone, a matter of a thirty-second hormonal eruption. And it wasn't really bad. In fact, she decided that it was a little like New York City summer heat— the more you fought against it, the worse it became. The only thing to do was to surrender yourself to it totally, let it flow through you. She began to imagine herself as the menopausal lady, taking London by storm with an outspoken acknowledgment of her condition. During the day her more modest acts were limited to flinging the windows of the office open, joking that it was another hot flush and she simply had to have air! She bought a beautiful blue Chinese fan, but at the appropriate moment it wasn't always easy to find at the bottom of her work-filled bag.

She was living on her own by now, leaving boys, home, and best-friend husband. She slept like a baby in a tiny, courtyard-facing, noisy, short-life flat in King's Cross. She was besotted with her small estate and, after the first shock of being on her own, enamored of that condition. Her life felt filled with possibility and a good amount of pleasure. She found her forties her most fulfilling decade yet. At the same time, she had some pretty spectacular relationship failures which left her curled in a ball on the floor sobbing through the nights, but in the end she recovered. Once, when the loss and betrayal and grief turned the world gray for a couple of months, she felt compelled to find a shrink, something she had never thought would be necessary or right for her. It was, and it worked, and she changed a tiny bit.

After six months or so of hot flushing, just as she was really getting serious about it all, the daytime flushes went, disappeared, vanished. The nighttime soaks remained, usually not extreme, but sometimes occurring up to ten or twelve times a night. The first time it had happened, with her lover lying there beside her, she felt embarrassed, but the woman was intrigued and interested. She was, as all her lovers had been, younger, and certainly not menopausal. They discovered that sex and flushes often went together, and that a good session of snogging could bring a little one on. Her girlfriend got blasé and was prone to say things like "Having a little flush, then, Susie?" which, while comforting, was occasionally irritating.

She told everyone she was menopausal, including her mother, who denied it. "No," said her mother, "you aren't." In a perfect continuation of their relationship, she found herself defensively arguing yes, it was happening to her, as if perhaps she was the one who had made a mistake. Then she decided to let it pass. Other people believed her, although they usually told her she was too young or went glazed in the eyes and pretended their attention was demanded elsewhere.

She wrote a secret poem called "Menopause Waltz" in which her ambivalences were expressed. She didn't dread the loss of her bloody cycle, but she did worry about getting a dried-up cunt. That more than anything else nagged and made her apprehensive. It was hard to admit because somehow it seemed self-obsessed and vaguely unimportant. But in fact, here she was, relatively late in life, getting off on slick vaginal secretions, sliding-sweet, sexy-wet. Her own and others'. Feeling sexual meant getting wet; getting wet meant fingers could open her up, and wanting more. Wanting more meant asking for it harder, and more and more. Getting sucked and licked was the best thing ever for fantastic orgasms, but fucking with a woman was different and amazing. Even if you were in a fantasy at home on your own, it was nice to reach down and push in and feel how warm and smooth and wet you were. Was this going to be lost? The descriptions were not reassuring: thinning vaginal walls, atrophied vagina, dry, possibly sore, cunts. Dreadful. It didn't seem to be happening at all during the menopausal process, but what about later?

It was double-edged, starting menopause early. It worried her when people told her she looked too young to be menopausal, because although she was a bit flattered, she then wondered what people would think when, inevitably, she did look old. Having never been particularly attached to her periods but being a worry-wort, she also puzzled that perhaps she was being a bit offhand about their loss. It was true that the few years of change had made her more interested in the real bloody discharge, more attentive to its smell, look and texture. When it was truly gone, would she have some sort of psychic crisis? Claiming that personally it had nothing substantial to do with feeling complete as a woman might be a huge denial. God, sometimes she wished she hadn't dabbled in psycho-analytic chit chat.

She kept a menstrual chart through all of her forties and that was how she finally figured out it was gone for good and that she was post-menopausal. It was quite a shock to realize that more than two years had gone by since her last period, because she still thought of herself as being in some sort of process. She remembered the series of dreams; they must have happened in the first year of an absence of blood. Each time she was sitting on the toilet; each time she reached down, tissue in hand, and came up with red stained paper. Each time she woke up feeling incredibly sad and then as consciousness returned, incredibly relieved.

There were no tampons in her flat; she had thrown away the last of them and expected her lover to provide her own. She rarely thought about periods. It felt entirely natural not to have them. No, more than natural, it felt wonderful. No mess, no fuss, no pain, no stains, no smell of warm blood, no lower gut ache or loosening of the bowels. Good-bye to all that.

She still had hot flushes at least a couple of times a week. She still felt the ebb and flow of bodily changes which seemed to be steered by hormonal patterns. Her emotions had never been at the total beck and call of her physiological processes, but they were still gratifyingly inconsistent, surprising and pleasurable. But this happened without the inconvenience of one whole bloody week a month taken up with periods. It was fantastic when she realized how absolutely freeing it was.

At the same time, she also realized that she felt considerably distanced and uncaring about other women's periods. She did try to be polite and interested when the conversation turned to who was having what sort of period. She made the right noises when a woman friend or lover complained of bad pains or something associated with menstruation. But really it was like trying to hark back to the Dark Ages. Of course it wasn't their fault. She certainly wasn't suggesting, if only to herself, that they should all go out and get hysterectomies. No, she wouldn't even have joked that way. It was more feeling sorry for them, but also feeling as if she'd done her time, it had had its moments and served its purpose, but now she was leaving it behind.

Her current and steadiest-ever lover, still in her thirties and regular as clockwork, was not one of her complaining companions. But she suspected that even she noticed her lack of interest. More difficult was the recognition that she wasn't really keen to fuck with her beloved when she was bleeding. In her thirties and much of her forties, she had spent a lot of time as a women's health activist and writer, talking with women about overcoming their self-disgust, their dislike of their own and other women's monthly bleeding. Oh, she could hear the times she had said, "It's not dirty. There is nothing wrong with having sex when you are menstruating. You may find you feel randy then." She had gently prodded women to engage with their partners' dislike of or ambivalence about their blood, and tell them if they were interested in sex at that time. In the past her own husband had communicated to her that he was not turned off at all by her bleeding and would engage in any sexual acts that she wanted during that time. She realized now that he had been more accepting than she was.

Back in the seventies and early eighties she had been aware of feminist critiques of hormone replacement therapy. She had been part of the women's health movement, taught women's health in

Holloway Prison, gained a diploma in Health Education, and finally ended up at Spare Rib magazine, where she was responsible for most of the health articles for the five years she stayed on the collective. She wasn't a hard-liner about health care; if menopause drove you nuts and made you miserable and HRT helped, she wasn't going to come on all judgmental. But she did think it was strange that after all the criticisms, all the exposés of how profit-driven and blandly disinterested in women drug companies were, anyone could merrily leap on the HRT bandwagon. Then there were the revolting paeans to the magical effects HRT had on women's ability to stay youthful and beautiful, with smooth faces and elastic cunts. When possible dangers associated with HRT began to come to light, it didn't surprise her at all.

Memories are short, time flies by, and drug companies are loath to give up. By the end of the eighties HRT was making a comeback, only now osteoporosis was the buzzword, striking terror in women's hearts. Suddenly every woman she knew was nervous about brittle bones, wondering if they too would end up cracking hips, developing dowager's humps, breaking wrists. Surely HRT was the answer and, not only that, it dampened hot flushes and made women feel happy! Several of her contemporaries who were not even menopausal asked her if she was on HRT when she talked about her menopause. When she answered no, they asked, "Why not?" To which she replied, "Why."

Why should she if she didn't find the flushes impossible, wasn't depressed, felt energetic and didn't believe HRT was the only way to stay fit and healthy? Thinking it over, she decided the subtext was almost always a fear of growing old, looking older. Strange that feminists, so confident in their more youthful twenties and thirties about the ephemeral nature of "attractiveness" and its male-defined meanings, began to waver and lose confidence in their forties and fifties. Sad and understandable, but maddening. She wasn't immune, especially alone at night. The more women she heard extolling the wonders of HRT with breathy sideways remarks about how good they felt—glowing skin, springy cunts—the more she wondered gloomily if she was making some sort of silly stand. Would she regret it in ten years' time? Then she would catch herself and think how ridiculous, she didn't look any different from the women who took HRT, she didn't need to medicalize her perfectly normal changes, she didn't have to bury the signals of change in her life. She had always celebrated change. Why stop now? She had no more reason to trust drug companies today than she had ten years ago. The difference now was that she didn't have a group of peers meeting together regularly to talk about their lives, committed to discovering the social roots of their private fears and confusions. She wasn't really hankering after those old days, but it helped to remember them.

In the last year or so, as she became more and more postmenopausal, she noticed more signs of aging in herself. Were they connected to being post-menopausal, or were they happening because she was older? Did it really matter? Her cunt was a little less wet. By this time she was deeply involved in AIDS work, running workshops and writing a lot for women about sex, sexuality, and safer sex. Familiarity with safer-sex techniques meant getting relaxed about lubricants. Lubes and latex go together like a horse and carriage. Her ex-lover in San Francisco sent her a plastic bottle of Probe, a water-based lube. It was wonderful. No more greasy gunk. What had seemed an admission of defeat, of sometimes needing help, of loss of spontaneity, was transformed into matter-of-factness and pleasure.

She thought, finally, that menopause was a wonderful thing. It gave women a clear hint of their mortality, and if they were receptive, it gave them a chance to reflect on their life. For her it was a signpost of change, and signaled that she had completed the longest period of her life. She read Germaine Greer on menopause, and wished that many other women could tell their tales as widely. For her the change was not about accepting a loss of sexual engagement, nor did she believe that lesbians necessarily experienced menopause in the same way as Greer claimed heterosexual women did. But she agreed wholeheartedly with her that any wishful desire for "no change" was desperately sad and horrible.

She felt differently passionate, differently engaged, differently but happily a woman, now that she was free of menstruation. She could still be blue and get depressed, but those were not conditions which typified her life. She could be deeply serious and self-sufficient at times, and laugh till her sides ached with a bunch of girlfriends at others. She could be pleased with her memories, filled with love for her grown-up children, and still fizz with expectation at a new idea for work or relaxation. She wept and raged at the grotesque levels of suffering and exploitation in the world, but she still considered herself committed to being part of changing that. She was sometimes confused and troubled by the end-of-the-century political scene, but she was confident in a way she had never been when she was younger. She was still the queen of second-hand shopping and still intended to get fit, but she fully understood that some possibilities were in the past for her. Each decade of her life had spun itself out at the time as the best. She saw no reason to think the next few wouldn't continue the tradition. Now if only she could shed those extra post-menopausal pounds...

A CHANGE OF MIND
Pele Plante

Few experiences in life can compare to going through menopause. Entering uncharted wilderness, perhaps, without a map or compass. Trying to find a way out without a trail.

As a lesbian who must be in charge of her body and her life and her libido, the hardest thing was not being in control and not knowing what to expect. Only a few years ago little information was available and no one talked about it.

The little I did know persuaded me to try to go through menopause naturally. The argument that it was a normal life occurrence, not an illness, made sense to me. But neither did I rule out hormone replacement. It would be my backup. If I couldn't make it naturally, help was as close as my friendly physician.

And that libido? A friend once said about me, "She sees life from the edge of the mattress."

In my own defense, this was during the 60s, a time of sexual revolution and freedom. Sex was freely given and received. I liked it a lot and wasn't a bit shy about multiple orgasms. Even into my thirties and late forties my sexuality was easy to arouse and easy to orgasm.

At age fifty, at menopause, all that changed.

There was much to distract me. For one, strange flutters developed, like a bird caught inside my chest. These sensations were like nothing I'd ever felt before, a syncopation of the beat, as though the heart were misfiring. They riveted my attention several times a day, forcing me to face my own mortality. I was sure this was the end of the line. The old ticker wasn't working right any more.

By then, thick menstrual clotting would cause me to go weak in the knees, followed by a dizziness that made for reflexive clutching of the nearest stationary object.

An unending flow demanded trips to the bathroom every hour on the hour, even in the middle of group therapy. Clients were on their own as I waddled down the agency halls with an extra thick pad between my legs.

Worst of all were the bouts of cold sweats and nausea that kept me in bed for a miserable twelve hours. They looked a lot like toxic shock symptoms. Now that was getting scary. I stopped wearing a tampon at night and, thank the goddess, the episodes ceased. Never did get an explanation for those little humdingers. A reduced immune system, no doubt.

I came to sympathize with our grandmothers. They knew even less than we did. Small wonder some took to their couches with Lydia Pinkham, or were put away in the attic.

By the time the electric tingling began somewhere at the base of my spine and ripped up into my brain, I was plain terrified. Until finally a more forthcoming elder told me this was it, this was a real hot flash.

Hallelujah! Deliverance at last. By now I welcomed the worst, if it meant nearing the end of it. To be free from the erratic gushes with periods sometimes back to back. To be free from cramps that could make a grown dyke cry, or at least moan and curse.

Miss my periods? Not on your life.

But it was not to be quite that easy. The first year was fierce.

We were living on the ocean's edge in Northern California where I was awakened every night, sweating and tingling with the flashes that left me buzzing, unable to go back to sleep. I learned that a cup of hot milk, flavored with a sprinkle of chocolate, would do the trick. A friendly arc of light from the South Caspar lighthouse kept me company, sweeping over the darkened house as I sat in the dining room, pondering the whithers and whethers of life. I came to realize that our busy lives allow few opportunities to merely sit and think. To meditate.

An improved health regimen also helped. Lots of water, walking, fresh fruit and vegetables, vitamins. At the very least it gave me the illusion that I was doing something to help make the some one hundred flashes a day bearable. Yes, I counted the damn things.

But something else began to happen. I began to write stories.

And my libido? Yes, that lusty, hair-trigger sexuality changed.

It wasn't that I lost interest, mind you. And it wasn't classic sublimation, either. It was something different, something more subtle and mysterious.

Slower to awaken with no more thunderous orgasms, but in their place, an ineffable kind of sweetness, a more peaceful release that paradoxically bonds me all the more to my partner.

But there's more. Something else. A sharpening of the senses to other pleasures—the diamond sparkles on a spider web, the sensuous curve of my beloved's thigh, the astonishing whir of a hummingbird's flight, the surprise of pleasing planes in a picture. An expansion of my attention and affections, a change of heart, a change of mind.

Merely hormones? Maybe so. With less estrogen pumping into the system, maybe one's focus widens as the biological imperative to caretake others lessens.

I even had the impulse to draw and have indulged it, with a promise of more to come. But mostly it is this new driving urge to tell stories. As though in a state of grace, regularly I am allowed to enter the page and dip from the stream bed of fable and metaphor, to bring back tales as yet untold.

What started out to be a determined negotiation of another of life's hurdles, menopause has become something else entirely. And I'm feeling my way along here, figuring it out by writing about it. Rather than landing on my feet again on solid ground, I have been lent wings to keep on soaring through the air.

Part of it is the quickened sense of how brief life actually is, an urgency about doing the things not yet done. Writing books, building a house, rendering service. And yet it is the quiet moments, the sensing of my kinship with other beings, that makes the self slip away, merging me into the deer, a kingfisher, the cat, or even a friend. I catch a glimpse of the power of the crone.

My long-time partner does not yet share my joy in this subtle diffusion of my sexuality. She was used to knowing in no uncertain terms when I had climaxed and how many times. Now it is much quieter, more like hers, I think.

But she is beginning to change, too. Her periods have worsened. Sometimes she thinks it's too warm. She is becoming a fine photographer. She goes into the landscape and, barehanded, grabs images out of the sky in which you can see the spin of the planet. She brings back pictures of rocks and waterfalls you can enter at the edge and climb right into, to lose yourself in the land itself.

She has already decided, with all the information now available, that she will use HRT as there is a history of heart problems in her family. She plans to use it for a year or so, as long as necessary, then go off it or go to a lower dose. If I had known then what we know now, that it isn't required to choose all or nothing, I might have done the same. A change of mind, yes. One thing for sure, menopause is not for the faint of heart. Though I confess to some satisfaction, even pride, at the risk of hubris, in having trekked into the unknown and returned to tell about it. And like a wilderness adventure, one returns with a different take on things. A change of heart and mind.

SOME THOUGHTS ON THE MENOPAUSE
Rev. Victoria Lee-Owens
Adapted from correspondence.

"In the midst of my tears and heartache, suddenly the Comforter will send a sweet mood, like a gentle kiss, to touch my heart." Surely that is what happened for me today. I write this from the deep, dark cavern of a blackness never visited before (and I sure hope I get to leave soon). I am encountering horrendous mood swings and emotional upheaval traveling onward through these adventures with the black candle of life known as menopause. Through The First Woman's Church, I have been taught to call it mini-pause. It has been quite a long time since I visited the darkness of fear and anxiety for this long, so I'm taking time to investigate what this all means for me in hopes that anyone else entering "the void" may be at least partially guided through. I believe that all does get finished in beauty, that all passes to make way for newness.

The point when I go into the dark, when all appears to be waning, is really the point of rest for renewed vivaciousness. Then the truest form of beauty comes pouring out. If I have invested the energy and courage to "know myself," all of the stages of my life will converge as an apex—my innocence as a toddler, my inquisitiveness of child-hood, my challenges fought during adolescence and my resulting self-knowledge of the woman I have become. Above all, it has become absolutely necessary that I push out all the ancient rumors and mistaken messages about this time. I don't have to go crazy, 'cuz I can tell someone how I feel, rather than act out how I feel. I don't have to get old, because I am freed to visit my "inner child" and share a meaningful relationship with her. I can stop acting like a grownup during those periods (no pun intended) when I really don't want to be an adult. I can even let someone hold and hug me as I re-experience being five, ten or fifteen-years-old. I can open my heart, my soul and let all the fears, anxieties, mixed emotions, embarrassments, hurts, and other painful things come forth, no longer being "needful things." I can re-create myself in the likeness of my highest ideal through Divine Comforter (Goddess within) who can mold "Me," the barren wilderness, into the Garden of Eden; who can drench "Me," the desert of bewilderment, with cooling waters sent from a heavenly taproot. And, I can become a vessel of joy and gladness found within as thanksgiving and the voice of melody (taken from Isaiah 51:3).

My life hasn't always seemed to flow successively from childhood to adulthood. I often surged too early into adulthood and then detoured backwards into emotional childhood and adolescence on my route to self-growth. But all was not for naught. Without those experiences I would have no need or appreciation for that which I've found through The First Woman's Church.

I am only able to write this while going through a personal reach for comfort in the midst of discomfort because I choose to learn from and emulate other spiritually empowered women, acquainted or not, who have walked this avenue before me in a positive way. Their encouraging words and examples wash my soul, teaching me the importance of getting out of my own mess by assisting another, even thought I'd rather sit and percolate. Thus, I wish to blend my words with those of other sister friends. That in itself is a testimony to how the bond of womanhood expresses. When most needed, we can and will move mountains of discouragement and valleys of depression to be available to one another, sharing a message of promise.

I say thank you to the empowered women who helped grow me up and even now continue to seed and water my growth. I've come too far in accepting myself as the Black lesbian I am to turn back now. My dark feelings push and probe my ego into wanting to "go somewhere, do something else, even turn back the hands of time." Turning a deaf ear to the lyrics of nonsense, I continue to hold high the banner of the Divine Inner Goddess "keeping cadence in my right place" as we move into the Aquarian Age, an age of knowing who I am rather than wondering. I know that I know all I will need to know when the time presents itself for expression.

Sometimes I have cried, sometimes been scared or feisty, sometimes needed to hold onto some mother essence hand, sometimes wiped my eyes on someone's skirt tail while hiding behind it. I have found a way to become friends with the womb darkness where all is being re-ordered. I have re-established new thoughts and new actions around new activity, the menopause (the mini-pause period).

Children often fight and then go back and make friends again. In my case, I need to make friends with who I am becoming and release the woman I have been. Before I know it, I'll be smiling, holding hands and sharing peanut butter and honey sandwiches and drinking herb tea with the rest of you as we play through our changing seasons in the sandbox of time.

NON-MENOPAUSE: A CHRONOLOGY
Susan J. Wolfe

In January, 1994, at the age of forty-seven, I did *not* go into menopause, at least according to the clinical definition. By June, though I had undergone as many uncomfortable medical tests as I ever care to have in this lifetime, I had *still* not gone into menopause. I had the word of a specialist in internal medicine, a family practitioner, and a gynecologist that, hormonally speaking, I was not—and, I suppose, am not—menopausal. But if this isn't the "change," I dread the real one.

That's why I resisted writing this piece. As I told the editors, I'm not menopausal, at least according to the doctors. Besides, the entire story sounds like a litany of trivial complaints, or (if you're Jewish rather than Catholic) kvetching. As a result of some of the symptoms of (what I still believe to be) menopause, I now know more about my body than I really wanted to know, and a lot more than you care to. On the other hand, every woman I've talked to who's my age or older and has had comparable symptoms has seemed to listen sympathetically, and then agree promptly that I have indeed entered menopause. So I'll share the kvetch list with you, and let you be the judge. And, if you ever wind up with similar complaints, by all means, go to the specialists—but don't surprised if they can't help you.

I first sensed that I might be menopausal in January, 1994. There were only twelve days during that month that I did *not* have my period, the 8th through the 19th. Now, I'm familiar with the theory that I should sing the praises of the goddess for all that blood, but the first time I put a large napkin on upside-down and yanked out a pubic hair or two cured me of song. Nineteen days of menstruating simply means nineteen days of rinsing out underwear and feeling as though one or two showers a day might not be enough.

Toward the end of the month and the second (thirteen-day) period, I developed a far more annoying symptom: cardiac arrhythmia...except I didn't know that's what it was. What it seemed to be was shortness of breath, accompanied by soreness of the muscle sheath over the upper chest. And as a person with allergic bronchial asthma, I'd had that feeling before. And tachycardia, racing of the heart, wasn't an unlikely accompaniment.

But this was different. Before my heart started racing, I had a funny feeling, as if my heart was turning over in my chest like a fish. Sometimes it felt like a very heavy beat, a thud, and then it seemed to stop. And it was worst at bedtime. I couldn't lie horizontally, or on my back at all. Eventually I took to sleeping with three pillows, two under my head and one under one or both legs, or alongside, whichever seemed to work. I smeared eucalyptus ointment all over my chest so I could ignore the feeling enough to sleep.

It started to wake me up nights. At the threshold between waking and sleeping, I would feel that large thud in my chest and I would be short of breath, my heart racing. I felt best standing up and walking around, so I began to do that whenever I woke up. Sometimes it was possible to fall asleep propped up on the sofa; often it wasn't. By March, I took to getting out of bed and just walking around, doing household chores or just pacing. Sometimes the only thing that seemed to stop the arrhythmia was taking a shower, and I'd take one for forty minutes, only to discover I'd have to get in the shower again. When I slept through two consecutive nights, I'd start to feel semi-normal, only to start the cycle all over again the following night.

I was almost one hundred percent certain it was not my heart that was causing the problem, an assertion that sounds stupid on the face of it. But hear me out. I had had a full heart work-up the preceding summer because I inadvertently gave myself an electrolyte imbalance, too little potassium in my system. In case you don't know it, that can cause heart spasms, and eventually lead to a heart attack. I wound up in a hospital where I had a treadmill test and a sonogram, and learned that I showed no evidence of heart disease of any kind. So it was extremely unlikely that I'd be having heart problems.

Knowing this, I attributed all of my symptoms to a combination of menopause and stress. Not surprisingly, I was starting to feel quite stressed. There were a lot of work factors I could've pointed to, and did...speeches in different states, theses I was directing, a student grievance committee, a new doctoral program that finally got approved in March and then needed to be implemented all in addition to my usual class load and chairing the department. But there'd been times in my life I considered far more stressful, and I had never experienced anything like this.

It was my partner Cathy, who'd been living with me for seventeen years, who noticed that I didn't seem to be wheezing, although my blood pressure, which had been under control since 1978, had suddenly gotten to be high again. I finally agreed to see her specialist, an internist with a specialty in kidney disease and hypertension, in the hope that something could be done about my blood pressure and the arrhythmia as well.

I went to see him in mid-April, by which time I had had the current menstrual period for fourteen days. I suggested that menopause might be a factor in the other symptoms I was experiencing. And that's when he did the magic test that told me and the medical world that I was not menopausal, and that all these symptoms were obviously in my *mind*...the FSH, follicle stimulating hormone test.

It seems that when you cease to produce enough estrogen, this hormone becomes elevated in a last-ditch attempt to convince your body you may still bear the young of the race. And if you have a low FSH reading, your estrogen should still be fine: ergo, you are not menopausal. But he suggested that if I were contemplating estrogen replacement, I should see my family practitioner or a gynecologist.

I didn't *have* a gynecologist. I imagine some dykes do, either because they've elected to have children or have "female problems" which I hadn't had, at least until the recent past. He also suggested that I see a pulmonologist to have my lungs tested, because he wanted to do a sleep test on me, to determine whether sleep apnea (stopping breathing when you sleep because your air passage closes) was causing my sudden high blood pressure (which peaked at 185 over 115 *while* on medication).

On April 28, I went to a pulmonologist and a gynecologist because I couldn't stand the discomfort anymore, and was willing to undergo virtually any procedure to make it stop. I had a full set of tests for lung functions, all of which were normal, a chest x-ray, a vaginal exam, and a sonogram of my reproductive system.

That last test, particularly for a dyke, is really annoying. When the technician came at me with an eight-inch rubber club four inches in circumference and asked me to insert it in my vagina, I thought she was joking. In fact, I asked her if she was. She pleasantly denied it. I inquired whether she meant me to insert all of it. She suggested in an encouraging tone that we would "see," and eventually, with her help, we did see...the entire inside of my uterus, my ovaries and my cervix—all in living black and white.

In 1993, I had discovered I had no heart disease, and now found I had no lung disease or reproductive disease either, that last despite the fact that by April 28, I'd been menstruating for twenty-four solid days, a period which, according to the gynecologist, still had "normal" flow. To deal with that, he put me on the pill. The period stopped within a few days, but not the arrhythmia. I also found it funny to be on birth control pills since I'd been a dyke for seventeen years.

In the meantime, the internist had tinkered with my blood pressure medication, Capoten, twice: once to raise it to three doses a day, once to drop it back down to two at the original dosage—which, not surprisingly, didn't lower my pressure either. (I should mention that this is a highly-respected man in his field.) Finally, on May 31, he substituted a new drug, which drove my pressure down to normal in two weeks—and below, but that's another story.

Needless to say, the pulmonologist and internist agreed that I had to lose weight. It is my belief that a woman my weight (a little under two hundred pounds) could go into an emergency room with a bleeding stump and her detached leg in her arms and the doctor on call would prescribe a diet. I eventually did lose a little weight but not enough, I think, to account for the difference in blood pressure. When I commented on the difference to the internist, he said, "Oh, well, Prinivil's a good drug."

On May 6, the arrhythmia started at two in the afternoon in my office and would not stop. By midnight, Cathy and I were beside ourselves, and I agreed to go to the emergency room. At first, after putting me on oxygen and slapping an oximeter and ECG leads on me, the technician declared everything was normal. Luckily, she pushed the wrong button on the machine which was printing the sample ECG readings and instead of copying her first strip (which indicated normal heart rhythm), produced a second which showed an abnormal ("borderline abnormal") rhythm. *Cathy*, looking over the woman's shoulder, noticed the difference. (Now perhaps someone would've read the hours' worth of cardiograms, but I'll never know, and I find it scary, personally, that my lover's inveterate curiosity appears to be the only reason we discovered the symptom when we did.)

What I was doing, what I had been doing every time I felt like this, was throwing a PVC (premature contraction of the left ventricle) every five beats, causing me to feel short of breath and causing my chest to hurt. Eventually, the state of anxiety brought on by all this would cause rapid heartbeats as well.

My family practitioner came to the emergency room. He reassured me that there was nothing to worry about, because people throw PVCs all the time—about every thirty beats—and don't notice them. They're "benign." (Silly me. An entire semester without sleep for no reason.) I could stop them by raising my heart rate and throwing myself out of them. (No wonder walking around felt better; the Nordic Track, presumably, would have been better still...but then, what if the doctor was wrong about the condition of my heart?) In fact, I was to discover, inhaling as deeply as I could and then forcing one small extra puff of air in would do the same thing. (When I questioned the pulmonologist, she said something about "negative pressure" in the chest cavity.)

I don't mean to imply that the last year has been all bad. The emergency room visit did more than convince me I wasn't imagining things; it prompted the family practitioner to take me off the antihistamine I'd been on for years, Seldane. Seems it's been known to cause this kind of arrhythmia. He also took me off the decongestant, which may have been contributing to the hypertension. The pulmonologist prescribed a steroid inhaler that has made it possible for me to go off the pills I was taking for the asthma. I breathe better than I have in years.

On May 18, I walked around with a twenty-four hour heart monitor on. A cardiologist confirmed that this was a benign condition...as long as I never throw a few PVCs in a row. (Of course, since no one truly knows whether I will or not, I'm not fully reassured...but then by now I am a hypochondriac.)

On June 16, just to make sure that sleep apnea wasn't contributing to my hypertension, I had an overnight sleep test. Twenty electrodes were taped to my body and four glued to my scalp; an elastic band was put around my thorax; a rigid piece of plastic was taped between my nose and lip; a firm clamp for the oximeter was placed on my right forefinger; and I was asked to sleep, with full knowledge the camera was on me.

I took six minutes to fall asleep. As I pointed out to the pulmonologist, I may have a little apnea, but I don't have insomnia except when my heart feels like a trout. It turns out my apnea's mild, too. I won't even discuss what my alternatives would have been if it had been severe.

On June 21, I returned to the internist. My blood pressure was down. He attributed it to the weight loss—largely due to involuntary exercise to stop the arrhythmia and lack of appetite from inability to sleep during episodes. Of course...Prinivil *is* a "good drug."

The arrhythmia? It's still here, but I've learned that breathing trick, and it really does work. (Lucky thing. A friend of mine who's something of a physical fitness nut said her menopausal arrhythmia used to strike *while she was running*...no way to get your heart rate up if you're that physically fit. And besides, it's hard to lecture or chair a meeting from a Nordic Track. Not that there's a real danger I'll become physically fit.)

As for menopause, I had no period during the entire month of November, and a light one in December. Looks like menopause to me, but then, I haven't had an FSH test this year.

POSTSCRIPT

I'd like to add a couple of observations on medicine and class. And on what appears to me to be the arrogance of the medical profession. I am middle class. Those of you with less money than I have, perhaps without insurance, undoubtedly started to add up the possible costs of all this. I am insured, yet wound up paying about two thousand dollars for doctors and medicines in 1994, with my insurance paying perhaps three times that, most of it for these batteries of tests. Without insurance, only the emergency room would have been covered...although, oddly, that's where the problem was finally identified.

Growing up working class, I spent hours in the free clinic at

Presbyterian Medical Center in New York, in pain with earaches, waiting with my parents to get waited on. I hurt, and I was also humiliated waiting on those benches with people who had lots of different illnesses and injuries. I felt powerless.

I still do when I'm dealing with the medical profession. I don't know what that specialist in internal medicine thought he was doing when he dropped my dosage of medicine to a level that had previously been ineffective. His nurse, the only person I got to talk to in a non-emergency without driving sixty miles and spending seventy-two dollars (only twenty four of which was paid by insurance) for a twenty-minute visit, was unenlightening. The doctor never told me why he didn't prescribe the Prinivil in the first place, and I still feel intimidated asking. Maybe that's my problem, or maybe I just have enough experience with this guy to know I'll either get little response or an overwhelming amount of data, so much that I won't be able to process it.

Apparently all the doctors have shrugged off the problem that really drove me to them in the first place. What if, in addition to the arrhythmia, I had no money to pay these people, and I'm right about stress contributing to the effects of menopause?

I'm also troubled by the implication that the drugs they've prescribed knowingly for years are a possible trigger.

I have to go to the doctor weekly for shots, and the allergist once a year. Whenever I go to the allergist or the family practitioner for another problem, I'm asked to list the drugs I'm taking. Why bother, since they never took/take me off potentially dangerous ones? (Incidentally, the information most of us had on Seldane warned about arrhythmia from overdose, not prolonged medication at the standard dosage.) I'm lucky my general practitioner did pick up on the possibility that Seldane might have been a problem when I was in the ER.

I'm sure some people would urge me to try herbal or holistic approaches. Since extract of horsetail is the herb that threw me into electrolytic imbalance in the first place while following the directed dosage, I'm inclined to ask an MD for a potassium-sparing diuretic the next time airplane travel and restaurant food cause me to bloat alarmingly. I'm sure a well-informed herbalist can work miracles, but I definitely recommend against dabbling.

SUMMERTIME
Lee Lynch

It's a muggy New York summer day. Her regulation white shirt clings to her like spider webs. In the alley out back of her store, she pries loose the corner of a plastic milk crate which has caught on her name tag: FRENCHY TONNEAU, ASS'T. MANAGER. She gives herself an admiring whistle as she tiptoes to jiggle the crate on top of several others. A twinge in her back brings her quickly down. As she absently rubs a stain from her store-issue cotton blazer, she breathes in the sweetish smell of produce composting in the dumpster. She could have Rosario take delivery, but it took her fourteen years to get promoted off the front end.

The door slams open. Mu Tan backs out, giggling, riding the narrow end of a grocery cart. Her blazer covers her shorts and makes her look undressed. Rosario is pushing, a grin on his face, jacketless, his shirttails flying.

"Off!" barks Frenchy, shocked at her own fury. A cloud of cooled air from the open door surrounds her.

Both clerks whip their heads around. Mu Tan's wide laughing mouth closes tight, Rosario's grin becomes a guilty grimace. Mu Tan climbs down. "We're on break," Mu Tan complains, her tone sullen.

"Your neck is what you're about to break. And we don't have the okay on shorts yet, summer or not." She wonders about herself. She never yells at her crew.

Rosario backs the wagon into the store. He's wiry, curly-haired and a damn good stock man. Mu Tan has a loving touch with the bakery customers, speaks a dialect that pulls people from Chinatown. Together, though, they're a couple of puppies, giddy with love. It's been a long time since she felt like they must, but she knows it's bad business to mix work and love.

"Just stop the rough-housing, guys, and watch the dress code," she orders, light on them, and brushes past into the store, ashamed of her initial outburst. She touches the keys that hang from her belt, afraid she'll misplace them again. She never loses things.

Usually, she revels in her job, especially the weekends. That's when she's top dog at Apple Cart Foods, downtown. It must be the heat that's getting to her. One of the fans in the walk-in dairy cooler whines like a meat cutter's saw. For the sixth time today she flips the switch off, then on again to get it to stop. She made out a repair order, but between the fan and the dentist music that's piped into the store non-stop, she's going bonkers.

She's in the detergent aisle when the feeling starts again. Like she's being scraped raw. Like her bones are rusting and flaking. Like a sunburn is slowly crawling up from her thighs to her head. The scented soaps make her queasy and she breaks into a clammy sweat. It was so bad last night she took her temperature. Her buddies in the AIDS visiting program, Alan and Cornel, both had night sweats when they were sick. The scariest part is that she can't ask if this is what they felt; they're gone.

By the time the front end is in sight, she remembers why she helped unload the milk truck—to get away for a while. In this weather, griping customers and grumpy cashiers can come to blows. Her mood sinks and as it goes, so does her courage to face the heat, the crew, her life. All she wants is to go back to bed and stay there.

A steady Sunday morning trickle of customers comes in: church-goers looking for Mu Tan's donuts, ragged-looking partyers bumping into one another as they grab tomato juice and aspirin.

Frenchy rips down last week's huge red, white and blue Memorial Day specials poster from the window, the twinge in her back making her feel like she might rip in two herself. One of the fluorescent bulbs flickers and sizzles. The dentist music drones on and on. She tells herself again that she's not getting sick.

"You just quit that cursing," the new cashier Clove is telling a stumpy guy shifting from one foot to the other. Clove is ringing out an old woman in churchy-looking clothes who's paying with a coin purse stuffed with change. The stumpy guy makes Frenchy nervous, but looks too strung out to be thinking about a hold-up or anything except where his dealer might be. Clove tells him, "Too bad you never going to get old and slow like her."

The customers who hear laugh. The jittery guy slaps a five dollar bill on the counter and pushes his way past the old woman. He tells Clove, "Screw you, bitch." Frenchy pulls into herself as he passes, leaving behind the stench of his unwashed clothing. She considers telling Clove not to push the crazy people.

"You see this, Boss-lady?" Clove calls laconically. She rings up the man's cigarettes and waves his five before slipping it in the drawer. "You make sure I get the nice man's tip when I cash out, hear?" The customers laugh again. Frenchy manages a grin.

Clove has close-cropped kinky grey hair that makes her cheekbones stand out like rocks along the Palisades at night, dark, naked, defiant. She's skinny, proud, accurate, takes nothing off nobody. Some rough customers come in the store, but they never give Clove a hard time twice. Frenchy's supposed to talk to her about dress code too, but she doesn't know if it's Clove's prickly attitude or if she's turning wimp in her old age; she hasn't been able to bring herself to do it. At least Clove is wearing her name tag today, but she's got shorts on and she's trying to pass off some kind of white tank top with lace trim as her white shirt.

Frenchy turns back to her posters and sips from the cardboard container of cold coffee she's been carrying around the store. Somebody told her caffeine gives you lumps in your breasts. Does cancer make you feel this way?

Later, when Clove is filling the bottom of her cigarette rack, Frenchy can't put it off any longer.

"Clove," she snaps, angry that she has to say it, "do you have any idea how far down that top of yours I can see when you bend over like that?"

"Not as far as you'd like to," Clove replies without a pause, then pops her gum.

Frenchy feels that rusty scraping crawl up the front of her rib cage. Fury, like a storm wind, surrounds her head. "It's not dress code, Clove, any more than the shorts are. At least put on your Apple Cart jacket. Don't make me write you up."

Clove stands slowly, like her joints are rusty. "I don't make you do a single solitary thing, Boss-lady. You want me to dress in black pants and long-sleeve shirt like you on this hot day? Na-huh. Not this gal."

"You're pushing me, Clove. And you want to know the truth?" The scraping inside her skin has stopped, but she's so hot, her face must look like a tomato about to explode. She'll fire this one, watch her. "You may impress the men, but you sure don't look professional."

"Maybe you don't think us man-hungry black women should get big important jobs like grocery clerk."

"This company has an image to keep up. It's got nothing to do with color."

"What kind of professional are you supposed to look like, the Marlboro man?"

The light pings and flickers overhead. She hears a cooler door open and imagines she smells that faint sour milk smell she's tried to scrub away. The fan whines like an ambulance all the way across the store. Mu Tan laughs over at the bakery. Rosario calls to her. Customers swarm the other registers. Clove glares. Frenchy's storm winds die and leave her in a desert of hopelessness. She manages to hold in her tears until she reaches the office.

* * *

Despite a terrific tromp through the twilight drizzle with Duchess III, her Sheltie mix, her eyes still sting from crying when she gets to the co-op meeting that night. She never cries.

"Is this the coolest place in the city or what?" asks Geoffrey, the photocopier repairman who lives next door.

She claps him on the back, surprised how good it is to see a friendly face. "You're the best neighbor I could ask for."

Geoffrey replaces a brief puzzled look with a smile. "It's mutual," he responds.

The broad damp basement room in Frenchy's pre-World War II building has an old air raid shelter sign at the door and small wire-reinforced windows just below its high ceiling. The two outside walls are cement and cool to the touch. She leans her forehead against one briefly, taking a shallow breath to avoid disturbing the fragile peace she's made with her back. Over the years, tenants have contributed ratty couches and chairs, scratched tables, faded posters, until the room has become a comfortable and familiar mix of histories.

Except for Frenchy, they all tell horror stories about the day's heat. She's chilly now, wishes she were back upstairs pulling the old string of silvery beads the cats like to chase, trying not to worry about what kind of sick she is.

"Anybody know a good doctor?" she asks without planning to.

Stephanie Lois Stephens sits so abruptly in the straight-backed chair next to her, Frenchy hopes she's bruised her scrawny haunches. Mid-fifties, a former actress turned cosmetics saleswoman, she's all solicitude. "You're sick?"

"I figure I need a physical once every twenty-five years," she jokes. Is the bitch angling to buy her apartment if she dies?

"You don't go annually?" The woman pats her stiff hairdo like a yellow cotton candy wig. She stinks of a lavender-heavy perfume.

"I'm never sick."

Stephanie Lois fleetingly touches the back of Frenchy's hand and lowers her voice, which does no good as everyone in the silent room, aware of their ongoing enmity, listens. "But women our age simply must have a check up every year."

Anyone else she might forgive, but she resents this flinty-eyed neighbor with fingernails the length of Long Island making like the two of them are birds of a feather.

Geoffrey's lover, a foot shorter, considerably wider and striking-ly more pale than Geoffrey, like a white chocolate chunk next to a semi-sweet Easter rabbit, has arrived. The monthly meeting can begin.

It's not a large building, twenty-nine apartments, all occupied, and Frenchy counts eighteen people, several of them couples. Mr. Meyerowitz, the school principal, who is newly single and a power-ful magnet to Stephanie Lois, slams his gavel on the coffee table to quiet the bickering between Geoffrey and Tony. They moved in about the time Mercedes moved out on her eight years ago, but she doesn't see what keeps them together unless they enjoy their screaming matches.

She reads the minutes of the last meeting. She never wanted to be a secretary, but an election forced her to find out she was good at it.

"You mean," corrects Stephanie Lois as soon as Frenchy begins, "1989, not 1988."

"Sorry," she says, embarrassed, but not a minute later the woman pats her cotton candy and cries, "Mr. M.! I move that the minutes be corrected to read one-thousand-three-hundred dollars not thirteen-thousand dollars."

"Of course," Frenchy admits, not quite snarling.

"Darling," Stephanie Lois interrupts with another error. "Are you sure you're not ill?"

She's rattled now and reverses words. She never makes mistakes in the minutes. Maybe it's a brain tumor. At the store she tells Rosario to fill the egg case when she means ice cream case, then yells at the poor guy. "But you told me to!" he wails and, these days, she has to believe it's not him dreaming of Mu Tan, but her, with early Alzheimer's. How will she pay her mortgage, take care of Duchess and the cats, if she's sick?

Mr. Meyerowitz takes them through the old business. She can see Stephanie Lois cross her legs for him. Will all the straights vote with that old battle-ax this time? Each of them looks like the lone hawk on the highrise across from the Apple Cart, watching for the weakest pigeon, gearing up to swoop.

"I'm willing to attach a grandfather clause," offers Stephanie Lois. "I'm aware that a few of our esteemed neighbors have formed a rather..." Her pause makes the words sound worse. "...queer attachment to their menageries."

"Hey!" cries Frenchy, half-rising, but her back pulls her down. "Watch what you're saying."

"Mr. M.!" Stephanie Lois yodels, her fake lashes framing genuinely alarmed eyes. "That woman is threatening me!"

With all the dignified authority that makes them call him Mister, Phillip Meyerowitz instructs, "Please moderate your language, both of you." He squirms around on the couch. "And let's get this issue resolved once and for all. It's been dragging on for the past two meetings."

"If I may," says Stephanie Lois, her voice high and strained. She pats her hair. "I propose no more than one pet per unit with the exception of current owners, who may keep two."

Frenchy's a seeping tomato again, bursting ripe under a noon sun. The hawks glower. She never has insomnia, but now she lies awake nights trying to resolve this conflict.

"This is what you call a compromise?" Frenchy rails. "I only have to choose between two of my animals and my home? Shit."

"Language," warns Mr. Meyerowitz.

Geoffrey's lover says, "Frenchy's right. We chose this building based on the rules when we bought in. I don't see where you get off wanting to change them in the middle of the game, Stephanie Lois, just because you're sensitive to barking."

"Maybe I should propose a noise rule instead. Barking isn't the only nuisance in this building," the woman snipes back.

The lover falls silent, but others squabble pro and con. Then mild Mr. Meyerowitz proposes, "We can write in a grandfather clause to keep the status quo. That way those of you who have more than two pets now lose nothing and can make plans for the future size of your household, or to leave the building."

"Leave the building! You don't understand, Mr. Meyerowitz," pleads Frenchy. Her scalp tingles. The sweat gathers. She thinks of Cornel's cat, willed to her. "When we converted, it was cheap, remember? It was a once-in-a-lifetime deal for someone like me. And now if a friend is dying and needs me to take in a guppy, I have to say no?" She can't talk any more. She's choking on her tears. Her back's on fire.

"It's not just me!" Stephanie Lois shrieks.

"You move!" Frenchy counters in a hoarse yell. "You move! It's my home!"

"Ladies, ladies," calls Mr. Meyerowitz.

"There's no working with her," accuses Stephanie Lois Stephens. "You want to know what's wrong with you?"

She steels herself for the words: pipsqueak, queer, riffraff.

The woman hisses, just loudly enough for every neighbor to hear. "You're going through the change, little lady, just like us normal women. Get some hormones if you expect people to put up with you."

* * *

Sometimes when the manager goes to the shore with his family for the weekend, he asks Frenchy to work a double for him Monday. Years of doubles were paying her mortgage, but she's relieved when he doesn't call the next morning. She takes Duchess to run through the playground sprinkler with the kids and when they get home. Cornel's cat, big gray Googie, licks the dog's damp, woolly-smelling feet like a fussy mother.

At work, Frenchy and Rosario haul most of the stock stored in the back room onto shelves out front. She builds a display of dog food, twenty-four can cases, twice her height. It's a damn good display, but her muscles feel like rubber bands ready to snap. She'll take another hour-long bath tonight. In the chilled meat room, she trades dirty jokes with the meat cutter while she sharpens knives.

It's nine o'clock that night before she sees Clove head for the break room. Though Frenchy never takes breaks, she follows.

Management has relented, with a little pushing from Frenchy, and okayed walking-style shorts and short-sleeved collared white shirts. Clove came in wearing culottes and a Hawaiian print shirt with a white background. She's got her blazer on, sleeves pushed up. Frenchy figures Clove's not earning enough to buy a whole new wardrobe. Management can just get over themselves this time.

At the table, Clove's peeling an orange. Its oils spurt in a sweet mist.

"What's the matter, you decide to rag me outside the public eye for once?" Clove asks with a sour look.

With the toe of her desert boot Frenchy tears a scrap of newspaper from a sticky spill on the concrete floor. "I don't blame you for being mad at me."

Clove stacks pieces of orange peel in the ashtray. "It's your job. I know that," Clove says.

"Then how come you give me so much attitude?"

Clove has one gold tooth way back in her mouth and it shows when she laughs. "Attitude's the only weapon I carry."

"What do you need a weapon for?"

"It helps."

"Helps what?"

"You don't know? I thought you were going through it too."

"What?"

"The change."

Just the words trigger one of those heat waves. She sits on a metal folding chair and presses her white shirt to her breastbone to soak up the trickle of sweat. "You're the second one to say I have it."

"How old are you?"

"I hit the big five-o this year."

Clove shrugs. "What can I say?"

"Say it isn't so," Frenchy half-laughs, half-groans.

"You'd be happier if your friend came to visit every month the rest of your life?"

"It's better than crazy time at the zoo."

"Who's crazy?" asks Clove, offering her a section of orange.

She holds the moist fruit with her fingertips and watches Clove eat. "This lady in my building, the one who says I have it. She's got it and everything drives her up a tree. And my mother. I had to take care of her, like she was dying, then she moves to Florida and gets a job. Go figure."

Clove pops another section of orange in her mouth and Frenchy remembers her own.

She can feel each tiny juice sac burst, sweet and sour, on her tongue. She looks away from Clove, speaks in a smaller voice than she'd intended. "And me. I'm coming apart at the seams. One minute life's gold in my hands, then it turns to shit." She looks at her hands in disgust. Swallowing a taste of fury as keen as orange she looks up. "And you, giving me a hard time."

"Me? I haven't lost anything I wanted to keep. I'm through with that monthly mess after all these years. It pisses me off, the kind of attention I finally get from you."

"What do you mean?"

Clove stretches to dump the ashtray full of peels into the trash. "Ask me out and I'll show you."

Frenchy feels herself gawk. "You're gay?"

"I never dressed for a man in my life."

"I feel like two cents."

"You ought to."

"But I can't ask you out," Frenchy proclaims. "I don't date anyone on my crew."

Clove's dark eyes flash that knife blade anger. "It's some boss-lady code of yours, right?"

"It never works out."

Mu Tan and Rosario, in their matching Apple Cart jackets, dark slacks and white shirts, come waltzing in the break room door, cheek to cheek in time to the dentist music. They stop at the sight of Frenchy, looks of horror on their faces.

"I know, I know," Frenchy says, "you're on break."

"We are and..." Mu Tan holds out her hand to display her ring finger.

Rosario clears his throat and with a silly grin announces, "We're getting married."

"Hey!" says Frenchy. She lunges at the soda machine, fumbling in her pockets for change. Going out with co-workers may not be part of her code, but it doesn't take much to make her misty-eyed these days. "Congratulations! I'm buying."

They stand around, pop their cans and sip. Frenchy presses the cold aluminum to her cheek, catches Clove's knowing smile.

"Did you set the date?" asks Clove.

"No," Mu Tan says, giggling. "He only just asked me."

"Right here? In the back room? On break?" Frenchy exclaims.

"And you said it never works out," taunts Clove.

"Listen to that attitude," she tells the kids and hears the admiration in her own voice.

She thinks about how it's been lately. Just her and the animals, her lost AIDS buddies, the co-op clashes, the middle-of-the-night staring-at-the-dark creeps. She sees Rosario and Mu Tan make eyes at each other over their sodas. She sees skinny, proud, defiant Clove, who knows about the sweat, the short fuse, probably the night creeps, and still rules her world. She never goes out with her crew, she reminds herself even as she steals a peek at the schedule on the wall.

"Maybe," she says, "this is why they call it the change."

NOW DON'T START THAT AGAIN!
Shelly Roberts

I think what surprised me most about menopause was the fact that I was in it.

Not out of some massive, generationally influenced denial about graying hair and immanent Geritol and Metamucil dispensure to follow, but, really, simply because in my family we didn't do that sort of thing. Have menopause, I mean. At least not at the comparatively infantile age of forty-eight. My foremothers forbore their bloody "curse" usually into their sixties. Way past the time that grandpa gave a damn, we continued to shout our particular, practical, fond announcement-euphemism, *"Dry Cleaning!"*

I expected to be bringing my wardrobe in for chemical peels for another decade. I mean, after all, what did I have to look forward to with its unpleasant onset? I had watched one lover start in at thirty-five. She taught me the joys of coping with what a fabulous/rotten person/pterodactyl I cyclically became, depending on what floor the hormone elevator landed. Another honey, to her dismay, had me lurking in Chinatown in search of infinite varieties of folding fans for her discomfort. I had watched libidos shrink, moods swing, and partnerships dissolve on a misunderstanding, blissful that I was a mere observer, and for a very long time would not become actively involved.

Isn't it easy to be smug when it's happening to someone else? Particularly when you are, if only falsely, confident that by the time it happens to you, scientific minds will have found an aerosol spray, or tiny, timely tablets that will make the entire adventure seem like a trip to an iron lung museum. Like Dr. McCoy reviewing twentieth century brain surgery. Antiquated. And quaint. When I got there, I fully expected it to be over.

Then one cranky day, I realized that I should be using the word "period" for what I was doing: which is to say, *coming to a full stop.*

I hadn't had a period for quite a long time. In fact, it had probably been months. How could that be?

I can't say that I had a lot of warning. When you live in the tropics, (South Florida only *seems* like it is the New York-New Jersey annex), dripping is not an unusual avocation, so it is hard, exactly, to pinpoint the actual onset of symptoms. Hot flashes? Oh, I just thought the entire neighborhood was swampy.

But I am pretty well convinced that what arrested the development of my case of terminal smugness was my decision to improve my health. I quit smoking. I had tried unsuccessfully dozens of times before, and couldn't break through the nicotine wall without some chemical assistance. So I asked my doctor (who used to be a pharmacist until she realized that her reward for all that work was getting to spend the rest of her life at Walgreens) if she would put me on the nicotine patch. She approved and wrote the prescription. And I found that, with some work, I had quit.

And with no work at all, I had quit something else. Being menstrual.

There has been scant confirmation of the possibility that, immediately following the Technicolor nicotine dreams starring all my best friends in scenarios never written by Freud, the nicotine patch could do such a thing. They don't do much medical research on women anyway, so it doesn't surprise me that most (male) doctors, even friends, look at me like I am suggesting that one day we could walk on the moon, or talk into unwired plastic boxes to people in other geographies. But I am convinced that cessation of Benson & Hedges marked the trigger of temperature roulette.

I have heard that the brain receptor sites that collect estrogen also find nicotine very attractive. With the continuous suffusion of the Winston/Salem stuff into my system, when estrogen tried to climb on board, there was no room. Sending such a signal to your synapses could easily, I maintain, have pulled the switch that derailed my monthly visitation rites.

No fool I, I phoned my pharma/physician and pleaded for Premarin. So, estrogen and no nicotine in the same year. Hey, who needs a waistline? Apparently I didn't, because within the time span of a box of cookies I wished my middle a fond farewell. Then, in the vainglorious expectation that I might yet have an indent, I wished the hormones and their effective sidekicks *"adios"*, and decided to go it alone. I had nightmares about inconclusive cancer concerns, and was never all that addicted to upping my risk factors anyway. So going off hormones wasn't all that difficult.

For months that have turned into years, I have adopted the folding fan fixation. At home, I glance heavenward in perennial gratitude (nearly every room in a South Florida house comes mercifully equipped with a variable speed ceiling fan).

I now work out at the gym, which hasn't done all that much for the indestructible tummy that came as a menopause accessory bonus gift with or without purchase. Three times a week I climb into clothing I wouldn't have worn to the beach in my old body, and stationary-cycle my way to Sandusky, Ohio and back. I pretend I don't notice being in the company of anorexic teenagers who can bench press their high schools while ingesting Pizza Huts whole. I grunt my way to minimal maintenance in the ongoing effort to avoid lifetime enrollment in the Girth and Mirth foundation, while cursing every Merit and Lark commercial I ever met.

And then one day it happened. For no apparent reason.

I started again.

Spontaneously.

(Are you sure you want to hear this? It seems so intimate. And intrusive. Well, okay. As long as we're both here.)

It was a particularly Florida kind of day. But I knew sweat didn't feel like that. Well, *later*, I realized that I knew that sweat didn't feel like that. And I usually didn't sweat *there*. Still, that didn't stop me from spending long hours at my computer without paying any attention. Until finally.

No question. I had "A Visitor." My underwear was going to have to be burned. My good linen shorts would have to go to the....omigod! *"Dry cleaners!"* I was doing *it* again. For no discernible reason.

I had completely forgotten about the nuisance. Not to mention the inconvenience. It's not like I was celebrating the cessation. It's hard to celebrate an event that never arrives. But suddenly there I was, scurrying for paper goods. Caught bloody unprepared in spoiled apparel. With crippling cramps. I headed out gingerly to the nearest 7-11 where I could effectively embarrass some male clerk by an armload of feminine premenopausal requirements.

I was temporarily buoyed by an origami'd washcloth jerry-rigged into my underwear (shades of junior high before the invention of the miraculous self-adhesive strip). If anyone tells you that it is easy to navigate city streets while alternately shifting gears and positions which allow you to keep your knees crossed, they need professional help. But I needed stuff to get through this bout, and if this were going to happen again, I was going to have to up my investment in Kimberly-Clark stock. Pads, inserts, Midol, liners, purse and car carriers, new underwear, all the discarded accessories again. All the inconvenient things that had been conveniently excised from under the sink would have to renew their lease.

And then...it stopped. Again. Never to return after that one nostalgic reprise.

I am convinced that my period returned just long enough to make me grateful it had gone.

It succeeded.

Oh, I still stick my head in the freezer on a regular basis. And contribute my share of the national debt to the purchase of potions, and lotions and Mexican plant extracts in thirty-dollar jars.

And I *am* taming my waistline by the elimination of anything remotely tasty from my diet and watching low-fat TV, which is also probably good for me. I do feel stronger for the pumping and grunting and pushing, even if it is mostly at the gym, and not for the private amusement of my nearest and dearest. (Who did, by the way, get her chance for some get-even gloating the very first time I uttered the immortal words, "Is it *hot* in here, or is it just me?") I also understand that in a few years I will endure a menopausal affliction referred to fondly by those who have grown past it as "CRS." (Can't Remember Excrement).

I'm sorry, what were we talking about?

Oh, yes. *"Dry Cleaning!"* Now I only have to worry about it when my S.O. has run out of clean things to wear to the office. Or when, due to another advantage of aging, the cutest grandchild ever created makes a religious peanut-butter and jelly offering to anything silk in my closet.

Menopause? I wouldn't have missed it for the whole bleeding world.

CHANGE OF LIFE
Sunlight

I'm from the era when we got "the curse," patriarchy's Biblical curse. It sounds like a disease and it felt that way, tainting every aspect of menstruation. The cramps that wracked my belly each month when I bled those quantities that verged on hemorrhage. And the pre-curser, PMS. We didn't call it that, we didn't call it anything, but I remember the swollen breasts, the heaviness, feeling mean.

By the time we took back our bodies and our words and began to celebrate our bloods, mine were dwindling, menopausing. I was sorry to miss this new-old way of seeing. If I had gone to the moon hut to dream and bedaub myself with that life blood and let it flow onto the earth instead of dragging to work, heavy with tampons and sanitary [sic] napkins, I'm sure everything about it would have been different. But it wasn't, and in this culture, even Lesbian culture, much of that is still to come. So when my bloods slithered to a stop, it was a release, a gift of freedom. However, the hot flashes, to some degree, have continued for years. I welcomed them while sitting in the subway on winter nights, but found them irritating when, in the heat of sex, hot flashes, my lover's or my own, touched off more heat, forced us apart to sweat it out on different sides of the bed.

The male medical establishment had branded menopause "an estrogen-deficiency disease" and recommended that it be treated by that hormone. At the time, I considered it. Long ago, before my bloods stopped and I was still acting heterosexual, a friend told me that estrogen keeps at bay the signs of aging—sagging breasts, wrinkled skin—marks that our child-bearing years are over, making us unattractive to men. I couldn't care less about that now, although since coming out I was saddened to notice that old women's bodies are unattractive to most younger Lesbians too, indoctrinated as we all were by the patriarchy. The loss is theirs. We old Lesbians are rediscovering ourselves and each other—interesting, vibrant, wise and beautiful.

For me, menopause was a vast change of life. Since it came slow-ly, erratically, over several years, it's hard to assign cause and effect or even a sequence to the events. But one of those years was the one when I came out. I stopped drinking, stopped having sex with men, stopped bleeding, started another life. I quit my job and moved from the east coast to the west, from city to country, from mainstream to fringe, and incalculable distances within my mind and possibilities. I made contact with my own inner wisdom and began to live accord-ingly. I became less, much less dependent upon others for my opinion of me as I grew to know myself. It was a time to step into another context, one of my own making.

Many of the tidal wave of Lesbians now beginning their second half century are gathering information about menopause. Nice that the silence has been broken. It must be great to talk about it with contemporaries. But instead of reading the travel books, I suggest going into it as the adventure it is—opening, exploring, discovering and experiencing it without other women's road maps.

For me, menopause was a powerful initiation leading to the threshold of cronehood, the door to another world.

HORMONIC CONVERGENCE:
con sangre/sin sangre
Terri de la Peña

Blood, la sangre, surged forth in thick torrents. It forced me awake at three-thirty a.m with the abrupt passage of massive clots. Shocked, I switched on the overhead light. I found myself ensangrentada, drenched with the gory evidence. Stumbling to the bathroom, I left behind a frightening, blotchy trail, red puddles on the linoleum.

I was forty-two when that unexpected episode happened. Until then, I had rarely experienced menstrual cramps or any other type of monthly symptoms, except for an occasional headache. While I cleaned up the mess and changed the bed sheets, I contemplated whether being in my forties would bring about further inconveniences. Before I fell into a restless sleep, I considered writing about that night. At the time I was finishing an erotic short story as well as editing the third draft of my first novel. Both were populated with characters twenty years younger than myself. With that in mind, I decided to postpone whatever ideas I had about documenting that hemorrhage-like incident. Yet I did not forget la noche de sangre; its memory seemed indelible.

* * *

At age thirty-eight, my mother gave birth to me. My brother and sister were nearly a decade older; I was "a surprise." By the time my mother was forty-four, she had had two more "surprises," her last daughter born with Down's syndrome. The realities of her life and my own of growing up with a mentally handicapped sister impacted my decision not to have children. Reared in a Catholic Chicano household, I knew my decision—not to mention my lesbianism—departed drastically from my mother's religious and cultural expectations. Here I was, forty-two years later, at the age when she had dealt with unplanned pregnancies, beginning at last to find something in common with my Mexican immigrant mother—the sudden hormonic changes and bodily symptoms, the ebbing and flowing of la sangre, the blood. After that frightful night, I wanted to know of her own experiences at the beginning of menopause.

She laughed as she always does whenever I probe. "Oh, that was forty years ago, honey."

"You must remember *something* about it," I insisted.

"I wound up having a hysterectomy," she reminded me. "How can you expect me to remember having heavy periods?"

I shrugged, feeling sheepish for asking.

Which, of course, explains the major differences between my mother and me. I am a writer; details, fragments of conversations from years ago remain vivid. I delve for underlying reasons, connections and explanations. She trusts in God and prefers to live in the here and now.

"You're starting to go through the change, that's all," she advised. "Don't worry about it."

Despite her nonchalance, I knew that bloody night was a milestone. It jolted me out of the complacency of trusting my body. No longer could I expect it to behave routinely, without any sudden transformations. After that unforgettable night, my womb became a willful stranger, ruled by hormones, unrestrained by the calendar. It began to bleed whenever it wanted to, tossing its former twenty-eight-day cycle to the winds of Change. It became erratic, manic, hysteric in the truest sense of the word. While it careened out of control, frustrating and exasperating me with its whims, my writing life continued on a steady track. I wrote short stories, book reviews, continued with my novel. My physical self seemed completely at odds with my creative self.

Physical self, creative self—to many women those terms are synonymous. To them, the physical self of the womb *is* the creative self: it represents the center of passion, it becomes pregnant and shelters a developing child until the moments of birth. Women wanting to conceive must have an intimate relationship with their wombs, alert to daily rhythms and secretions.

To me, passion resides in the mind; creativity originates in the brain, not in the womb. That could be why headaches are more familiar to me than menstrual cramps. As long as I can remember, I have lived "in my head." I tend to exist from the top down, hardly solicitous of the rest of my body. The grey matter between my ears is where my identity lies; it is home to daydreams, developing characters, unwinding plots. Sexual desire occasionally visits my thoughts, and fantasies focus on fictional characters, rarely on myself.

From late teens to mid-thirties I was a closeted lesbian. Those mostly celibate years enabled me to dismiss "female" functions. Without the distraction of heterosexual experimentation, I also remained blissfully ignorant of birth control methods. I knew nothing of "procreative" matters, even less about pregnancy scares. I was in favor of reproductive rights, yet felt removed from that issue. Why educate myself about something that did not apply to me? When heterosexual sisters spoke of childbearing issues or told childbirth horror stories, I would grimace and disappear. Why listen to their melodramatic cuentos? And when the lesbian baby boom erupted, I veered even further out of the loop.

Without question, my particular case is extreme. Yet maybe some lesbians have similar tendencies. How many of us disregard our so-called reproductive organs except for a few days every month or when planning schedules and vacations? After all, if given the choice, who wouldn't prefer to keep tampon supplies out of a knapsack, to forget about that scribbled red letter "P" on the calendar? Wouldn't a couple of books and a notepad make more fitting companions?

However, plunging deeper into my forties, I began to find it impossible to ignore my unpredictable womb. I became ever more conscious of its vagaries. By age forty-four, my periods grew so heavy they eventually lasted weeks at a time. I was diagnosed as borderline anemic. A D&C ruled out cancer. That in-patient procedure scared me enough to make me slow down a bit. *Margins* was in its final stages that year. I decided to refuse any other writing assignments and concentrate on finishing the novel.

For several months following the D&C, my periods became regular again; my womb settled into "normal" routines. When the novel was published a month after my forty-fifth birthday, life became increasingly hectic with book promotion, readings and signings. A fifty-two-day bloodless interval occurred in tandem with that fast-paced time. In summer and early autumn a calmer schedule returned. My periods reverted to shorter cycles. Then the days between them lengthened throughout the winter until I had forty-two days of bloodless freedom at the beginning of the next year.

* * *

The morning of my forty-sixth birthday, I awakened to a gentle snowfall outside Fir Cottage at Hedgebrook Farm. While the skies opened to swirling snowflakes and my mind filled with soaring thoughts, I knew that my womb was in a dormant stage. Somehow it seemed fitting that the ebbing of the blood, la sangre de mujer, coincided with the most creative interval of my life: that seven-week residency at Cottages at Hedgebrook, a retreat for women writers on Whidbey Island. I had taken a leave from my university staff job to accept the residency and begin my second novel.

To celebrate my birthday, I hiked into the woods that snowy morning, my boots crunching on the slippery path. I trekked deeper into the groves of fir and red cedar, marveling at shiny crystals sprinkling the low-lying branches. Although I had been at Hedgebrook Farm for only ten days, already its slow pace had soothed me, allowing me to escape from city stresses, particularly the smoldering aftermath of the Los Angeles uprisings months before.

In the forest, I relished the solitude yet soon sensed another presence. My eyes flickered to a slight rustle beyond the trees. I suspected shy bunnies, their cottontails white puffs in the bushes. Instead I glimpsed the vague outlines of three deer. Shadowy figures etched in the mist, the trio of does gazed at me momentarily and vanished. Symbols of gentleness and innocence, they seemed like sylvan muses, welcoming me into that peaceful haven of women's creative space.

During that winter and early spring, in the cozy cottage near Useless Bay, I drafted the early versions of *Latin Satins*. Surrounded by five cottages filled with other creative women, two of them menopausal, one not quite perimenopausal, one wanting to be a mother, one pregnant with twins, I was at my most productive stage. Although among women, I did not menstruate at all; their company did not affect my hormones or my cycle. Instead, I concentrated on my work and turned out six to ten pages a day. My sister-writers marveled at my discipline, my drive. I would smile at their comments, yet would not waste a moment. I relished being able to write all day and into the night. My overactive mind spewed months' worth of pent-up fiction while my womb expressed nothing.

Not surprisingly, the writing focused on fictional counterpart

Jessica Tamayo, a singer-songwriter so emotionally stressed that her periods halted before returning with a vengeance on one of the most important nights of her life. Too young to be menopausal, Jessica nevertheless found herself at odds with the unpredictability of her body. Her ensuing bewilderment definitely paralleled mine.

On those grey Northwest mornings, I encountered another new experience: hot flashes. The first time I awoke drenched with perspiration, I suspected the flu. Most of the other writers had been ill; so far, I had managed to avoid it. However, after several sweaty awakenings, I realized the flu was not the culprit. Groggy with sleep, I would pull off my flannel nightgown and hurl it aside. I would doze off, only to wake up shivering a couple of hours later when the heat from the wood-burning stove diminished. Slipping into the damp nightgown, I would hurry downstairs to relight the fire. And, of course, by then I would be fully awake, energized by the unexpected "power surge," ready to work, not sleep.

The hot flood of perspiration became a substitute for the absent menstrual flow. A particularly wet night seemed to guarantee a productive day with the novel. During the seven weeks at Hedgebrook Farm, I never experienced writer's block. The structure, the plot, the dialogue of the novel sprang from me in whole chunks, in rapid succession, while my womb continued to rest. I felt freer than ever— without job responsibilities, away from tense everyday realities— living a truly creative life, at least temporarily.

When I left Hedgebrook Farm as winter bloomed into a brilliant spring, I knew I had been transformed, too. The former week-night writer had evolved into a dedicated novelist, the regularly menstruating woman into one with increasingly sporadic periods. I rejoiced in the mental metamorphosis, and hardly gave any thought to the latter.

* * *

Back in California, I returned to the harsh reality of working for a living and scrounging for a few creative hours. Yet because of the discipline gained at Hedgebrook, I managed to finish my second novel despite the interruption of the Northridge earthquake. That cataclysmic event actually prompted a menstrual period before my forty-seventh birthday, though I had not had one since the previous autumn. For a few months afterward, I had regular periods before they again trickled into sporadic events.

Before the publication of *Latin Satins,* I traveled to the Northwest to teach a week-long fiction workshop in the company of sister-writers. By then my periods were virtually non-existent. That forty-seventh summer, though creativity flowed through and around me, I did not bleed.

During the book promotion tour in autumn, the blood—la sangre—did not appear. It eluded me throughout my travels with *Latin Satins.* I habitually tucked tampons into my luggage, "just in case." As time went on, I grew more and more accustomed to living without la sangre.

At the end of December, between Christmas and the New Year, I took a few days of vacation to begin my third novel. I had at last decided to write about a fictional character close to my own age, a woman dealing with growing older. Ironically, as I began the novel, la sangre returned. Once more, reminiscent of that bloody night years ago, I experienced an extremely heavy flow. Fortunately, I was home that whole week, moving from laptop computer to bathroom every hour. Because my energy level dwindled, I would write in the mornings until early afternoon, take a nap, and continue to write in the evenings. That cold, rainy week I was alone with my characters, and la sangre. Somehow it seemed appropriate.

* * *

During my forty-eighth summer, I returned to Hedgebrook Farm for a reunion of former residents. Two and a half years had passed since those heady days of unlimited writing time. Because of university downsizing, my office workload had increased, and I found myself with less and less energy to work on my third novel. I had taken on several non-fiction projects (including this one) to substitute for my lack of productivity with fiction.

Being at Hedgebrook for the weekend reunion revived my creative spirit. I spoke with current and past residents about the daily tensions of balancing the necessity of working for a living with the difficulty of maintaining a writing schedule. The enthusiasm, the honesty of those sister-writers inspired me to discipline myself again, to overcome nagging distractions, to carry on with the novel-in-progress.

Before leaving Hedgebrook that weekend, I walked along the beach with two of the writers who had been in residence with me. The day was cloudy, the tide low enough for us to tread far off the shoreline. We conversed about our writing projects, the changes in our lives over the past two years. While we spoke, we glimpsed three bald eagles soaring above us. They skimmed over the bay, hunting for fish, then darting and gliding overhead. We were awestruck by their majestic beauty.

I remembered observing the three does in the woods the morning of my forty-sixth birthday. From reading about animal symbolism, I had learned that the number three represents new birth and creativity. I knew that because they are birds of the water, eagles represent "an awakening ability or need to learn to walk between worlds. They are also symbols of the rediscovery of the inner child."*

Watching them high above me that forty-eighth summer, I marveled at their aerial agility, swooping suddenly, then resting on the large firs on Double Bluff, at home at sea, on land. Their sudden appearance, their rapid movements from air to water to earth, reminded me of my own resilience, my abilities to cross over, to reach those like and unlike myself through my writing.

While my friends continued to converse, I sat on a thick log apart from them, pondering the significance of sighting the eagles. Not having bled for seven months, I knew for certain that menopause had become an unavoidable reality. My body had begun to change, no matter how much I preferred to ignore that; I was greyer, heavier, sometimes sleepless due to hot flashes.

Following the examples of the eagles, I determined to be more flexible, alert for opportunities, cognizant of the need to be vigilant for any unhealthy signs during this time of rebirth, renewal. Like other transformations in my life, I would have to adapt. And with the cessation of the blood, la sangre, came a profound realization that no matter what further physical vicissitudes occurred, I would celebrate my private hormonic convergence and continue to create with my mind, not with my body.

---

*The quotes about eagle symbolism are from *Animal-Speak: The Spiritual and Magical Powers of Creatures Great and Small,* by Ted Andrews, Llewellyn Publications, 1993, pp. 138-139.

BOOKS

Barbach, Lonnie. *The Pause: Positive Approaches to Menopause*. NAL Dutton, 1994.

Brady, Maureen. *For the Change: 365 Meditations on Menopause & Other Life Passages*. Harper S.F., 1995.

Brown, Ellen H. & Walker, Lynne P. *Breezing Through the Change: Managing Menopause Naturally*. Frog, 1994.

Cabot, Sandra. *Smart Medicine for Menopause; Hormone Replacement Therapy & Its Natural Alternatives*. Avery, 1994.

Coney, Sandra. *The Menopause Industry: How the Medical Establishment Exploits Women*. Hunter House, 1994.

Consumer Guide Editors Staff. *Medical Book of Remedies: Fifty Ways to Cope With Menopause*. NAL-Dutton.

Doress, Paula Brown, Siegal, Diana Laskin, and the Midlife and Older Women Book Project. *Ourselves, Growing Older: Women Aging With Knowledge and Power*. Simon & Schuster/Touchstone, 1987.

Fincher, Susanne F. *Menopause: The Inner Journey*. Shambhala.

Gittleman, Ann Louise. *Super Nutrition for Menopause*. Pocket Books, 1993.

Greenwood, Sadja, M.D. *Menopause Naturally* (updated). Volcano Press, 1992.

Greer, Germaine. *The Change: Women, Aging and the Menopause*. Knopf, 1993.

Gross, Amy & Ito, Dee. *Without Estrogen*. Crown, 1994.

Henkel, Gretchen. *Making the Estrogen Decision*. Fawcett Columbine, 1994.

Henkel, Gretchen. *The Menopause Sourcebook: Everything You Need to Know*. Lowell House, 1994.

Hudson-Ferman, C. Sue. *Turning Point: The Other Side of Menopause*. OUP, 1994.

Hunter, Myra and Cooper, Jean. *Time of Her Life: Menopause, Health and Well-Being*. Parkwest, 1995.

Jacobowitz, Ruth S. *150 Most Asked Questions About Menopause: What Women Really Want to Know*. Hearst, 1993.

Jovanovic, Lois, M.D., with Levert, Suzanne. *A Woman Doctor's Guide to Menopause*. Hyperion, 1993.

Lark, Susan M., M.D. *The Estrogen Decision*. Westchester, 1994.

Lark, Susan M., M.D. *The Menopause Self-Help Book* (revised & updated). Celestial Arts, 1990.

Landau, Carol. PhD, Cyr, Michele G., M.D., Moulton, Anne W., M.D.

The Complete Book of Menopause. Perigee, 1994.

Notelovitz, Morris, M.D. & Tonnessen, Diana. *Menopause & Midlife Health* (35 p. booklet). Woman to Woman America (222 SW 36 Terrace, Gainsville, FL 32607) 1995.

Perry, Susan and O'Hanlon, Katherine, M.D. *Natural Menopause: The Complete Guide to a Woman's Most Misunderstood Passage.* Addison-Wesley, 1993.

Ryneveld, Edna C. *Secrets for a Natural Menopause: A Positive, Drug-Free Approach.* Llewellyn, 1994.

Sang, Barbara, Warshow, Joyce, Smith, Adrienne J. *Lesbians at Midlife: The Creative Transition.* Spinsters, 1991.

Sheehy, Gail. *The Silent Passage.* Fawcett Columbine, 1992.

Smith, Trevor. *Homeopathy for Menopause: A Guide to Health for the Middle Years.* Atrium, 1995.

Taylor, Dena & Sumrall, Amber Coverdale, editors. *Women of the 14th Moon: Writings on Menopause.* Crossing, 1991.

Villarosa, Linda. *Body and Soul: The Black Woman's Guide to Physical and Emotional Well-Being.* Harper Perennial, 1994.

Weed, Susun. *Menopausal Years The Wise Woman Way. Alternative Approaches for Women.* Ash Tree, 1992.

Wolfe, Honora L. *Menopause, A Second Spring: Making A Smooth Transition With Traditional Chinese Medicine.* Blue Poppy, 1993.

ARTICLES

"Acupuncture & Menopause Where Has All the Yin Gone?" J. Lisberger. *Sojourner*, V. 20, p. 1, Mar '95.

"Bisphosphonates: A New Class of Drugs—Medical Breakthrough in Treatment of Osteoporosis," C. Chestnut, M.D. *Women's Health Digest*, V. 1, p. 280, Fall '95. (This publication almost always has up-to-date information about menopause. Please see Organization section.)

"Brittle Bones" [debate over h.r.t for osteoporosis] A. Elash. *Maclean's*, v. 108, p. 389, JL 17 '95.

"Decline & Conquer "[countering effects of aging with hormones], N. Wade. *New York Times Mag*, p. 22, Ag 20, '95.

"Estrogen Benefits May Outweigh Risks: Two Feminist Doctors Speak Out." J. Lisberger. *Sojourner*, V. 20, p. 1, Mar '95.

"Estrogen or Not—How Did They Decide?" [interviews]. D. Bozzo. *Sojourner*, V. 20, p. 12H, Mar '95.

"The Forgotten Hormone." Dr. David G. Williams. *Alternatives for the Health Conscious Individual*, V. 4, #6, p. 41, December 1991.

"Menopause Naturally." L.M. Willeford. *New Age*, v. xii, Oct '95.
"Mid-Life Woman's Right to Choose, or Collective Threat to Women's Health and Wellbeing?" S. Coney. [feminist Response to HRT]. *Broadsheet*, p. 25, Winter '95.
"New Therapy For Menopause Reduces Risks". J. Brody. *New York Times*, Nov '94.
"Progestin Fails to Cut Breast Cancer Risk" [study by Graham Colditz]. T. Adler. *Science News*, V. 147, Je 17 '95.
"Protection in a Pillbox" [Estrogen replacement therapy may prevent colon cancer; research by Eugenia Calle]. M. Munson. *Prevention*, v. 47, p. 26, Ag '95.
"What Risk Hormones?" [breast cancer risks]. L. Seachrist. *Science News*, v. 148, p. 94-5, Ag 5 '95.

ORGANIZATIONS and PERIODICALS

Boston Women's Health Book Collective (pamphlets, factsheets & workshops). 240A M Street, Davis Square, Somerville, MA, 02114. (617) 625-0271.

HOT FLASH: Newsletter for Midlife & Older Women, Jane Porcino, ed. Health Technology Management, POB 816, Stony Brook, NY, 11790-0609.

Menopause Management, magazine endorsed by the North American Menopause Society, 9 Mt. Pleasant Turnpike, Denville, NJ 07834.

Midlife Women's Network, 5129 Logan Ave., S, Minneapolis, MN 55419. (800) 886-4354 or (612) 925-0020. Newsletter: "Midlife Woman."

National Institute On Aging, POB 8057, Gaithersburg, MD 20898-8057. (800) 222-2225 or (301) 496-1752. Publishes booklet "Menopause."

National Menopause Foundation, 222 SW 36th Terrace, Gainesville, FL 32607; (904) 372-9990. Magazine: "Women's Health Digest."

National Women's Health Network, various publications. 1325 G St NW, Washington, DC 20077-2052.

North American Menopause Society, c/o University Hospitals, OB/GYN, 2074 Abington Rd., Cleveland, OH 44106; (216) 844-3334. Refers individuals to physicians who specialize in menopause.

Older Women's League, 666 11th St. NW, Suite 700, Washington, D.C. 20001. (202) 783-6686. Newsletter: "Women's Health."

Oregon Menopause Information Network Newsletter, 1253 SE 32nd Place, Portland, OR 97214. Subscription $15.00/year. Ann Kopel, editor.

The Woman's Medical & Diagnostic Center, 222 SW 36th Terrace, Gainesville, FL 32607; (904) 372-5600. Newsletter: "Transitions."

VIDEO

"Menopause: Dispelling the Myths, Telling the Truths, Exploring the Possibilities." Moondancer Productions, POB 7823, Fremont, CA 94537-7823. (from Lesbian Connections)

RED JORDAN AROBATEAU is a butch dyke of mixed race heritage, age fifty-two, author of forty street dyke novels currently being published by Richard Kasak's Masquerade Books. Available through local queer-friendly bookstores, and thru Red Jordan Press, 484 Lake Park Ave. #228, Oakland, CA 94610.

PAIJ WADLEY-BAILEY, an African American radical lesbian eco-feminist, educator / activist Crone, runs a diversity consultant firm and an archive of media on People of Color and women. JUDITH BECKETT is a European American writer, cartoonist and artist as well as a feminist philatelist and registered nurse. Her work has appeared in *Lesbian Ethics*, *Women of Power* and most recently, *Front Line Feminist*, and numerous philatelic journals.

HENRI BENSUSSEN lives momentarily in the San Francisco Bay Area and plans to retire by 1999 to Bandon, Oregon to concentrate on writing and gardening. She's in a state of transition from middle age to old age, and from a past of limitations to a freer, more creative future.

BARBARA FIEBIG BENNETT, MD is an out lesbian physician in rural Alabama by choice. As the only physician in town, she is very welcome. Her coworkers and family asked that she wear a bra when she went to Washington, DC to lobby, because "the people up there didn't know her." She didn't comply. Please don't tell them.

SANDY BOUCHER is a writer, teacher and writing consultant in Oakland, California. She is presently living with cancer, and writing a book for women interested in Buddhism. She has published two books of fiction and two of nonfiction.

MANDY CARTER was born in Albany, New York in 1948. She is currently making her home in Durham, North Carolina and is director of North Carolina Mobilization '96 working to defeat Jesse Helms. She formerly worked with the Human Rights Campaign in Washington, DC.

BEATRIZ COPELLO was born in Argentina and migrated to Australia in the early seventies. Beatriz dedicates every free minute she isn't working at the NSW Public Service to her passion—writing. Her poetry and fiction include the poetized novel *El Encuentro y Mi Esencia* and *Women, Souls, and Shadows*, poetry.

LAUREN CRUX, at any given moment, is a writer, photographer, backpacker, cyclist, surfer, storyteller and adventurer. Her poetry, prose and photography have appeared in numerous journals and anthologies. She is currently enrolled in the MFA program at UC Irvine and is gladly accepting donations of kindness or money or both.

SARAH DREHER was born in Hanover, PA in 1937, graduated from Wellesley College and earned her Ph.D. from Purdue University. She is a lesbian activist, award-winning playwright, the author of the popular Stoner McTavish mystery series, and a clinical psychologist in private practice in Amherst, Massachusetts.

MATTIE FAST worked as a secretary in the San Francisco Bay Area most of her life until she recently retired. She was one of the first members of the Daughters of Bilitis. After five permanent relationships ranging from two to sixteen years, she's single now and feels she probably will be forever.

CAROLYN GAGE is a lesbian-feminist playwright and activist. Her recent collection, *The Second Coming of Joan of Arc and Other Plays,* was a National Finalist for the 1995 Lambda Literary Award. She lives in Northern California.

SALLY MILLER GEARHART lives on a mountain of contradictions with a pit bull and many cats in Northern California. She is a child of the white Southern water-treading middle class, the penny postcard and the ten cent movie, and the author of *The Wanderground* and co-author of *A Feminist Tarot.*

CANDIS GRAHAM lives and writes in Ottawa. Two collections of her stories have been published and she is working on her second novel, a collection of creative nonfiction, and one of poetry. She teaches creative writing to women in small workshops and finds it one of the most satisfying things she has ever done.

KARLA JAY has written, edited, and translated nine books, the most recent of which are *Lesbian Erotics* and *Dyke Life: From Growing Up to Growing Old, a Celebration of the Lesbian Experience.* She is editor of *The Cutting Edge.* She has written for many publications, including *MS Magazine, The New York Times Book Review, The Village Voice,* and *Lambda Book Report.*

TASHA ANTHONY JOHNSON is a young queer person  whose writing has appeared in g/b/l/trans publications including *Out and About* and a womyn's newsletter that she founded. While not writing, she is working a production job, going to college and playing pinball games.

REV. VICTORIA LEE-OWENS has authored five books of poetry, including *May I Touch Your Satin Softly?* She presents workshops for the *African American Women on Tour* and *LEO II;* produces and hosts the cable TV show, *Rhythmic Keys;* designs and sells ceramic figures and African-style hats; and edits a newsletter about spiritual empowerment especially for lesbians.

LEE LYNCH has ten books published, including *Cactus* *Love, Morton River Valley* and *The Swashbuckler.* Her column *"The Amazon Trail"* appears in over a dozen newspapers. She is enjoying her postmenopausal years with Akia Woods in rural Oregon where she earns her living in social service work.

MARÍA (pronounced "Moriah") lives on Wildwood, twenty acres of woods near Roseburg, Oregon with her dog, Amber, her cat, Sydney, and a variety of wilder plant and animal people that sometimes includes her five-year-old grandson (RJ), trying to make a living and remain true to herself. Writing is simply a necessity.

MARIWYNNE was born in 1942 in Pontiac, Michigan and graduated from NCSU in 1965. LYNN was born in 1943 in Columbus, Ohio and graduated from Ohio U in 1973. They live with their two dogs, two cats, an African gray parrot and a horse on forty-seven acres in Southeastern Ohio. They teach school, garden in the summer and feed birds in the winter. They walk for exercise, read for relaxation and give each other a trip to England every summer.

PEARLIE McNEILL returned to Australia in 1994 after thirteen years in England. She has been a creative writing tutor for most of that time. Her recent titles include: *One of the Family* and *Because You Want to Write*. She has co-edited *Women Talk Sex* and *Women's Voices, Refugee Lives—Stories from Bosnia*.

MEREDITH MORE used the Outer Banks of her native North Carolina as the setting for her well-received mystery-romance *October Obsession* (Naiad, 1988). Living in the Tidewater area of Virginia since the 60's, Meredith, a former teacher, works at home with her life partner, Kay, as a writer/editor.

JEAN MOUNTAINGROVE is a Libra 'people-person.' Twenty-five years in Southern Oregon mountains, she gardens on sunny days and writes on the wet ones. A rebel, a visionary and a pioneer in feminist spirituality via *Woman Spirit* magazine, she writes to understand life or when an idea amuses her.

MARILYN MURPHY has been a feminist activist since 1969. Her essays have appeared in many Lesbian and feminist publications and anthologies. Over the years she has taught courses in women's history and feminist issues for colleges and community organizations. Her book, *Are You Girls Traveling Alone? Adventures in Lesbianic Logic*, is a collection of her columns.

MERRILL MUSHROOM is now fifty-four, and the worst of all this is behind her. She is considerably less dense than she was thirty years ago. She still has an occasional hot flash in the Tennessee hills where she lives.

JOAN NESTLE, fifty-six, is co-founder of the Lesbian Herstory Archives. Her publications include: *A Restricted Country, The Persistent Desire: A Femme-Butch Reader, Women on Women 1,2, and 3, Sister and Brother: Lesbians and Gay Men Talk about their Lives Together*. She is working on a collection of her writings, *A Fragile Union*, and an anthology of international lesbian fiction. She retired from Queens College, CUNY, as a teacher of writing in 1995.

SUE O'SULLIVAN, originally American, spent over thirty years in London and now resides in Australia. Her most recent writing includes *Lesbians Talk (Safer) Sex* with Pratibha Parmer. A collection of her writing called *I Used to Be Nice* was published by Cassell in June 1996. She's alive and kicking.

CONNIE PANZARINO is a Boston lesbian, author, activist and psychotherapist with a severe physical disability. Her autobiography, *The Me in the Mirror* (Seal Press, May '94), serves to educate persons with and without disabling conditions.

TERRI DE LA PEÑA recently celebrated the first anniversary of her final menstrual period. She realizes now that the eagles were beckoning her to go back to Whidbey Island where she drafted *Faults*, her third novel. She is the author of *Margins* and *Latin Satins* (Seal Press), and contributor to *Another Wilderness*, *Night Bites*, and *Out for Blood Two*.

JULIA PENELOPE resigned her academic position in 1987 and now earns her living as a freelance editor and proofreader. In addition to her collaborations with Susan Wolfe, she is the author of *Speaking Freely: Unlearning the Lies of the Fathers' Tongues, Call Me Lesbian* (a collection of her essays), and *Crossword Puzzles for Women*.

PELE PLANTE began writing at menopause. She is the author of the lesbian mysteries *Dirty Money* and *Getting Away With Murder*. She also writes reviews for *The Lesbian Review of Books* and a bi-weekly column for her local newspaper. Pele lives and works on the beautiful Oregon coast.

LAURA POST is a left-handed Jewish writer of mixed-class heritage whose fiction, poetry, features, column and reviews have appeared in *Ms, Out, Deneuve, Advocate, Outlines, Washington Blade,* and over one-hundred and fifty other publications. Her essay on lesbian battering won first prize in the 1995 Arizona Authors' Contest; her anthology of interviews with women musicians will be released soon by New Victoria Publishers.

MARY CLARE POWELL writes poetry and non-fiction when she is not teaching teachers at Lesley College in Cambridge, Massachusetts how to (1) recover their own creativity (2) integrate the arts into their classrooms. The arts and social change is the theme of all her work, including *The Widow* and *This Way Daybreak Comes: Women's Values and the Future.*

SHELLY ROBERTS is a nationally syndicated lesbian columnist, speaker and author.

AZALIA RODRIGUEZ is a health education director for a nonprofit clinic in San Jose, CA. She shares her life with her partner (Lucy), cat (Calamity) and volunteers at Billy DeFrank Lesbian and Gay Community Center. She considers this the best time of her life and is looking forward to the wisdom that comes with age.

ELENA SHERMAN is happily writing her first best-selling Lesbian mystery.

SUNLIGHT is an old lesbian, off the rag for twenty years, each better than the last. She left cities and molecular biology to live in the coastal hills of Northern California where she writes, gardens and has just built a house together with ten other dykes.

VALERIE TAYLOR began writing at eight and published her first book at thirty-nine. A Quaker, feminist, bisexual, anti-war activist and lifetime socialist, she has published fourteen books. Her work was recently remaindered by Naiad and is banned in South Africa. Now eighty-two, she is still writing, seeking a new publisher and a new typewriter.

NAEKO WAKABAYASHI was born in Tokyo in 1947 and has lived there all her life except for one year spent working as a health counselor at the Feminist Women's Health Center in Oakland, California. She has been involved in the women's and lesbian movements since 1970 and is one of the founders of the Asian Lesbian Network Nippon.

JULIA WILLIS is the author of *Who Wears the Tux?* and *We Ought To Be In Pictures,* and her work appears in numerous anthologies. A Southern lesbian by birth, she's thrilled that menopause allows her to get good and mad for the first time in her ladylike life. Her cat baby book, *Meow-Mories,* is available from Laugh Lines Press.

SUSAN J. WOLFE co-edited *The Coming Out Stories, The Original Coming Out Stories, Lesbian Culture: An Anthology,* and *Sexual Practice, Textual Theory: Lesbian Cultural Criticism* with Julia Penelope. An English professor at the University of South Dakota, she is now completing a book on feminism and linguistics.

AKIA WOODS, one-time singer-songwriter and frontline activist, now lives with multiple chemical sensitivity and fibromyalgia. Weekdays she interprets Medicaid policy relating to seniors and adults living with disabilities and has also managed to carve a niche for herself as a teacher and troubleshooter in the use of personal computers. Weekends she's usually found enjoying a good book and the birds at their feeder.

zana is forty-eight, jewish, disabled, living on desert land. a book of her poetry and art, *herb woman,* is available for seven dollars from zana at MSC 044, HC04 box 6872-44, tuscon, az 85735.

"Flossie's Flashes" by Sally Miller Gearhart originally appeared in *Women of the 14th Moon, Writings on Menopause*, edited by Dena Taylor and Amber Coverdale Sumrall, published by Crossing Press, 1991.

"Hot Flash To Warm Glow" by Jean Mountaingrove originally appeared, in part, as "Nature's Plan" in *Women of the 14th Moon, Writings on Menopause*, edited by Dena Taylor and Amber Coverdale Sumrall, published by Crossing Press, 1991.

Joan Nestle's "Desire Perfected: Sex After Forty" appeared in *Lesbians At Midlife: The Creative Transition*, edited by Barbara Sang, Joyce Warshow and Adrienne J. Smith, 180-183. San Francisco: Spinsters Book Company, 1991. Available from Spinsters Ink, 32 East First Street #330, Duluth, Minnesota 55802. Reprinted by permission.

Sandy Boucher's "Half of a Map" was published in Sinister Wisdom 28, Winter 1985 and in *Long Time Passing: Lives of Older Lesbians*, edited by Marcy Adelman, PhD., Alyson Publications, 1986.

"Menopause Waltz" by Sue O'Sullivan was first published in *A Certain Age—Reflecting on the Menopause*, edited by Joanna Goldsworthy, Virago, 1993.

"Lesbian Menopause" by Mary Clare Powell was included in *My Lover Is A Woman*, edited by Lesléa Newman, Ballantine Books, 1996.

ALL ARE REPRINTED BY PERMISSION

Photographs are credited as follows:

Joan Nestle—Susan Fleischmann Photography
Jean Mountaingrove—Kathleen Buckalew
Terri de la Peña—Carol Peterson
Valerie Taylor—Tee A. Corinne
Julia Willis—Laurel Blanchard
Red Jordan Arobateau—Louise Hogerheide
Sunlight—Tee A. Corinne
Carolyn Gage—Newman-Brittingham, copyright 1995
Mandy Carter—Kristi K. Gasaway
Karla Jay—Jill Posener
Julia Penelope—Linnea Johnson
Lauren Crux—Lauren Crux
Sue O'Sullivan—Jill Posener

FROM NEW VICTORIA PUBLISHERS
PO BOX 27 NORWICH VERMONT 05055
CALL 1-800 326 5297   EMAIL newvic@aol.com
Home page   http://www.opendoor.com/NewVic/

TALES FROM THE DYKE SIDE Humorous Essays by **Jorjet Harper**
Lesbomania author Jorjet Harper, in her unique blend of humor and wry commentary, continues her exploration of the growing lesbian cultural panorama.
Jorjet Harper is smart, hilarious and seriously depraved. –Alison Bechdel
    $10.95   ISBN 0-934678-71-5

I CHANGE, I CHANGE Poems by **Barbara Deming**.
Edited and forward by Judith McDaniel. Preface by Grace Paley
Barbara Deming, was one of the most dearly loved and respected activists and essayist of our time. *I Change, I Change* is a collection of previously unpublished poemsdedicated to women with whom she shared a significant relationship. $12.95 cloth ISBN 0-934678-72-3

A FIRE IS BURNING, IT IS IN ME The Life and Writings of **Michiyo Fukaya**. Edited by Gwendolyn L. Shervington
Michiyo Fukaya was a young Japanese American lesbian poet/activist who lived in Burlington, Vermont in the 1970s and '80s. She was a single mother of a mixed race child, living on welfare, who struggled with mental illness and a history of sexual abuse. $9.95   ISBN 0-934678-78-2

WINDSWEPT by **Magdalena Zschokke**
A beautiful novel of women's adventures on the high seas. Three women sailing the open oceans, sometimes together, sometimes apart, their letters, dreams and their connection to the stars keeps them going, moving toward a goal of an all-women crew.
    $10.95   ISBN 0-934678-73-1

EVERY WOMAN'S DREAM by **Lesléa Newman**
Newman brings a sharp yet playful style to these tales of sex, monogamy, fantasies, the future, and the possibility of lesbian motherhood. Who else can write about lesbian life through the story of a traveling sock? She's compassionate with her characters yet doesn't flinch from confronting hard issues faced by communities, gay and straight alike. $9.95   ISBN 0-934678-62-6

A PERILOUS ADVANTAGE The Best of Natalie Clifford Barney
Edited and Translated by Anna Livia with a Forward by Karla Jay
Finally, the writing of one the century's most notorious lesbians is
available in English. Natalie Barney was the center of the lesbian
universe in Paris in the 1920s and 30s. Read her impressions of
Gertrude Stein, Colette and many others of her day.
$10.95 paper ISBN 0-934678-38-3 $19.95 cloth ISBN 0-934678-45-6

RADICAL FEMINISTS OF HETERODOXY by **Judith Schwarz**
An account of Heterodoxy, the club for unorthodox women that
flourished in Greenwich Village from 1912 through the '30s. Among
its members were many of the most dynamic women of the times.
Revised edition. $8.95   ISBN 0-934678-08-1

ALL THE WAYS HOME—Parenting and Children in the Lesbian
and Gay Communities—A Collection of Short Fiction
A unique collection by such well-known authors as Beth Brant,
Ruthann Robson, Jane Rule, Julie Blackwomon, Jameson Currier, writing about the experience of being part of lesbian and gay families.
*"This is a powerful, inclusive collection, and oh so very real. We've been
waiting a long time for a book like this."*   —Irene Zahava
     $10.95 paper $19.95 cloth

SATURDAY IS PATTYDAY A book for children by **Lesléa Newman**
When Frankie's two mothers break up, he feels hurt and confused.
Patty assures him that even though she and Allie, Frankie's other
mom, can't get along, she still loves him and will always be his
mommy and that he will be able to visit Patty every Saturday, This
is Lesléa's fourth children's book focusing on children whose parents are lesbian.
$6.95   paper ISBN 0-934678-51-0 $14.95 cloth ISBN 0-934678-52-9